# Angels

### Arthur Frederick Ide
With the assistance of John Paul Smith

Introduction by Decherd Turner

Las Colinas, TX
Monument Press
1997

Published by
**Monument Press**
Las Colinas, Texas

*First Edition    First Printing*

Copyright © 1997, Arthur Frederick Ide

**Library of Congress Cataloging-in-Publication Data**

Ide, Arthur Frederick.
    Angels / Arthur Frederick Ide ; with an introduction by Decherd Turner.
    p.   cm.
    Includes bibliographical references and index.
    ISBN 0-930383-49-4
    1. Angels.   I. Title.
BL477.I34  1997
291.2'15--dc21                                                      97-28268
                                                                                             CIP

All rights reserved including the right to reproduce this work in any format by any means to any length save for quotation in a professional, scholarly or news review by any mechanical, electronic, or other format, in serial or *en toto*. Permission is granted exclusively by the author or publisher.

For
**John Paul Smith**

काङ्क्षन्तः कर्मणां सिद्धिं यजन्त इह देवताः ।
क्षिप्रं हि मानुषे लोके सिद्धिर्भवति कर्मजा ॥१२॥

iv

# Illustrations

Satan and Belzebuth, illustration for *Paradise Lost* by
John Milton (Haley)....................................................cover
*Icarus Reborn* by D. Jonathon Miller..................title page
Assyrian winged cherubim (guardian) c. 860 BCE................iv
Pair of 8th century BCE Persian Sphinxes.............................10
Seraphim, 8th century Spain...................................................34
Demon, Etruscan tomb painting, 5th century BCE................38
Hell's Jester............................................................................42
Fall into Hell (William Blake)................................................44
Kairos of Tragir, 3rd century BCE..........................................48
Aristocrats of Hell..................................................................49
Lilith, goddess of death, bas relief from Sumer,
  c. 2000 BCE........................................................................50
Fall of Angels (William Blake)..............................................56
Gold Rhyton. Achaemenid, 5th-3rd century BCE
  Archaeological Museum, Teheran (Iran)..........................64
St. Michael, medieval altarpiece............................................78
St. Gabriel (stained glass window at Mare Island
  Naval Base, California)....................................................94
Douris, *Eos and Memmon* (interior of an Attic red-
  Figured kylix) c. 490-480 BCE, The Louvre
  Paris..................................................................................110
Uriel wrestling Jacob, 19th century (Eugène Delacroix)......113
Metatron staying the hand of Abraham, 1401 by
  Filippo Brunelleschi (Florence)......................................116
A Power (a defecting angel who goes to Hell) from
  *Hierarchy of the Blessed Angels* (Heyward)..................122
Ezekiel's ride into heaven....................................................124
Rebellion of an Angel by Gustave Doré..............................126
Choirs of Heaven..................................................................134
Angels of Light of Heaven...................................................136
Two Faces of Priapus (Angel of Lust).................................146

Charon the Etruscan God of the Dead
  *Tomb of Ocrais– Tarquinia* 5th century BCE ............... 169
Assyrian winged genii, c. 855 BCE ................................ 184
The Creation of Adam (c. 1430 CE)
  by Jacopo della Queriia
  Marble. Main Portal, S. Petronio. Bologna ................ 201
Angel of Death ................................................................ 204
The Flood by Michaelangelo
  (Fresco, Sistine Ceiling) Rome .................................. 207
Marduk battling with Tiamat (from a wall panel in
  the palace of Ashur-nasir-apal II, c. 885-860 BCE;
  original in the British Museum, London) ................. 208
*The City of Sodom* (book cover; Monument Press)
  by Arthur Frederick Ide ............................................. 218
Jacob's ladder (18th century) by Heyley ........................ 226
Jacob wrestling an angel (St. Uriel)/god
  by Gustave Doré ......................................................... 229
Temptation of Jesus ........................................................ 240
War in Heaven (a series of illustrations)
  by Gustave Doré ......................................................... 256
Advent of Apocalypse
  by Gustave Doré ......................................................... 259
Muhammad's night journey to heaven on the mare Buraq
  (detail from Persian manuscript in the Bibliotheque
  Nationale, Paris) ........................................................ 261
Moroni (son of Mormon) ............................................... 265
Fertility ride (bas relief in Museum of Nimes) ............. 268
Queen Mahamaya conceiving the Buddha
  (railing medallion at Bharhut Museum, Calcutta) ... 270
Three Deities (Mycenae, c. 1500-1400 BCE)
  Ivory, National Museum, Athens ............................... 291
Cowboy angel (contemporary study) ............................ 296

# Contents

Introduction by Decherd Turner ............... 1

Chapter 1: *Angels: An Introduction* ............... 5
Chapter 2: *Angels in Hell* ............... 41
Chapter 3: *Angels and Sex* ............... 57
Chapter 4: *Angels and Symbols* ............... 63
Chapter 5: *Angel of the Lord* ............... 65
Chapter 6: *Archangels* ............... 71
Chapter 7: *Michael* ............... 79
Chapter 8: *Gabriel* ............... 95
Chapter 9: *Raphael* ............... 105
Chapter 10: *Uriel* ............... 111
Chapter 11: *Metatron* ............... 117
Chapter 12: *Rediyao* ............... 123
Chapter 13: *Sandalphon* ............... 125
Chapter 14: *The Other Archangels* ............... 127
Chapter 15: *Semil* ............... 135
Chapter 16: *Samael* ............... 137
Chapter 17: *Shamshiel* ............... 145
Chapter 18: *Satan* ............... 147
Chapter 19: *The Sons of God & The Daughters of Men* ............... 169
Chapter 20: *The Watchers* ............... 185
Chapter 21: *Adam* ............... 201
Chapter 22: *Noah* ............... 205
Chapter 23: *Abraham* ............... 209

Chapter 24: *Sarah* ................................................215
Chapter 25: *Angels at Sodom* ..............................219
Chapter 26: *Hagar and Ishmael* .........................223
Chapter 27: *Jacob* ...............................................227
Chapter 28: *Jesus and the Angels* .......................233
Chapter 29: *A Miscellany of Angels* ...................259
Index ......................................................................297
About
    Arthur Frederick Ide .......................................317
    John Paul Smith .............................................319
    Decherd Turner ..............................................321

# Introduction

## By Decherd Turner

The great poet T. S. Eliot declares in his *Four Quartets*

> human kind
> cannot bear very much reality.

And the chief channels of escape get personalized into angelic creatures — good and bad. Man through many generations of concentrated mental masturbation has created armies of imagined creatures dancing around out there or over there or up there or in front of him or behind him or beside him whose role is to sanction and enhance his escape from reality and responsibility. No tribe or culture is immune. Each group produces its own hierarchy of angels, yet when placed in the broad historic perspective, as Dr. Ide has done, it turns out that the profiles of the angelic corps produce astonishingly similar clone-like configurations. Through this declension we view the astonishing unity of man — whether cave dweller or twentieth-century corporate head or prince of the Church.

Angels are parasitical vines enveloping us sucking the juice of reality and responsibility out of our bodies. We have experiences but we surrender the meaning to the angelic host because we don't want to face the meaning. Mankind continues to exist century after century in a kind of grey monotone learning little: hostility and hubris renew their dominion with the dawn of each day. Reality and responsibility are thus daily handicapped.

Dr. Arthur Ide shows what creeps some angels are. He shows us that some angels are "angelic", and some angels are long overdue for retirement. His wide linguistic abilities take us into exotic places and thought patterns — and there we meet the most familiar of angels! Widely different and strangely the same!

I find this experience of writing about Dr. Ide's text on angels one of the strangest of my life. Although I am Irish and I never really believed in the "little people" or the clouds of angels hovering over the church. My mother was inclined to declare that some gene had been left out of my makeup. On the other hand, reading an Ide book is one of the verbal delights left to man. The text above the footnotes is important, but not the best part. It is that collection of massive footnotes below the text that stretches the mind.

No, I don't believe in angels, but I enjoy some of the problems of those who do, especially the discussion as to whether "real" angels have wings or not. I'll never forget encountering the issue some years ago when a group of religious prints was being offered for sale by a noted art dealer. I was discussing the qualities of these wonderful prints with him, and learned the astonishing fact that one of the major denominations in the United States would have nothing to do with the prints because the angels shown had wings! Goodbye Gabriel! Or, shed those wings and walk, but getting to the next pregnant virgin can be complicated.

Prodded by Dr. Ide's presentation, I decided to do a little "man on the street" survey. I first turned to a genuine prince of the Church, a man who has served his Christ with devotion and intelligence, a man revered by his colleagues and friends. I asked him if he believed in angels. His answer: "No."

I later met a young clergyman who became so tense when I asked him about angels, and who looked at me with such distaste for asking, but answered that he did indeed believe in God's messengers, as well as the Devil's. My dubiety must have been so apparent that he shook the dust off his feet, and departed quickly.

And then, I had a genuinely pleasant and heart-warming experience. I met an attractive lady, a mother of four children, who had experienced some of life's most rugged edges, and had come through it like fine metal refined by fire. She most graciously agreed to give her testimony about angels: she felt that she could not have survived her difficulties without the conviction that supportive angels took care of her. So sincere were her words and expression that for a while I was almost persuaded to re-examine my negative position.

Hold on! To enter that path will only lead to larger celestial citizenship than I am prepared to deal with. Next thing will be UFOs, and then Saints, and then....!

To believe or not to believe in angels is not the question Dr. Ide addresses. What he does with mature scholarship is to deal with written records stretching over many cultures and centuries and from those sources report the maturation of the angel-scene. The result is a wonderful rocky ride a bit on the wild side.

Who was the creep who first said: "History is dull"?

—Decherd Turner

Austin, Texas
July 5, 1997

# Angels: An Introduction

Angels.[1] They're a part of most world religions and myths long before the Hebrew[2] or the

---

[1] F. Saurez, *Summa Theologiae de Deo Rerum Omnium Creatore*, pars secunda, 'De Angeles,' (Lyons, 1620) is still a solid work on angels. It has later support in J. Turmel, "Histoire de angélologie des temps apostolique à la fin V$^e$ siècle," in *Revue d'histoire et de littérature religieuses* III (1898), pp. 531-552; J. Turmel, "L'angelologie depuis le faux Denis l'Aréopagite," in *Revue d'histoire et de littérature religieuses* IV (1899), pp. 217-238, 289-309, 414-434, 537-562.

[2] There are only two "eye-witness" accounts to the existence of angels in the Hebrew bible. They are: Ezekiel 1, and Elijah's record in 2 Kings 2:11. Enoch 14:8VB also recounts the presence of angels. The accounts, however, must be approached with caution. Enoch is spurious as an individual, fleshed out only in Apocalyptic literature. The only record of his lineage is found in Genesis 5:18-24, and Jude 14. His existence is suspect, since he "walked with the gods" who ultimately took him to heaven (see: Sirach 44:16, 49:14, and Hebrews 11:5). These records have strong Babylonian parallels. For example: Enoch is accounted the "seventh from Adam" (Jude 14; cp. Enoch 1:9, 5:4, 27:2). This parallels the seventh name in the list of the antediluvian kings given by Berosus in *Evedoranchus*. The list most likely is a corruption of Enmeduranki, a king of Sippar who was received into the fellowship of the Sun God Shamash and Ramman. Under these Babylonian deities, the Enoch-prototype is inducted into the "mysteries" of creation and heaven and earth. Mastering

Christian bibles were written or even conceived.[3] Some of the angels were considered gods. Others were seen as demigods. They were thought of as having slightly less power than the gods have. A few were associated with the "upper world" (life), while others were thought to control the "under world" (death). Still others were seen as being in charge of this world and the lives of mortals. But in each case, as time lapsed and a priestly class was invented by those opposed to manual work and preferred to dedicate themselves to mental activities, the angels were considered to be messengers. They were seen as agents of death and life, seducers of men and women, boys and girls, as well as champions of mortal beings. They were acclaimed as potentates, until the arrival of henotheism and monotheism. They were both ben-

---

this divine material he is made the founder of a guild of priestly diviners, so that his life would last for 365 years (the same number of days in a solar year). Enoch has the rare distinction of being titled "Son of Man" and also "Son of God." *Ethiopic Book of Enoch* 60:10 ff; 71:14, 17 ff. Cf. Douglas R. A. Hare, *The Son of Man Tradition* (Minneapolis, MN: Fortress Press, 1990). Cf. Josephus, *Apion* 2.203; *IQM – War Scroll* xii.7-12 (154).

[3] James Hastings, *Dictionary of the Bible*, rev. ed. Frederick C. Grant and H. H. Rowley (New York: Charles Scribner's Sons, 1963), p. 32.

evolent (always styled as "angels") as well as malevolent (always styled as "demons"). For this reason, especially in Egypt and the Mesopotamian kingdoms, magic became a part of the worship ritual. New rites were invented. Water miraculously changed into wine. Bread, it was preached, was transmogrified into flesh, and the sport of blood-letting was sanitized through the mutilation-torture of circumcision. In each situation, the draconian act served as a guarantee of winning the favor of the messengers and the god(s) the angels represented.

In the Old Testament angels are called *mal'ākh*. The Hebrew word goes back to the Ugaritic *mal'ak*. They are referred to as "divine ones."[4] Some are styled "sons of divine beings."[5] Then there are "mighty ones,"[6] as well as "saints" or "holy ones."[7] They are the "host" of the "host of Yahweh": guards,[8] the martial and militant "host of

---

[4] *Elohim* in Psalm 8:6(5); 82:1, 6; 97:7; 138:1.

[5] *b$^e$nê elohim* in Genesis 6:2, 4. Job 1:6; 2:1; 38:7; and as *b$^e$nê elim* in Psalm 29:1; 89:7(6).

[6] *'abbīrîm* in Psalm 78:25.

[7] *k$^e$dhōshîm* in Job 5:1. Psalm 89:6(5). Zechariah 14:5. Daniel 4:14 (17) and 8:13.

[8] Joshua 5:14, 15. Host in this case concerns warfare: צבא.

heaven,"[9] who assemble around god (Yahweh).[10] They do this in the very same manner as do the celestial beings fleshed-out in the Ugaritic texts. For in Jewish and Christian mythology, they are a revised version of the Ugaritic *ilm*, the *bn ilm*, and the *bn qds* that were a group of young men who stationed themselves around the god *El*[11] in a sexual

---

[9] 1 Kings 22:19.

[10] 1 Kings 22:19-22. Job 1:6, and 2:1. Psalm 89:7(6).

[11] El translates as "The Lord." He was the greatest of all the Old Testament gods. In part, his fame grew because of his exceptional fecundity. Records show that El was the biological father of most of the gods who would rebel against or be challenged by Yahweh. Chief among these gods that El spawned was Baal (along with at least seven brothers and seven sisters). Together with his brothers and sisters, Baal (his name means, and translates as, "Master" and "Possessor") and his squadron of kin were the greatest threat to Yahweh, although Yahweh's most fierce competitor who won the hearts of all Canaanites and most Israelites was Baal's sister Asherah. To conquer Asherah, Yahweh married her, bedded her, and kept her occupied as did her priests and worshippers. Both of the Canaanite deities are given in the plural with the definite article prefixed to indicate their strength, grandeur and support by the other deities. See: Numbers 22:41. Cf., their major rivalry with Yahweh in Judges 2:11, 13; 3:7; 6:31-32; 8:33; 10:6, 10; their support among the Israelites is captured in 2 Samuel 7:4, 12:10; 1 Kings 16:31, 32, also 18:18-19, 21-22, 25-26, 40, and 19:18 with 22:53. Other references include 2 Kings 3:2, 10:18-28, 11:18, 17:16, 23:4-5; 2 Chronicles 17:3,

rite of passage to increase the country's fertility. Since the young men held tight the shafts of spiritual renewal, they had bargaining power with the god El and those deities who followed him.[12]

---

23:17, 24:7, 28:2, 34:4; Jeremiah 2:8, 23, also 7:9, 11:13 and 17, 12:16, 19:5, 23:13, 32:29 and 35; Hosea 2:8, 13, 17, and 11:2, 13:1; Zephaniah 1:4. The Canaanite god is even mentioned in the New Testament: Romans 11:4. As for Baal's famous sister Ashtaroth (it means "wife"; she was also known as Ashtoreth (the singular form), among other names; her Greek name is Astarte, and she was the goddess of fertility, love and war). See: Judges 2:3, 10:6; 1 Samuel 7:3-4, 12:10, 31:10; 1 Kings 11:5 (noting that Solomon also worshipped her) and 33; 2 Kings 23:13. Solomon's Temple was hardly unique. It was patterned after Canaanite temples. For example: in the Orthostat Temple there are two pillar bases at the entrance from the porch into the main hall (cp. 1 Kings 7:21). The small Stelae Temple in Area C featured upright slabs like the מצבה (*maṣṣēbâ* or cultic pillars) mentioned and condemned (Exodus 23:24; and so forth) in the sanctuary of the moon god where there was a statue representing the mood god. Cf. Yigael Yadin, *Hazor: The Rediscovery of a Great Citadel of the Bible* (New York: Random House, 1975). Later many of these gods became Hebrew angels.

[12] Job 25:2, 21:22; cf. Isaiah 24:21. The Canaanite god El (*el olam*: the eternal god) dwelt in a tent-shrine on a mountain. This is identical to the god of Moses whose presence was on Mount Sinai. See: Exodus 19:20; cf. Richard J. Clifford, *The Cosmic Mountain in Canaan and the Old Testament*; Harvard Semitic Monographs 4 (Cambridge, MA: Harvard University Press, 1972). A stele was found at Ras Shamra and dated to

Heaven's angels are ferocious in appearance. Their wings (those who had wings) were weapons, as depicted in Persian art and reliefs, and on Sumerian cylinder seals, Assyrian bas-reliefs, Babylonian vase paintings and eighth century Persian Sphinxes.

The Greek god Mercury was one of their direct descendants and stood like them in protective order on Mount Olympus. The angels did not become the insipid soft and fat figures that we

---

the thirteenth century; it represents El seated on a lion-footed throne, with his feet on a footstool, wearing a long robe and a high crown with horns. He raises his hand in benediction over a lesser figure holding a vase and an animal-headed scepter (possibly the king of Ugarit). Behind him are subordinate gods, including Zebul (meaning Prince) Baal. This later becomes the foundation for additional biblical stories, people and places with various deliberate distortions. Cf. 2 Kings 1:6, 16; Josephus, *Antiquities* 9.19. Matthew 12:24 turns Zebul Baal into Beel-zebul as another name for the "prince of demons." See: T. H. Gaster, "Baal-zebub," *Interpreters Dictionary of the Bible*, ed. G. A. Buttrick (4 vols.; Nashville, TN: Abingdon, 1962), vol. 1, p. 332. The ancient Hebrews will use this to feed their wars of the angels, and set themselves aside as a Chosen People divinely separated from the Canaanites and those around them.

know today until the end of the Middle Ages and into the Renaissance. All were naked.[13]

Some of the angels tired of their puny god who didn't have the strength to withstand the entire heavenly host and challenged him. This led to war and ultimately the expulsion of some of their number when they were defeated, after which many "fallen angels" hurled themselves, or were hurled by the avenging deity, to the earth.[14] The closer the Jews came in contact with the Gentiles, the more complete did their angelology become until it was unsurpassed. In the end, most Jewish angels were strictly of pagan origin.

In the New Testament, angels are styled *angelos*. It is the same word used in ancient Greek texts to recognize mortals who served their ancient kings as ambassadors, envoys and messengers. New Testament records aren't that much different than the Old Testament accounts. Good angels and bad

---

[13] Cf. Manfred Barthel, *Was Wirlich in der Bibel Steht* (Econ Verlag GmbH, 1980).

[14] Genesis 6:24 *cum* Jude 6, 2 Peter 2:4. Cf. Isaiah 27:1, and 34:4-5. In these incidents we know that the angelic choirs were not in song but in war maneuvers. For example, in one passage one angel is styled a "captain" (*sar*). See: Joshua 5:14; cp. Daniel 10:20, 21. The style of being a captain originally meant the head of a unit in the army of the pharaoh.

angels[15] are clearly segregated and marked.[16] The good angels are fiery spiritual beings.[17] Under normal conditions, they dwell in heaven where they attend to prayer and praise, glorifying god.[18] Yet these angels are equally ready to form and fight in armies,[19] both in heaven and on earth. Some angels "come down" to earth[20] to help men: Jesus, in particular,[21] and others in general.[22] They continue as communicators and messengers of the intent and

---

[15] Bad angels are referred to as "evil angels": Psalm 78:49; cf. Job 33:22. Although evil, they are sent "from the Lord" with the full permission of the deity to do what is allowed or commanded; see 1 Samuel 16:14-23; 1 Kings 22:20-23.

[16] Revelation 12:7; cf. Matthew 25:41.

[17] Hebrews 1:7.

[18] Matthew 18:10; Luke 1:19, 2:13-15, 12:8-9; John 1:51; Revelation 5:11.

[19] Revelation 7:12, 9:14.

[20] Matthew 28:2; Luke 2:9; Acts 10:3; Revelation 18:1.

[21] Matthew 4:11, 26:53; Luke 22:43.

[22] John 5:4; the magical property of this angel is seen in his ability to "trouble" (ταράσω) the waters to cure impotency (John 5:7) for example: Acts 5:19, 12: 7 ff; Hebrews 1:14 ff.

wishes of their god.[23] They prophesy what will be in the form of revelations[24] as they are charged to protect men[25] and oversee their salvation.[26] They help in man's salvation, by carrying man's prayers to god,[27] and after man dies, convey his soul to an undefined resting-place.[28]

To ensure that man has the opportunity of salvation, the angels in the New Testament are charged even with chastising man.[29] This is divine punishment which all who would be saved must accepted in the manner Job endured his tribulations.

"Evil angels" are similarly charged. On god's instruction they are sent to the earth to test

---

[23] Matthew 1:20, 2:13, 28:5 ff; Luke 1:11, 28, 2:10 ff; Acts 8:26 ff, 10:3-7 and 30-32, 27:23-26; Revelation 21:9.

[24] Revelation 1:14, 14:6, 22:16; cf. Acts 7:53, Galatians 1:8, Hebrews 2:2.

[25] Matthew 18:10 exemplifies the angel's power of protection because of their immediacy with the "Father." Cf. Acts 12:15.

[26] Luke 15:10; cf. 1 Timothy 5:21.

[27] Revelation 8:3-4.

[28] Luke 16:22.

[29] Matthew 13:49, 50; Revelation 9:15, 16:1, 21:9.

man.[30] They visit and reprimand anointed kings on the expressed order of their god-leader.[31] They persuade others to go to places they would have been exempt from visiting.[32]

As in the Old Testament, New Testament angels appear to men in dreams, and always in the form of radiant, beautiful males.[33] They wear garments,[34] and speak with human voices in the language of the dreamer.[35] Yet, they are of limited

---

[30] Job 2:1 ff.

[31] 1 Samuel 16:14-23.

[32] 1 Kings 22:20-23.

[33] Matthew 28:3; Luke 2:9; Acts 1:10, 10:30; Revelation 18:1. *Testament of Abraham* II.2 records the Lord of the Universe ordering the Angel of Death (Sammael) to "cast aside thy terrific aspect and thy impurity and assume the radiant and lovely form of a shining angel. In the garb of a bright and beautiful angel of light, in the shape and form of a handsome youth, exhaling the beauty of regions celestial, go and appear to Abraham...."

[34] Luke 24:4; John 20:12; Revelation 19:14. There is a problem with the angels wearing garments. Clothing, from aprons to robes, was a sign of sin and the avenues to sin (cf. Genesis 3:7). Before the mythical fall in Eden, mortals were naked as were the angels (Genesis 3:11).

[35] Matthew 1:20, 2:19-20; John 12:29; Revelation 7:2.

knowledge.[36] Only some gods are granted complete wisdom. Their rank and station define the enlightenment of angels: archangels are considered the wisest.[37] The New Testament even adds new groups of angels. These celestial groups include Powers, Dominion, and Principalities.[38] Some of the early Christian churches even worshipped these new angelic groups as if they were gods.[39]

New Testament angels have assigned duties as they did in pagan literature. One angel is set over the bottomless pit.[40] Others are in charge of the phenomena of nature.[41] In the Last Day, they will have tasks that they will share with others.[42] Angels who rebelled against god will be judged,[43] along

---

[36] Matthew 24:36; Mark 13:32.

[37] Jude 9; 1 Thessalonians 4:16.

[38] Colossians 1:16; Ephesians 1:21, 3:10; 1 Peter 3:22.

[39] Colossians 2:18; cf. Revelation 19:10, 22:8-9.

[40] Revelation 9:11.

[41] Revelation 7:1, 14:18; 16:5; 19:17.

[42] Matthew 13:39 ff, 16:27, 24:31; 2 Thessalonians 1:7-10.

[43] 2 Peter 2:4; Jude 6.

with the Principalities and Powers and lesser angels who flocked behind their banners.[44] The ruler of this evil lot is singled out as The Satan.[45] The only legitimate Satan was imported from ancient Babylonian myths. He is the "Divine Son," the "Prince of Light" as well as the "Prince of Darkness," "the Morning Star" and the "Beloved Son." Satan is one of the $b^e ne\ ^e l\bar{o}him$, because he is hostile to traditional piety and those who appear as pious people, from Job to the high-priest Joshua.[46] He scorns these seemingly saintly servants of the Lord for he feels that they are acting piety and not living it, and so becomes the Divine Advocate to test them, *completely* with the will and permission of the godhead.

At first, Satan was considered an important Son of God, and remained subject to the will of the god(s). It was only when it became necessary to make the tribal god Yahweh supreme did the writers of the myths of angels take deliberate action in making all angels subordinate to Yahweh. With the

---

[44] 1 Corinthians 15:24; Ephesians 6:12.

[45] Revelation 12:7 and especially 9: διαβολος και ὁ Σατανᾶs being a composite; cp. 20:1-3, 7, 10.

[46] Zechariah 3:1-2.

rise of the priestly class, evil was seen no longer as the will of Yahweh. Instead it was heralded as the connivance of certain angels. Actions that were previously attributed to the god(s) became transmogrified into the actions of angels.[47]

Even though he is the divine prosecuting attorney for the godhead in all matters concerning mortals, as seen in the epic poem of Job, the Satan is particularly singled out for the libel of being the "instigator of evil."[48] Not until the mythical meandering of the writer(s) of Wisdom, or the hallucinatory presentation of "John" was he associated with the evil serpent in the Garden of Eden.[49] It occurred when the writers were charged with making moral distinctions. Their distinctions were clumsily based on the ethics the venal priestly class determined would best meet their needs in controlling the "chosen" people of Israel.

Priestly connivance wasn't new or unique. On the contrary, it was fitted around popular rival pagan mythologies in an effort to keep the Israelites loyal to them. For this reason, priestly phraseology

---

[47] Compare 2 Samuel 24:11 ff with 1 Chronicles 21:18.

[48] 1 Chronicles 21:1; cp. 2 Samuel 24:1.

[49] Wisdom 2:24; Revelation 12:9.

included such fantasies as "dark forces" of chaos, "chaos introduced at creation," and so forth.[50] It is the "dark forces" of chaos that demonstrate that not everything was peaceful or celestial in heaven. Instead, we read that there were battles over suzerainty and sovereignty in heaven, as the various armies of the heavenly hosts battled for primacy.[51]

A minor god, Yahweh, tried to keep the peace. Not surprisingly, he wasn't successful, given his lack of character, strength and command.[52] Yahweh's message wasn't welcomed. The heavenly hosts wanted a more stringent set of laws than man had, even though some of their number would deal closely in assorted wickednesses. Their wickedness centered on sexuality and the natural pleasure sex brings participant(s). Since sex was seen as a part of non-Yahwhistic worship exercises, it was abruptly condemned and legislated against in the form of

---

[50] Psalm 74:12 ff, 89:9(8); Job 26:12; Isaiah 51:9-10. While Old Testament writers saw creation as a synthesis of chaos and the ending of rebellion, early Christian apologists argued that creation occurred in harmony with all the elements working together; see *The Letter of the Romans to the Corinthians* (*First Clement*) 19-20.

[51] Job 25:2; Daniel 10:20.

[52] Genesis 6:2-4.

commandments, insipid injunctions and priestly pronouncements prohibiting the carnality of the chosen people. Here, too, neither the priests nor their god (Yahweh) were successful in turning the people from carnal pleasure. Realizing their own celestial ineffectiveness and the resistance of the people who saw human sexuality as a normal function and a positive good, to shore up their claims prophets wrote (and preached) at length that Yahweh and his righteous angels would deal with all recalcitrant beings.[53]

Some writers became so disgusted with the entire emerging mythology of angels that they ignored these fantasies completely. The priestly writer of the Document P[54] doesn't mention angels.

---

[53] Isaiah 27:1, 24:21-22; Psalm 82:1; cf. Jude 6.

[54] P is the abbreviation for the Priestly source in the Pentateuch. The role of the priest is highlighted, as seen in its celebration of Aaron and his priesthood, even at the expense of Moses. P is described as a creation of the exilic or postexilic period (eighth to the fifth century BCE), and stresses Israelite ritual and religious observances. Its narratives are etiological, providing explanations for numerous functions such as circumcision (Genesis 17:9-14), dietary laws (Genesis 9:4), the Sabbath (Genesis 2:2-3). It describes in detail vestments of the high priest, the Passover ritual, the tabernacle and its furnishings, and more. Most of it is taken from far older manuscripts (J and E). P's god is more transcendent and less anthropomorphic than J's.

The books of Proverbs, Esther, and Ecclesiastes give angels little or no mention. Ezekiel, which seems to belong to the period of transition, has many problems for scholars, for redactors of his work have added "angels" where the original text talks of the actions of men. The only authentic inclusion of angels in Ezekiel is where he names various groups of celestials: Seraphim, Cherubim, Ophannim (wheels), Hayyôth (living beings), and a certain Spirit.[55]

The concept of angels being spirits is an old one. Out of this concept came the development of ghosts as angels.[56] For some faiths, ghosts became

---

[55] Ezekiel 2:2, 3:12, 9:5 and 24.

[56] Etymologically, *ghost* is linked to the German word *geist* (meaning "spirit"). The Hebrew has two words for spirit: נפש (*nephesh*) which is equivalent to "breath" and the energy of a soul (Job 11:20 and Jeremiah 15:9), which is from Persian antecedents. The New Testament offers ρνεῦμα (*pneuma*) being a form of life within the body ("spirit") which activates and sustains the body (Matthew 27:50 and John 19:30). The "Holy Ghost" is a New Testament invention that has no biblical precedence or justification in keeping with the Old Testament and other Hebraic writings. Cf. Matthew 1:18, 20; Mark 1:8; Luke 1:15, 35, 41, 67; John 1:33; Acts 1:2, 5, 8, 16; Romans 5:5; 1 Corinthians 2:13; 2 Corinthians 6:6; 1 Thessalonians 1:5, 6; Titus 3:5; Hebrews 2:4; 1 Peter 1:12; 2 Peter 1:21; Jude 20; and so forth. All evidence points that these lines were added to the original texts for impact or

the incarnation of evil. For others, ghosts represent a special spiritualism and the systematic approach to mediumship. It is this communication of intermediaries with various spirits that mediums become special entities who remain on earth to aid loved ones in various capacities. In some situations the medium's spirits reveal various truths (such as revealing who took a missing object or uncovering the nefarious plots of villains). Still others remind loved ones of the location of a misplaced object. The medium's spirits (or ghosts) are earthbound angels.[57] They include gnomes (dwarf fairies[58]),

---

instruction and have nothing in common with the actual text or message. See: *The Five Gospels: The Search for the Authentic Words of Jesus* a new translation and commentary by Robert W. Funk, Roy W. Hoover, and the Jesus Seminar (A Polebridge Press Book; New York: Macmillan Publishing Co., 1993).

[57] Rosemary Ellen Guiley, *The Encyclopedia of Ghosts and Spirits* (New York: Facts on File, 1992).

[58] Fairies were lesser spirits in ancient Arabia, and rivaled angels in kindliness, and venerated by Muhammad's tribe, the Quraysh. Fairies were considered children, and were praised as being without evil, in contrast to the desert-ranging jinn (a predominantly demonic group) who struck terror in Arab hearts as the active agents of evil. The jinn consorted with ghouls who lay in wait where men were destined to perish that they might satisfy their depraved appetite for feasting on festering human flesh in the full stage of decomposition.

gremlins, brownies, and other minor denizens of forests and wooded areas.

Gnomes are charged with maintaining the earth in an inhabitable fashion. Working with elementals and devas (an angel who works within nature), they build up forms in the natural world: dunes, natural grottos, and the like. They are under the rule of the archangel Uriel.[59]

Gremlins are technological fairies. They readily adapt to the age that is current. Throughout history they are pictured as naked beings one foot tall, green in color, with fuzzy ears and webbed feet. Today they are associated with airplanes following precedents where they held on to the wings of other angels in a successful effort to hitchhike a ride to the place they were to live and work.

Angels don't become a part of the official Hebrew/Christian pantheon until the appearance of Daniel and Zechariah. This becomes even more pronounced with the writing of the Apocrypha and Pseudepigrapha. Yet there is no general agreement.

---

Sometimes ghouls robbed graves to feast on bodies in midnight orgies; only fairies could preserve the sanctity of the grave with their own innocence.

[59] Ted Andrews, *Enchantment of the Faerie Realm: Communicate with Nature Spirits & Elementals* (St. Paul, MN: Llewellyn Publications, 1993).

Angels become a fluid force in Jubilees, Fourth Ezra, Tobit, the Testaments and the Enoch literature. Angels make scant claim for the attention and musing of the readers of Ecclesiasticus, Judith, Maccabees (I-IV), and Psalms of Solomon. An increasing divergence of opinion began to take its toll on the Hebrew people, with classes separating over belief and practice. The Sadducees were skeptical about the existence and activity of angels,[60] while other groups, especially the Essenes, made much of angels.[61] Since angels figure prominently in the Dead Sea Scrolls, those who began to decipher the scrolls erroneously concluded that the Essenes lived at Qumrân and wrote the documents.[62]

---

[60] Acts 23:8 Σαδδουκαῖοι μὲν γὰρ λέγουσι μὴ εἶναι ἀνάστασιν μήτε ἄγγελον μήτε πνεῦμα reflects the split in the Jewish community at the time.

[61] Josephus, *War of the Jews*, II.viii.7 [142].

[62] The debate over the Dead Sea Scrolls has been extensive, exhausting, and encompassing. The best account of the difficulty with the scrolls and the Essenes is Michael Baigent and Richard Leigh, *The Dead Sea Scroll Deception* (New York: Summit Books, 1991). The various works authored by John M. Allegro should also be consulted. The primary apologist for the Roman Catholic viewpoint is J. Danielou, who formulated much of his hypothesis in his *The Dead Sea Scrolls and Primitive Christianity* (Westport, CT, 1979).

Angels in Hebrew lore lived in heaven.[63] They traveled freely to earth when they wearied of living in the stars (or in some instances, as stars).[64] They were in most instances either invisible or in a fiery appearance.[65] They had superhuman powers,[66] had exceptional wisdom and insight,[67] yet were easily corrupted, and failed.[68] They appear to mortals in human form.[69] They are men who have the power of speech and articulation as men have.[70] They stand and they sit,[71] walk about,[72] eat,[73] wear

---

[63] Genesis 28:12; 1 Kings 22:19; Job 22:7; Nehemiah 9:6; cf. Deuteronomy 17:3.

[64] Genesis 32:2(1). Exodus 14:9; 23:20, 23; Job 1:7; Isaiah 6:6; Zechariah 4:1; cp. Daniel 10:10, 11.

[65] Psalm 104:4; Judges 13:20; 2 Kings 6:17; Daniel 10:6.

[66] Psalm 103:20; Genesis 19:10, 11; Judges 6:20, 21.

[67] 2 Samuel 14:17, 20; Daniel 10:21.

[68] Job 4:18 shows that the angels were not perfect.

[69] Genesis 19:1 ff. Joshua 5:3. Judges 6:11. Daniel 8:15.

[70] Joshua 5:15. Judges 6:12; 13:3, 11; 1 Kings 19:5; Zechariah 4:1, 5.

[71] Daniel 8:16; Judges 6:11.

clothes,[74] brandish weapons,[75] and even ride horses,[76] when not having sex.[77] A few had wings, although the number of wings varied according to station and religion.[78]

The angels had leaders (archangels)[79] and followers (angels) among their own kind. Angels, of

---

[72] Genesis 32:2(1); Job 2:2; Zechariah 1:10, 11.

[73] Genesis 18:8.

[74] Ezekiel 9:2; Daniel 10:5.

[75] Numbers 22:23; Joshua 5:13; 1 Chronicles 21:16, 30; Ezekiel 9:2.

[76] Zechariah 1:8, 6:1ff; cf. Revelation 9:16.

[77] Genesis 6:2, 4. Usually it was coitus with women, but occasionally the angels had sex with men as in the case of the dog-priests.

[78] *Qur'an* Al-Fātir [35]:1. Cherubim: Exodus 25:20, 37:9; 1 Kings 6:24, 27 and 8:6, 7; 2 Chronicles 3:11, 12, 13 and 5:7, 8; Ezekiel 10:16,19, 22; Revelation 9:9. Phoenix or seraphim: Ezekiel 1:4-9, 11. Cp. *Beth HaMidrash*, ed. Adolph Jellinek (6 vols.; Leipzig, 1853-1877; photostat reprint, Jerusalem, 1938), vol. 2, p. 52. *Zohar Hadash*, compiled by Abraham Halevi Berokhim (Warsaw (Levin-Epstein), no date), p. 41.

[79] The word "archangel" appears only twice in the New Testament. Once in Jude 5:6, where Michael is referred to as "the Archangel," and the second time in 1 Thessalonians 4:16

all levels, are messengers (or "ambassadors") and compose an innumerable multitude.[80] In the earlier books of the bible (extracanonical Jewish and Christian writings) only their mission is discussed. In the *Qur'an* (the Moslem bible), angels are never sent out of heaven without a purpose.[81] They are in the middle ground between the god(s) and mortals. They are to warn mortals of their sins, to detail that there is only the One True God, and to fear god.[82] They were intermediators between the god(s) and man; even in the New Testament they are considered to be the promulgators of the Law.[83]

---

where it's written "the voice of the archangel" but no specific archangel is mentioned. According to traditional angelology and Pseudo-Dionysius the Aeropagite, archangels belong to the third and lowest hierarchy of the angelic beings.

[80] Genesis 32:2; Daniel 7.

[81] *Qur'an*, Al-Hijr [15]:8.

[82] Exodus 14:31; Leviticus 19:14, 32 and 25:17; Deuteronomy 6:2, 13 (all passages denoting a reverence). In the New Testament, fear is considered a phobia or terror, and fear is coupled with "not" as in Matthew 10:31; Luke 8:50; Colossians 3:22. Both definitions are adapted in the *Qur'an*, An-Nahl [16]:2.

[83] Acts 7:53; Galatians 3:19; Hebrews 2:2.

Jesus considered them spiritual beings.[84] Yet, Jesus qualified his comments, by declaring that they would accompany him during his Second Coming.[85] The same hidden terror that this message fosters is prevalent in the *Qur'an*.[86] In both cases, this is in keeping with the ancient Hebrew tradition. Tradition holds that the angels, like the god(s) of Abraham, Isaac and Jacob, were physical entities as well as spiritual beings. They were engaged in a variety of occupations, tasks, and requirements: all of which match vocations and jobs on earth.

New Testament writers argue that angels were with Jesus at the most critical times in his life and death and pay them special attention. The angels were present at the announcement of his conception (the "incarnation")[87] and birth,[88] served as ministers when he is in the desert,[89] and when he

---

[84] Matthew 22:30.

[85] Matthew 16:27.

[86] *Qur'an* Al-Furqān [25]:22, 25.

[87] Matthew 1:20, 24.

[88] Luke 2:9-15.

[89] Matthew 4:11: τότε ἀφίησιν αὐτὸν ὁ διάβολος.

was in the garden agonizing over his destiny.[90] They are ready to defend him when he is captured,[91] and are the first witnesses to his resurrection.[92] Angels get the most attention in the *Book of Revelation*, written, allegedly, by the Apostle John. Their worship is considered a prototype for the early church, yet the rise of a cult worshipping angels was denounced by Saul of Tarsus (St. Paul) in his letter to the Church at Colossae.[93]

In what became the Old Testament and its apocrypha, the nature of angels is more precisely discussed. The authors of the Book of Isaiah[94] and Job, placed angels in choirs to praise the god(s) who made mortals. Daniel has the angels performing the god(s) work for nations and mortals.[95] It is in the canonical books that the names of three of the angels are recorded.[96] The remainder of angelology

---

[90] Luke 22:43.

[91] Matthew 26:53.

[92] Matthew 28:2-7; John 20:12 f.

[93] Colossians 2:18.

[94] Isaiah 6.

[95] Daniel 10:13, 21; and 12:1.

[96] Daniel 8:16, Gabriel; 10:13, Michael; Tobias 7:8, Raphael.

is developed in Jewish apocryphal writing, especially in the *Book of Enoch*.

In some Hebrew mythology, the archangel Michael is a priest. He offers sacrifice in the Temple in the Heavenly Jerusalem that spins in the sky above its earthly counterpart in a ring known as *Zebhul*.

A pair of angels are millers who grind grains for manna. They are in *Shehaqim*.

The gods ruling various heavens populated by angels were arrogant, cruel and totally uncertain of themselves. The deities keep a host of ministering angels in *Ma'on* to sing their praises all night. The angels fall silent with daybreak so that the gods can hear their praises sung by mortals.[97]

Other angels in ancient Hebrew myths live in more obscure heavens. They include angels who watch the stars that are storehouses of snow, ice and dew. They were known as Watchers (*'îrîn*) and are considered good angels.[98]

---

[97] Bavli (Babylonian Talmud), Hagiga 12b.

[98] Daniel 4:14, 17. The term or name "Watchers" first appears in the *Second Book of Enoch*. It is a composite of two Aramaic words: *irin* (the *ir* is actually the deity Eloah: see: *Midrash Tehillim* on *Psalm* 1; cf. Daniel 4:10, 14, 20) and *qaddishin* ("holy ones"). A better translation is "guardian angels." It is from this that the concept of celestial watch-over is created.

The Watchers were good angels. They are not like the angels in Genesis 6 who came down to earth to have sex with women in the guise of giants.

Bad angels are in the fifth heaven. They couch there in silence and agony. They remain miserable throughout eternity.

The sixth heaven is filled with angels who are astrologers and farmers. They are radiant.

The seventh heaven houses the archangels. It also contains the bulk of cherubim, seraphim, and divine wheels.[99]

Cherubim are considered to be the highest order of angels in the nine divisions.[100] They are the god(s) immediate attendants.[101] Surrounded by a strong Assyrian influence which generated the first cherubim, Old Testament cherubim guard the godhead so he doesn't hear profanity,[102] and in gratitude

---

[99] 2 *Enoch* iii-ix; cf. Louis Ginzberg, *The Legends of the Jews* (7 vols.; Philadelphia, PA: JPS, 1909-1946), vol. V., pp. 158ff.

[100] Psalm 18:11 (10); Ezekiel 9:3.

[101] J. Petersen, *Cherubim. Kurze Zusammenstellung der wichtigsten Ansichten und Erklärungen seit Luther* (1898). O. Vincent, "Les Chérubims," in *Revue Biblique* 35 (1926), pp. 328-358 and 481-495.

[102] Genesis 3:24; Ezekiel 28:14.

had representations of their likenesses crafted to set in Solomon's Temple at Jerusalem to guard the Ark of the Covenant.[103]

Myths fleshed out the cherubim. At first, they were winds that the gods of creation rode across the heavens.[104] Later, when the gods had the cherubim under their control (usually by breaking them like wild horses[105]) they appointed them to be messengers to other gods, angels, and various celestial entities.

Seven cherubim were set aside with the special distinction of living in the Sixth Heaven along with seven Phoenixes. There they spend eternity signing endless praises to the gods. They remain assembled before the Divine Throne of the Gods in ineffable light.[106] Their only pleasure is a

---

[103] Exodus 25:18-22.

[104] Psalm 18:10 and 104:3-5, cp. Proverbs 30:4; Isaiah 40:12.

[105] Psalm 65:7 speaks of the "calming force" of the gods in their riding the elements. In many ways, the taming of the cherubim can be seen as analogous to Zeus' ride on Ganymede.

[106] 2 Enoch 3-9; cf. Louis Ginzberg, *The Legends of the Jews* (7 vols.; Philadelphia, PA: JPS, 1909-1946), vol. V., pp. 158 ff.

"joyful noise" so the gods will know that they are great and good.

Seven cherubim were dispatched to Eden after Adam's expulsion. Their duty was to see that neither he nor his mate returned to the Garden. To that end they were transfigured into "the Flame of Whirling Swords" and entrusted into the hands of Michael and other angels.[107] One cherubim stood sentry before each of the seven gates[108] leading into the walled park.[109] Tall, strong and flushed red with

---

[107] Philo, *De Mundi Opif*, 60.

[108] Some records claim they only guarded two gates, but this does not fit within the Jewish concern for spiritual numbers such as seven. The argument in favor of there being only two cherubim guarding two gates is made on the assumption that the "Flaming Swords" were swastikas (fire-wheels). This, however, has come under attack as it would require the swords (swastikas) be painted on the gates as a warning to mortals that the garden lay under taboo. Some scholars of the Hitler era argue that it is on this premise that the Nazis adopted the swastikas to warn the Jews that they were unwelcome within the Third Reich. There is another argument that the cherubim were posted only at the East Gate to Eden since it was through that gate that Adam allegedly left when ordered out of the paradise. See: Genesis 3:20-24.

[109] *Beth HaMidrash*, ed. Adolph Jellinek (6 vols.; Leipzig, 1853-1877; photostat reprint, Jerusalem, 1938), vol. 2, p. 52. *Zohar Hadash*, compiled by Abraham Halevi Berokhim (Warsaw (Levin-Epstein), no date), p. 41.

fire, the cherubim gyrated and grew thick and menacing while the angels stroked him to perpetual vigilance, for the gods would not give up what they created.

We know only of one of the seven gate-keepers. He is the angel Hadraniel. Once a god, Hadrani-El was assigned to the second gate in heaven. He was an imposing sight. Sixty myriads of parasangs (2.1 million miles) tall, he was a frightening figure to face. He was the first angel to speak to Adam,[110] and he figures closely in the Moses myth. In the lore concerning Moses, Hadraniel was the angel that struck the Lawgiver speechless when he caught sight of his tremendous size and countenance. Hadraniel jarred Moses back to reality when he spoke. His voice was so strong and cutting that it penetrated through 200,000 firmaments (which, in the *Revelation of Moses*, "with every word from his [Hadraniel's] mouth goes forth 12,000 flashes of lightning"[111]) startling anyone who could hear.

---

[110] Zohar I: 55b. Cf. Yehuda Liebes, *Studies in Zohar*, translated by Arnold Schwartz, Stephanie Nakache, and Penina Peli (Albany, NY: State University of New York Press, 1993).

[111] The voice of a god being lightning is reflected in older texts, such as that of Job 37:2-3 where the keyword is אוֹר (*or*) encompassing both sound and light. Since thunder follows

Seraphim[112] are supernatural creatures, each with six wings. According to Isaiah, they are near the Throne of God, standing guard and keeping the air cooled and moving.[113]

The seraphim are monsters. They are shaped like fiery serpents and became the prototype of dragons.[114] There is no biblical or historical foundation to associate the seraphim with the cherubim, even though they are so positioned in the Preface of the Roman Mass, and in the *Te Deum*. Christians have ranked them highest in the nine orders of angels, with cherubim following second.

---

lightning the sound of it was believed to be the voice of angels.

[112] Isaiah 6:2, 6. Isaiah notes that the seraphim fly using the wings not as a propelling force, but rather to cover their face and feet. This is to hide their monstrous appearance (v. 2). The seraphim of this prophet are fire-handlers (v. 6).

[113] Isaiah 6:2-7.

[114] Numbers 21:6 ff; Deuteronomy 8:15; Isaiah 14:29, and 30:6.

Ancient fables concerning the seraphim don't agree with this ranking. Instead they are considered to be equals residing in the Seventh Heaven, along with the Archangels, Cherubim, and Divine Wheels (known as the Ophannim).[115]

The Phoenix are among the most unusual of the choirs of angels. Throughout early Jewish history and into the late European Middle Ages, sages and scholars use to ponder the labor and destiny of these strange beings of light. Two of the most frequent questions written were: "Was there a Phoenix on Noah's ark?" or "Without a Phoenix, how did Noah have light to see?"

The light of the Phoenix came from their constant closeness to the Divine Throne and to the sun. This was because a Phoenix was harnessed to a cherubim (reflecting the Pegasus legend) to pull the Sun and the Moon across the Fourth Heaven. In this instance the cherubim is seen as a brazen serpent with a face like that of a lion having a strange luminosity about their faces as lightning sparked from their eyes and teeth.

Seven Phoenix who won the favor of the gods live with seven cherubim in the Sixth Heaven

---

[115] 2 Enoch 3-9; cf. Louis Ginzberg, *The Legends of the Jews* (7 vols.; Philadelphia, PA: JPS, 1909-1946), vol. V., pp. 158 ff. Cp. Daniel 10:4-6.

where they sing with other choirs the gods' praises eternally.[116]

Other groups of angels include the Hayyôth (living beings), and a certain Spirit.[117] The Spirit is the prototype for the Holy Ghost, an addition populated and popularized by the invention of Christianity. Names of select angels don't fully appear until the writings of later books such as Daniel and Zechariah. These are enhanced in the Intertestamental period by the formation of such books as Tobit, Jubilees, Fourth Ezra, the Testaments, and the Enoch literature. They are absent in Ecclesiasticus, Wisdom, Judith, the Maccabees, and the Psalms of Solomon. The Sadducees were skeptical about the existence of angels,[118] although the Essenes were among their greatest proselytizers and advocates.[119] They figure prominently in the Dead Sea scrolls of the Qumrân

---

[116] *Ibid.* The Phoenix has no biblical support in Judaism or Christianity. Prior to the current era, they have been confused with Thrones and other angels "in the immediacy of God."

[117] Ezekiel 2:2, 3:12, 9:5 and 24.

[118] Acts 23:8.

[119] Josephus, *Bellum Judiacum* [hereafter cited with the translated English title *War of the Jews*] II.viii.7 [142].

community, which saw them as numerous beings,[120] who tirelessly sing and praise the Lord,[121] when not busy with men to whom they appear with Divine Aid.[122] The Divine Aid appears as specific angels serving as guides (as with Tobit), martial guards[123] or security agents protecting individual property[124] or nations.[125] They remain teachers,[126] and savage instruments of the divine wrath to punish transgressions that defy their god.[127] It is in this period that the "Sons of God" become clearly identified with Fallen Angels. This definition or resignation had not existed earlier, but quickly

---

[120] Enoch 40:1, 60:1, 71:8; Apocalypse of Baruch 48:10, 56:14, 59:11; Jubilees 2:18.

[121] Tobit 8:15; Enoch 61:7; Song of the Three Children 36.

[122] 2 Maccabees 11:6, 15:23; 3 Maccabees 6:18; Bel and the Dragon 34-39; Tobit 3:17; Jubilees 4:21.

[123] Jubilees 35:17. 2 Maccabees 10:29-30.

[124] 4 Maccabees 4:10.

[125] Baruch 6:7; Jubilees 15:31.

[126] Jubilees 4:15, 32:21; 4 Ezra 5:31 ff; 7:1 ff; Tobit 6:3 ff, 12:6 ff.

[127] Enoch 53:3-5, 56:1, 62:11, 63:1; Testament of Levi 3:2.

catapulted the concept of evil being a creation of a lesser god. This concept of sin gained strength.[128] It is also at this time that the most trusted and beloved Son of God, Satan, is libeled to be the chief of the Fallen Angels and the deviant planner of a heavenly rebellion. Satan is crowned with new names of disgust: Belial and Mastema,[129] names which clearly set him and the other Fallen Angels apart from the truly good angels,[130] so that the latter can be separated from the fabrication of demons.[131]

---

[128] Enoch 6-15; Jubilees 5:1, 7:21; Apocalypse of Baruch 56:11-13.

[129] *Mastema*, in Hebrew, translates as "animosity." It is also spelled Mansemat. Although he is frequently lumped in with Satan, this angel was once a god and considered the father of all evil. He is described as the Angel of Adversity (cf. Jubilees), and is the Lord who attempted to kill Moses (Exodus 4:24).

[130] Tobit 5:21; 2 Maccabees 11:6.

[131] Tobit 6:14; Jubilees 10:3; Enoch 99:7.

It is also during this time that archangels are clearly addressed.[132] Male names are given to the angels since they are defined as men, portrayed in masculine roles and occupations, and reflect the male virtues and carnal interests. Definite assignments and duties are recorded for different angels and groups of angels.[133]

In all the early legends, throughout the Torah and Talmud, and into the Qur'an (Koran) of the faithful Moslem, all angels are male.[134] While Jews and Christians feel comfortable to call upon angels to intercede for them with their god, the Moslem is cautioned against it. The Qur'an reads: "Many as the angels be in heaven their intercession will not avail in the last without Allah's [God's]

---

[132] Testament of Levi 35(a); cf. Tobit 12:15; Enoch 20:1-8, 40:2-10.

[133] Some are placed in charge of controlling nature (Jubilees 2:2; Enoch 60:14-21; 4 Ezra 8:22) while others are intercessors for man (Enoch 9:3, 15:2, 40:6, 99:3, 104:1; Tobit 12:12, 15; Testament of Daniel 6:2; Testament of Levi 5:6). This reflects the animism current in the civilization of the Middle East.

[134] Females exist only in the heaven where the saved believers go, and then only to serve men if they are "maidens with swelling breasts" (*Al Qur'ān*, An-Nabā [78]:33, cf. 31-36). These celestial maidens are known as the *houris*.

permission for whomsoever He please and approve."[135]

The issue of gender is critical to orthodox Jews, Christians and Moslems. Unanimously they agree that the angels are male in gender. While the Jews and Christians merely write as if the knowledge of the gender of angels is a given, for pious Moslems the gender issue is an article of faith for those seeking heaven. The Qur'an is specific on this point. The chapter entitled "The Star" (*An-Najm*) reads: "Those who do not believe in the Hereafter give the angels names of females."[136]

إِنَّ ٱلَّذِينَ لَا يُؤْمِنُونَ بِٱلْآخِرَةِ لَيُسَمُّونَ ٱلْمَلَٰٓئِكَةَ تَسْمِيَةَ ٱلْأُنثَىٰ

Allah [God] condemns those who believe angels are women as a feeble, mortal conjecture. It is a conjecture that will separate the learned faithful from the lax and lazy, the infidel and the ignorant. "Surely your Lord alone knows best who has strayed away from the path and who has come to guidance."[137]

---

[135] *Qur'an*, An-Najm[53]: 26.

[136] *Qur'an*, An-Najm [53]:27.

[137] *Qur'an*, An-Najm [53]:28-31b, esp. v. 30.

## Angels in Hell

Heaven isn't the only place to house angels. Hell was equally open to receiving angelic guests.[1]

---

[1] Enoch gives the most grotesque account of hell, and spells out which angels were consigned to its fiery liquid by number: "first of them [is] Semyaza, and the second Artaqifa, and the third Armen, and the fourth Kokabiel, and the fifth Turiel, and the sixth Ramiel, and the seventh Daniel, and the eighth Nuqael, and the ninth Baraqiel, and the tenth Azazel, the eleventh Armaros, the twelfth Batriel, the thirteenth Basasael, the fourteenth Ananel, the fifteenth Turiel, the sixteenth Samsiel, the seventeenth Yetarel, the eighteenth Tumiel, the nineteenth Turiel, the twentieth Rumiel, the twenty-first Azazel." *Ethiopic Book of Enoch* 69:2. Several things need to be noted in Enoch's indictment. The list is a later insertion by a zealous scribe, who repeats 6:7. In this redaction, some of the names are misspelled, others are derived from corrupt versions of other names, as is the case with the first Turiel which should have been Tamiel; Nuqael is a corruption of Ezeqiel; Azazel is corrupt for Azael; Basasael is an addition (cp. 6:7); the second Turiel should be listed as the eighteenth angel damned; Yetarel is corrupt for Satarel; Tumiel doesn't exist in the original; Rumiel is undoubtedly corrupted from Yomiel; and, the second Azazel is a corruption for והר׳אל that could be understood to mean either "light of god" or "moon of god." (The Greek edition is even more confusing, for the twentieth angel is called Σαριήλ which appears as a transliteration of שהר׳אל, than of והר׳אל. Furthermore their consignment to Hell was because of their status as *el* (god-warriors) than for any moral infraction.

To make the angels comfortable, Hell even employed a jester known as Nasr-ed-Din.

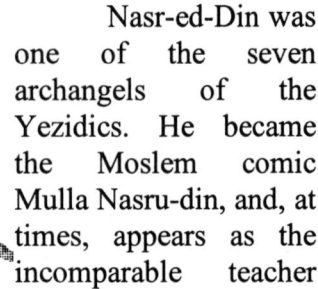

Nasr-ed-Din was one of the seven archangels of the Yezidics. He became the Moslem comic Mulla Nasru-din, and, at times, appears as the incomparable teacher Mulla Nassr Eddin. His name figures in the Koran (Qur'an), for in the Book of Noah, he is one of those whom followed "him whose wealth and children only added to his ruin. And they contrived a plot of great magnitude, And said, 'Do not abandon your gods, and do not abandon Wadda or Suwa, or Yaghuth, Ya'qu or Nasr'."[2] The punishment for their transgression was to be "drowned and sent to Hell, and ... not find any helper other than Allah."[3]

Nasr-el-Din was not alone in entertaining the angels and keeping them comfortable during their stay in Hell. Nisroc, the chief chef of Hell joined him, for Hell was to become a place where mortal delights were available but in such quantity

---

[2] *Al Qur'an*, Nūh [71]:21-23.

[3] *Ibid.*, 1, 25.

and frequency as to become painful and dreaded. Nisroc was originally an Eagle-headed deity who was of the Order of Principalities, and worshipped by Sennacherib, the ruler of Assyria (714-696 BCE).[4] When Sennacherib's troops were slaughtered by one of the angels of the god(s), Nisroc became so angry that he joined in the rebellion of his brother angels. Yahweh was cursed as a cruel, heartless, vindictive, selfish and mad monster god so heartily that Nisroc left his post as one of the guardians of the Tree of Life and Immortality.[5] When the rebellion was crushed, Nisroc was reassigned to Hell and placed in the position of feeding the Princes of Hell. To make the food of the princes most pleasant he was allowed to liberally spice their food with the fruits of the Tree of Immortality, thereby ensuring that they would live forever.

Enoch gives a different interpretation of Hell and how angels fared. They were weighted down

---

[4] Sennacherib invaded Judah in the days of Hezekiah unsuccessfully: his army was destroyed in one night. He was slain by his two sons in Nineveh in the temple of Nisroc. See: 2 Kings 18:13; 19:16, 20, 36; also, 2 Chronicles 32:1, 2, 9-10, 22; and, Isaiah 36:1, 37;17, 21, 37.

[5] Genesis 2:9. The tree of life (ה״ים : *chaiyimi*) is only one of the trees in the Garden. It is near the tree of knowledge (דעה : *daath*). This reflects the evolution of the tree of gnosis.

with an iron and brass chain.[6] They lived in a fiery furnace.[7] Dante's *Inferno* comes closest to his tale.

The Princes of Hell were seven in number. All were angels. All were male. All were warriors. And like the other angels consigned to Hell, all enjoyed sex.[8]

Baal-beryth, known originally as the Lord God of the Covenant and worshipped by the Israelites as their god,[9] was once a prince of the

---

[6] *Ethiopic Book of Enoch* 54:4, 56:1.

[7] *Ethiopic Book of Enoch* 54:6.

[8] *Ethiopic Book of Enoch* 69:4-7 ff.

[9] Judges 8:33, 9:4.

cherubim. After the rebellion he was consigned to Hell and made the Grand Pontiff and Master of all Infernal Ceremonies. He is frequently recorded in legend, as he always appeared as the counter-signatory in pacts made between mortals and devils, and mortals and demons. Baal-beryth, like all other Princes of Hell was subordinate to Dumah.

Dumah was known as the angel of the "Silence of Death." He was the guardian of Egypt, and chief demon of Gehenna. In the Old Testament, he was the son of Ishmael, son of Abraham by Hagar.[10] In reality the name comes from the deity who ruled over the city of Dumah[11] that was a part of the land holdings of the tribe of Judah.[12] He was displaced as a god and later consigned to Hell with the rise of the Yahwists and the entrenchment of Yahweh as titular god of the Hebrews.

One of the strangest Princes of Hell was Sariel. While there are claims that he was an archangel, he seldom left Hell. He was registered in Hell for the sin of teaching Canaanite priestesses the tides and courses of the moon to help them

---

[10] Genesis 25:14; 1 Chronicles 1:30.

[11] The cite of this city is doubtful; see: Isaiah 21:11.

[12] Joshua 15:52.

understand the seasons, direction of natural phenomena, and how to "enchant" the land to greater fertility. This rose a burning jealousy in the breast of the Hebrew God of the Sun who was always threatened by the Canaanite goddess of the Moon. The Hebrew god plotted to destroy Sariel and his priestesses, but Sariel learned of the Hebrew god's duplicity and evil intent and quickly slipped out of the heavens to take refuge in Hell. Once there, Sariel made Hell a delightful place for his followers, offering them *haute cuisine*, comedies and a gentler life than they knew in heaven.

Mephistopheles was grateful for the opportunity to find lodging in Hell. While he is often styled the "deceitful destroyer," this title is inappropriate. Mephistopheles name means "he who hates the light." He shunned the sun to protect his eyes that were weak. At one time he was an archangel, but he chose to leave heaven as the Sun God (Yahweh) became an intolerable bore. Still there are records that detail that he was frequently invited back to join the heavenly host in the Holy Presence. Mephistopheles is sometimes confused as being Satan. He wasn't, although he selected tasks for this great archangel when impeccable manners, an urbane disposition, a smooth and glib tongue were needed. Mephistopheles was the ultimate ambassador, the every vigilant messenger and crafty political emissary: the one being who most deserved the title angel.

Mephistopheles was instrumental in helping the prime minister of the entire Infernal Region, Rofocale, control any unruliness of its inhabitants. Rofocale eventually had complete control over Hell, all of its treasure, worldly wealth and the talents of all its angelic hosts and guest. Rofocale unreservedly called upon the talents of all angels, especially Mephistopheles and Meririm, the Prince of the Power of Air.

Meririm shared his title as Prince of the Power of Air with Lucifer. He is the angel of the Apocalypse charged with keeping the other four angels from hurting the earth and its waters until they had "sealed the servants of our god in their foreheads."[13]

Meririm's gentleness was not shared with his brother Rahab. As his name describes, this angel was "the Violent One." Originally a god of primordial waters, he took it badly when the Creator gods ordered him to give up his absolute rule and work the oceans at their demand. When they ordered Rahab to separate the waters, Rahab refused. In anger, the Creator gods destroyed him, but one of their number resurrected Rahab. This

---

[13] Revelation 7:2.

enabled Rahab to continue his good work in helping people. For instance, he appears at the time the Israelites attempt to cross the Red Sea, offering his help to the Pharaoh who wanted the migration stopped.[14] The god(s) of Moses' band became angry and destroyed him a second time for his effort. He returns as Christianity begins to blossom, this time as the Angel of Insolence and Pride.

---

[14] Rahab (רהב) is a symbolic and poetic name for Egypt and means "tumult" which is to be destroyed by the Hebrews. See: Psalm 87:4, 89:10; Isaiah 51:9. It is also the name of the Harlot of Jericho; see: Joshua 2:1, 3; 6:17, 23, 25; Hebrews 11:31; James 2:25; as well as the mother of Boaz and wife of Salmon (Matthew 1:5). In all cases, the name reflects the Hebrew concern for the sale of oneself for an immediate end, a finish coupled with evil and drenched in sin.

Some of Hell's angels are stationed in Hell so as to have less distance to travel to punish mortals who offended the Israelite god(s). Dumah, brings sudden ("silent") death. Ksiel (whose name translates as "Rigid one of God" was as merciless as Yahweh, and punished whole nations with a whip of fire. In this Lahatiel ("The Flaming One") who is the Angel of Punishment, and presides over the gates of death matches Ksiel. Lahatiel opens the gates of death after Shaftiel ("Lord of the Shadow of Death") pronounces judgment on the damned. At times he is styled as the "judge of God" and accorded absolute powers when a god becomes ungodly. Makkiel ("the Plague of God"), however, exercises most of his functions. Chitriel ("the Rod of God") joins him when they are ordered to take action from the most pitiless angel of all: Puriel ("Fiery and Pitiless Angel of God"). Puriel delights in probing and tormenting the soul. It is from the legends surrounding Puriel that many of the cruelest representations of Hell are based.[15]

Unlike in heaven, women are commonly found in all the levels of Hell. Some are special beings. They are known as Satan's Brides. They include the two angel prostitutes Agrat-bat-Mahlabt and Eisbeth Zenunim. Lilith,[16] the wild first wife of Adam who spurned both

---

[15] For example, *The Last Judgment* by Giotto, and *Inferno* by Dante.

[16] Originally, Lilith was a Mesopotamian night demon with a penchant for destroying children; when she is incorporated into *Habiru* mythology her crime is construed as attempting to dominate Adam and ruining children (usually by introducing them to masturbation) and eating them (fellatio and cunnilingus).

Yahweh and the other Creator Gods, frequently bests them and Adam to be one of Satan's favorite. By Satan, Lilith had hundreds of *lilin*: female demons. They became the succubi of Jewish and medieval Christian legend.

Lilith maintained her evil beauty and actions by engaging in forbidden oral sex, riding on top of a man who was made to assume the supine sexual position. This transgression was compounded by delighting in examining the size and breadth of his penis that she fondled in public at every opportunity.

While Lilith may be the most uninhibited wife of Satan, the one he sexually enjoyed the most was Naamah (it translates as "Pleasurable"). She was, at one time, the sister of Tubal-Cain and Noah.[17] She left them for Satan and became the mother of the great Asmodeus, and, as the fourth angel of prostitution, is accounted as the greatest seductress of both men and demons. Since there is

---

[17] Genesis 4:22 states that she is the sister of Tubal-Cain, but not the wife of Noah. Instead, she is the daughter of Zillah, wife of Lamech (son of Methusael; see: Genesis 4:19, 22-23), who descended from the lineage of Cain (c. 3874 BCE). Zillah translates as "screen" indicating some form of subtle dealings or espionage. Naamah is also a city in the southwest of Judah, near Beth-dagon bears her name (Joshua 15:41), and may have been the antecedent for her legend and consignment.

no adultery in Hell, Naamah frequently had sex beyond the confines of her marriage to Satan. He had no objections, however, welcoming the respite offered by her unexcelled promiscuity. She frequently performed her art in the company of the Jester of Hell, and at times with the arch-she-demons of Hell. The latter group includes Astarte (originally the creating and destroying goddess of the Indo-Europeans). In Egypt she is known as Athtar ("Venus in the Morning"). In Aramaic she is "The Morning Star of Heaven" which gave rise to ancient fiction that there is a woman in heaven with the stars overhead and the moon at her feet. The moniker, instead, was an indicator of power and tasks: she was the "Queen of the Stars" who ruled all dead spirits whose "astral" bodies were transformed into stars. Athtar would ultimately be desexed and transgenderized by the evolving, intolerant group known as early Christians, who made her into the Duke of Hell.

Athtar had congenial companionship in Hell. She was close to and the confidant of Proserpine, the original Greek "Queen of the Underworld." Much of Proserpine's legend comes from India. In India she is the destroying goddess Kali. Early Christians equally libeled her by declaring Proserpine as the "Queen of the She-Demons" in their opposition to any dissenting view, expression, worship or lifestyle which was generous, uninhibited, open and happy.

While Proserpine comes from a Greek background, another arch-she-demon is of a Gnostic background. This is Barbelo, the daughter of the female aeon, Pistis-Sophia who was the procreator of superior angels. Barbelo's only transgression was that she was so beautiful she outshone the Creator God. Her mother attempted to champion her daughter, and told the Creator off in very unpleasant language when he declared that he was the only true Creator. He wasn't, for without Sophia (wisdom and learning) his feeble attempts at creation would have fallen as lax as his creating rod.

In the angelology of Hell, there is one last arch-she-demon. That is the Leviathan[18] who was a coiled dragon eager to spring out and cause chaos. She was despised by Yahweh and his henchmen

---

[18] The name has various definitions, but has come to mean any formidable or monstrous creature. In the Judaeo-Christian bible, the Leviathan is a multiheaded monster defeated by Yahweh who crushed her heads (Psalm 74:13-14; Job 41). The tale of the Leviathan is originally from a Ugarit story in which the god Baal defeats a seven-headed monster with the aid of the god Mot. It was undoubtedly taken from the Babylonian myth of Marduk's defeat of the sea monster Tiamat. See: Egerton Sykes, *Who's Who: Non-Classical Mythology* (New York: Oxford University Press, 1993).

because of the beauty and glow of her fins and scales which were so bright that they obscured the rays of the sun that Yahweh delighted in riding. To keep her beauty suppressed, the gods ordered Jehoel (also spelled Jehuel, and sometimes considered to be Metatron) to "hold the Leviathan" from moving.[19] The Hebrews made the Leviathan into a great water animal (הןֹ ילןֹ).[20] Medieval Christian writers ultimately emasculate and transgenderize the Leviathan into a "king" over all children who exhibit any pride in their personal accomplishments.

In Islam, Malik is the wicked angel who guards the gates of hell. He is assisted by nineteen other angel guards known as *sbires* or *zabayniya* who show no mercy and delight in torturing the inhabitants who are sent there to suffer.

Malik delights in the sound of suffering. When his sinful residents beg him for help, he shouts that they must stay in hell forever[21] because they denied the Truth (the Koran) when it was shown to them. He then heats up the fires that were

---

[19] Gershom Scholem, *Jewish Gnosticism, Merkabah Mysticism, and Talmudic Tradition* (New York: The Jewish Theological Seminary, 1960).

[20] Job 41:1; Psalm 74:14, 104:26; Isaiah 27:1.

[21] *Al Qur'ān*, Az-Zukhruf [43]:77.

kindled by Allah[22] and makes bad jokes. The only relief that those who suffer in hell[23] have is to be able to recite the creed: "Allah, the Compassionate, the Merciful." Malik knows that those who do are true believers, who will, one day, be freed through Muhammad's intercession.[24]

---

[22] *Al Qur'ān,* Al-Humazzah [104]:6-9.

[23] Hell is to be in this world; *Al Qur'ān,* Al-Kahf [18]:101-102; Al-`Ankabūt [29]:54-55; cf. Al-Qiyāmah [75]:35-39.

[24] The Koran details that hell is not everlasting; see: *Al Qur'ān,* Hūd [11]:107-108.

56

## Angels and Sex

Sex has long been considered evil since it "distracts men from their prayers." However, in the beginning, when the adiaphora of religion came into its own (complete with myths, superstitions and assorted deceits), sex was an intricate part of religion and religious expression. Angels must be given the credit for this event.

When Adam swore never to have intercourse[1] with Eve after the death of Abel, incubi (who not only gave him dreams but nocturnal emissions and the desire to masturbate) tempted him.[2] Succubi (or *Meri'im*) seduced Eve and built in

---

[1] Vows of sexual abstinence were applauded by Christian ecclesiastics as a sign that a person wished to affiliate with the faith; such a declaration, however, was never common nor encouraged in Judaism. See: Stevan L. Davies, *The Revolt of the Widows: The Social World of the Apocryphal Acts* (London: Feffer and Sons, 1980). Augustine of Hippo wrote that no one could become a Christian until after a period of sexual abstinence, fasting, and baptism, in *Sermo* 210; cf. *Sermo* 224.

[2] *Genesis Rabba*, ed. J. Theodor and Ch. Albeck (2 vols.; Berlin, 1912-1927) p. 54. Masturbation was condemned as an act of idol worship (1 Kings 15:13; 2 Chronicles 15:16; Ezekiel 16:17; cp. Abodah Zara 44a) as it was seen as the celebration of the phallus.

her a wild abandonment and a desire for sex in its rawest form.[3]

Angels, like gods and goddess, that populate ancient scriptures loved sex. One of their number was designated to be the mentor, benefactor, guardian and intercessor for young girls. Another was the intermediary for young boys. A third listened to the prayers of women. A fourth was in charge of handling the petitions of men. None of these angels escaped the oversight of the writers of the Hebrew or Christian bibles or epigraphia.

The most colorful Angel of Carnal Knowledge appears in the story of Tamar, the wife

---

[3] One of the great problems theologians have struggled with in the case of Eve is her sexuality. Martin Luther worried that without women to take as wives, men would be bisexual. Luther concluded: "Therefore, we [men] are compelled to make use of this sex [women] in order to avoid sin." See: Martin Luther, "Lectures on Genesis," in *Luther's Works*, vol. 1, p. 116. Luther maintained these views to support his contention that woman was not man's equal (*ibid.*, p. 69). The one rare writer who understood woman, woman's sexuality, and the impact woman had on human sexuality was Hildegard of Bengin. See: Hildegard, *Causae et curae*, trans. by Peter Dronke, in *Women Writers of the Middle Ages: A Critical Study of Texts from Perpetua to Marguerite Porete* (New York: Cambridge University Press, 1984), p. 176. Women have been singled out for condemnation because of their sexuality and use of sex with the rise of patriarchies.

of Er[4] and Onan,[5] who would be the wife of Shelah.[6] Yet she conceived and bore twins to their father Judah.[7]

In the apocrypha, the tale of Tamar[8] goes beyond the pasteurized and flavored account found

---

[4] Er was slain because of unspecified wickedness (his name translates as "wicked"). See: Genesis 38:3, 6-7. Er reappears as the son of Shelah (1 Chronicles 4:21). Records indicate that Er was a tribe that had taken on some importance at least by the time of the Babylonian Captivity.

[5] Onan was the alleged second son of Judah (Genesis 38:4, 8). He was killed by his father's god(s) because of *coitus interruptus* or masturbation (the text isn't clear; see: Genesis 38:9). Both sex acts were seen as a crime against the gods and against the state as both limited the number of children that might be born who could defend the state. Onan's name, which translates as *strength*, gives a clue that Onan was more into building his body than siring a son by Tamar (an acknowledged temple whore). Extrabiblical records indicate that Onan was a tribe (like Er) that existed as a warring state. Onan disappeared when defeated by the Babylonian empire. Its armies killed off most of the soldiers of Onan. Its youth and women and young men were sold for sex within the Babylonian temples and homes of the wealthy.

[6] Genesis 38.

[7] Genesis 38:24-26.

[8] The name Tamar translates as *palm-tree*. The palm was sacred to the Love-and-Birth goddess Isis (Ishtar), who the

in the Hebrew scriptures. The apocrypha adds the required points to flesh out the New Testament: Tamar is possessed by the gift of prophecy; using this gift she sees that the Messiah will be from her loins. This prescience, more than the desire to remain in the house of Judah and have a son by her dead husband's brother, prompted Tamar to obey a more ancient Amorite law. That law required every young girl, before she married, to spend seven days outside the city gate selling herself to strangers if she was to mother a son. When she caught sight of Judah she wanted him: he was a man. He, being "righteous" refused, and passed by.[9]

---

Arabs style as Lät (or Ilät). Worship of the palm tree was centered at Nejran, where the great palm was annually draped with women's clothes and ornaments. Lät's son, Apollo of Delos, and the Nabataean god Dusares, were both born under palms (Apollo on Ortygia [Quail Island], and Dusares at Nabataean). The scarlet thread mentioned in the Genesis account is a mark of a prostitute's calling.

[9] Sex with temple prostitutes, like the *q'deshim* (dog-priests) was common in Israel from the later Judaean monarchy (1 Kings 14:12, 22:47; 2 Kings 23:7) through the time of Jesus (Revelation 22:15). Special quarters were assigned to the *kelebites* on Mount Zion. That Judah enjoyed the *q'deshim* is apparent in his offering the sacred prostitute his jewelry which was forbidden in Deuteronomy 23:18. The problem with Temple Prostitution was centered on patriarchal objections to sodomy since it failed to generate life.

Judah's refusal tore at Tamar's heart. She prayed to God to change Judah's mind. God commanded the Angel of Carnal Desire to fly down and whisper into Judah's ear to have sex with the young girl for the sake of Israel and that the people of Israel would have kings and redeemers. Because Judah was righteous, he felt his loins burn for the faith, and his religion became hard and pulsed beneath his earthly clothing. He turned and found Tamar, and had sex, but only after he assured himself that she was unmarried, an orphan, bodily pure, and a true servant of the Living God, putting out her body for righteousness and in testimony to the true faith. His strong faith pushed through any corrupt doubt until it was within the folds of religion, there to work its way until it erupted in a hozanna of praise. Tamar was made instantly pregnant.

Since Tamar conceived out-of-wedlock, she was damned to death.[10] She was given a chance to

---

[10] This inclusion antedates Deuteronomy 22:23-24 which condemns a wife or betrothed woman taken in adultery to be stoned; burning, in the Mosaic Law, is reserved for erring daughters of priests (Leviticus 21:9). Tamar was obviously not married and fell under the second prohibition. Following the evolution of chauvinism within the male population of Israel, men were not included in this prohibition, as long as the prostitutes weren't the property of a husband or father, or in a state of ritual impurity (menstruating). There was no clear

save her life by telling the Temple priests who sired her children. Tamar told no one who had fathered her children. When the twin boys were born, in a manner similar to the nativity of Jacob and Esau, Judah acknowledged his parenthood, and "continued to cheer Tamar in her widowhood" by applying the rod of salvation to her body and soul.[11] This action the angel concurred with.

---

distinction between sex with a *zonah* (lay prostitute) or a *q'deshah* (sacred prostitute). The prohibition against prostitution lay not in the act but in the intent, which was defined as the quest for or to do evil (pagan worship), and reflects the Jewish abhorrence of its neighbors whose society reflected laws coming from the days of Hammurabi (see: Code of Hammurabi paragraph 181:2). Still such worship remained through the days immediate before the appearance of Christianity (see: Hosea 4:14).

[11] Genesis 38:27-30. Genesis Rabba, ed. J. Theodor and Ch. Albeck (2 Vols.; Berlin, 1912-1927). 1042, 144; Tanhuma Buber Introd. 129; Midrash Hagadol Genesis 569, 572, 574; *Testament of Judah* 12 and 14:3-5. Bavli (Babylonian Talmud) Sota 10a-b. Cf. Arthur Frederick Ide, *Battered & Bruised: All the Women of the Old Testament* with an introduction by Decherd Turner (Las Colinas, TX: Monument Press, 1993), pp. 316-319, 427.

## Angels and Symbols

Talmudists have had a wide birth in creating numerous symbols to represent angels singular and plural. Foremost among the symbols are the Ark of the Covenant, and the various cups used to divine honesty, trust and valor.

The tale of Joseph is filled with symbols. The most graphic symbol is the cup that was hidden in Benjamin's sack.[1] It was placed in the sack to determine if his father still loved him, and because it was a common belief that the cups had guardian angels (*sare hakos*). This same metaphor is used in the Last Supper in the New Testament. As a chalice, it contained the wine that represented the blood of Jesus.[2]

---

[1] Genesis 44:2, 12, 16-17. *Genesis Rabba*, ed. J. Theodor and Ch. Albeck (2 vols.; Berlin, 1912-1927), p. 1124; *Midrash Tanhuma*, ed. Solomon Buber (Wilna, 1885; reprint, 2 vols., New York, 1946), Genesis, 203. *Sepher Hayashar*, ed. Lazarus Goldschmidt (Berlin, 1923), p. 186.

[2] Matthew 26:27; Mark 14:23; Luke 22:20; John 18:11 makes it emphatic that the cup was personally given to Jesus by his spiritual father. Legend records that the cup (known as the Holy Grail: a corruption of *cratella* being a bowl) was later used by Joseph of Arimathea to collect drops of Jesus' blood when the latter was crucified. Because the keepers of the cup were morally impure, angels were sent to earth to retrieve it.

Inheritance was determined by the amount placed in a cup,[3] as cups were vessels of Lords, gods and angels.[4] Being the chalices of divinities, those who drank from cups were granted salvation:[5] political,[6] spiritual,[7] personal,[8] legal;[9] as well as fury, vengeance[10] and cruelty.[11] Such cups had wings.

---

[3] Psalm 16:5.

[4] Psalm 75:8.

[5] Psalm 116:13.

[6] Genesis 40:11. Nehemiah 1:11.

[7] Matthew 20:23.

[8] Matthew 26:39.

[9] 2 Samuel 12:3.

[10] Ezekiel 23:33.

[11] Jeremiah 25:15. Isaiah 51:17. Zechariah 12:2. The wings symbolized the cups belonged to angels and gods.

## Angel of the Lord

People of all civilizations see themselves as unique. It is common throughout the world's religious literature that they are "the chosen people" of a god/dess. The ancient Jews made much of this concept in an effort to leaf a special patina on their troubled status in the Middle East. An entire mythology was developed around their being chosen by a tribal deity, and the announcement of their election being sent by the "Angel of the Lord."

The "Angel of the Lord" figures prominently in major Judaeo-Christian accounts. He is the one who has the special mission to protect Israel as a people, and stays the hands of Abraham from slaying his son Isaac in a sacrifice demanded by his god.[1] The same angel-god appears in Jacob's dream when he sees a ladder descend from heaven so that angels can climb up and down it without purpose or reason.[2] In the account of Moses, the "Angel of the Lord" appears "in the shape of a flame of fire" in a burning bush.[3] Moments later, when Moses turns

---

[1] Genesis 22:11.

[2] Genesis 28:12.

[3] Exodus 3:2.

aside, the god of the burning bush addresses Moses, proclaiming in muted words that he and the angel are one.[4] And the "Angel of the Lord" leads the Children of Israel through the "Red Sea,"[5] and appears to Balaam,[6] Joshua,[7] Gideon,[8] the parents of Samson,[9] and more.

This "Angel of the Lord" had powers nearly (if not totally, according to some accounts) equal to the deity (Yahweh), and played a major role both in heaven[10] and on earth.[11] His task was to be the personal representative of the god of the Hebrews, and in many ways had the powers of an Egyptian

---

[4] Exodus 3:4, 6.

[5] Exodus 14:19. There is cause to consider that the Angel of the Lord was created to clear the God-figure (God the Father) of all humanness. This would take away from the God Father all need to stand accountable for human suffering.

[6] Numbers 22:5-10 ff.

[7] Joshua 1:1, 3:7.

[8] Judges 6:22.

[9] Judges 13:3-22 ff.

[10] Zechariah 3:1 ff.

[11] Judges 6:11 ff.

ambassador.[12] Sometimes the angel appears in human form.[13]

The Angel of the Lord's human shape comes in regard to his earthly duties and responsibilities. His duties are both civil and military. He pronounces divine judgment,[14] and inflicts punishment on those who have displeased the god or his earthly representative(s),[15] when not defending the faithful from those who worship different than they.[16] This angel, like all angels, didn't receive a specific name or acquire a unique personality. It comes only in the Book of Daniel.[17]

While later-day Jews and Christians argue that the Angel of the Lord is a messenger for their god, their Bible doesn't support their claim. On the

---

[12] Isaiah 63:9 ff.

[13] Genesis 16:7-13; 22:11 ff. Exodus 3:2. Numbers 22:22 ff. Judges 6:11 ff; 13:3 ff. 2 Kings 1:3, 15.

[14] 2 Samuel 14:17; 19:27. Zechariah 3:1 ff.

[15] 2 Samuel 24:16. Cf. Numbers 22:22 ff.

[16] 2 Kings 19:35. Psalm 34:7; 35:5 f.

[17] Gabriel acquires human form in Daniel 8:16 and 9:21; Michael becomes a military captain and fights "the angel of Persia" in Daniel 10:13, 21 and 12:1.

contrary, the Bible clearly shows that the Angel of the Lord is equal to the deity Yahweh.[18] The Angel of the Lord frequently preceded Yahweh's visits to Earth. He met with Abraham before Sarah was impregnated by the Angel of Fertility, and with Lot before Sodom was destroyed. He was always cloaked and his face hidden, as was Yahweh's. The argument concerning this hiding is that both faces were so hideous (filled with fire) that no one dared look upon it/them lest he be consumed in that fire. To visually see the face of the Angel of the Lord is as dangerous as any attempt to look upon the "face of god [Yahweh]."[19]

What is unique about the fear of seeing the "face of god" is that it has distinct druid antecedents. In all instances, when the Angel of the Lord or Yahweh himself appears, they do it under or near a sacred oak or terebinth tree. For example, Yahweh (or, more probably the Angel of the Lord) appeared to Abraham at the oracular oak (or terebinth) of Shechem, where, after the meeting, Abraham built an altar in honor of the Divine Person.[20] This occurred, again, beside the oaks or

---

[18] Genesis 16:7-13. Zechariah 3:1 ff.

[19] Judges 6:22 f; 13:21 f.

[20] Genesis 12:1-12.

terebinth of Mamre at Hebron, and another altar was erected once the "three men" had eaten and rested "under the tree" before proceeding to Sodom.[21] So too, it happened at the hamlet of Ophrah in Manasseh,[22] and other areas protected by oaks, as trees were sacred from the earliest days when Yahweh's wife's image was carved out of oak.[23]

---

[21] Genesis 18-1-4 ff.

[22] Judges 6:11, 24 ff.

[23] The impact and significance of the polytheistic nature of ancient Judaism is lost in the contemporary rush to maintain its rubric that it is a monotheistic faith. In part this is substantiated by modern translations of אשׁירה (*asherah*) into the word "grove." This is patently wrong. At best the word *asherah* must be translated as "shrine," with the proviso that the shrine and its sacred phallic pillars (Deuteronomy 12:3. Cp. 1 Kings 14:15, 23; 15:13; 2 Kings 17:10) were frequently in a grove. The ancient Hebrews worshipped Yahweh's wife openly until wide-eyed bellowing prophets charged the groves and had them hewed down (Exodus 34:13; Deuteronomy 7:5; Judges 6:25, 28; 2 Kings 23:14-15; 2 Chronicles 14:3 and 31:1, 3, 19; and so forth). This was because the groves were considered places of sexual excesses and sinful sexual acts (Judges 3:7; 2 Kings 18:4) including ritual sodomy and the use of dildos (sexual stimulating toys). See: Arthur Frederick Ide, *Yahweh's Wife: Sex in the Evolution of Monotheism; A Study of Yahweh, Asherah, Ritual Sodomy and Temple Prostitution* (Las Colinas, TX: Monument Press, 1991. For a vignette on

Because early redactors created the Angel of the Lord as an equal to Yahweh, later scribes had to soften their arguments. They did this by articulating a strange and foreign concept that the Angel was only a messenger and then only delivered the message that the deity determined.[24] This novel idea became a hallmark of the Hebrews and was ultimately defined as "corporate personality." This means that the might and authority of the Angel of the Lord was subject to the deity since the Angel was nothing more or less than an extension of the personality of the godhead.[25]

---

the worship of the oak tree by ancient Israel, see: James G. Frazer, *Folklore in the Old Testament; Studies in Comparative Religion, Legend and Law* (New York: Macmillan, 1923; reissued by: New York: Avenel Books, 1988), p. 333. The issue of the Tree is covered generously in Ioan P. Couliano, *The Tree of Gnosis: Gnostic Mythology from Early Christianity to Modern Nihilism*, translated into English by H. S. Wiesner (San Francisco, CA: HarperSanFrancisco, 1992), pp. 77, 111, 113, 136, 162, 164, 175-176, 210 ff.

[24] Genesis 48:15 f. Hosea 12:4. Zechariah 12:8.

[25] A. R. Johnson, *The One and the Many in the Israelite Conception of God* (2d ed.; 1961), pp. 28 ff.

## Archangels

History knows archangels as Angel Princes. They were the sons of the gods and stood to inherit their fathers' thrones. Frequently impatient, they warred against their fathers, tumbling some from the high daises on which they sat; at other times losing and being banished from the Great Garden in which the thrones were placed,[1] or on mountain tops where they preferred to reside.[2]

Unlike angels, archangels were not ministers. They were guardians of their fathers' thrones. In Hebrew lore, there are four primary guardian archangels: Michael, Raphael, Gabriel, and Uriel.

All of the four primary guardian archangels are gods. This is seen in the root of their names (אל: *el*) Micha-El, Rapha-El, Gabri-El, and Uri-El. El translates as "Mighty."[3] It indicates martial and

---

[1] Ezekiel 28:13.

[2] Exodus 3:4; Ezekiel 28:14.

[3] The title *El* has a complex etymological history. In Sumerian, it means "brightness" or "shining." In Akkadian (spelled *Ilu*) it means "radiant one." In Babylonian (spelled *Ellu*), it translates as "shining one." It has numerous non-Middle Eastern similarities, but there is no evidence to point to their dating nor to the direction the term took: from or to the

personal strength and command of loyalty. Thus each of the four archangels had his separate band of followers, and priests who worshipped him as "the Most High God" or "the Mighty God." Yet the archangels could never rest easy, worrying that their worshippers wouldn't stay true to them, for mortals are fickle and change deities easily. Especially if they assume that there is a mightier god with a stronger army of avenging angels.[4]

---

Middle East (for example, Old Welsh is *Ellu* and translates as "a shining being"). What is common among all ancient languages is that it was used only in reference to a deity who had power equal to any other god. Since their powers were equal, one would make war upon another god, and if the aggressor was successful, he would banish his foe by throwing him out of his house (the term in this regard is "fall from heaven"). For the Jews heaven was defined as anything "thrown up" (such as a fort, or a structure built high on a mountain so that it appeared to be built within the clouds). Similarities exist in other religions, such as with the Greeks looking to Mount Olympus as the home of their gods (who were originally superior warriors).

[4] Exodus 15:11. Monotheism comes late to the Hebrews, migrating to Judaism only through the original monotheism preached by Zoroaster (c. 1000 BCE). It is not a part of the Torah until after Exodus 34:14, yet the Hebrews continued to slip back into the worship of various gods between that uncertain date and the coming of the Romans (cf. Jeremiah 10:11; Daniel 2:11; 2 Kings 1:1-3; and so forth). The Egyptians considered monotheism much earlier.

Because the father gods didn't trust their angel-princes, the angel-princes were kept within the *pargod* (veil) where the patriarchs sat. All others had to petition these distant potentates while standing outside the veil.[5]

The primary guardian archangels had three other brothers. Their combined number corresponds to the seven *Amshaspands* of ancient Persia. The Amshaspands were fashioned after the seven Babylonian gods of the planets. Their names change frequently, in keeping with their particular functions.[6] For example, when the star of Marduk is in the zenith, he is called Ninib.[7] Micha-El, Gabri-El, Rapha-El, and Uri-El's brothers are named Metatron, Sandalphon, and Rediyao.[8] When they are together they have a definite place to stand near the throne. Michael stands to the right; he is the

---

[5] Hagigah 5b. Pirqe de Rabbi Eliezer, chapter 4.

[6] Genesis Rabba, 78.

[7] A, Jeremias, *Das alte Testament in Lichte des alten Orients* (1904), p. 78.

[8] There is debate over whether or not the seven is an absolute number. There are other claimants for the position of archangel. These include Ana-El, , Ragu-El, and Razi-El, Remi-El, and Sari-El. They are discussed in a separate chapter entitled: "The Other Archangels."

titular angel of Israel and must intercede for it.[9] Gabriel stands to the left.[10] Uriel stands in front of the throne. Raphael stands behind the throne.[11] Metatron, Sandalphon and Rediyao are allowed to be near them. Each of these brothers is discussed in separate chapters in this book.

In the Zoroastrian religion, there are six archangels. They are:

Ameretat.........Immortality
Armaiti...........Piety (or Harmony)
Asha ...............Righteousness (or Truth)
Haurvatat........Prosperity (or Salvation)

---

[9] Yoma 77a. While the Hebrews have considered themselves to be a chosen people, set aside by their god from other mortals, they acknowledge that all other nations equally have guardian angels. Uza is the guardian angel for Egypt (see: Midrash Abkir, quoted in Yalkut, § 241); of course, when a guardian angel protecting other nations is in dispute with Michael, the lesser angel always loses.

[10] In Moslem lore and tradition, Gabriel is their national angel. He is also the angel of revelation who brought the Qur'an to Muhammad (see: *Al Qur'an*, Al-Baqarah [2]:97), and thus they place him, not Michael, to the right hand of god (Allah) where he intercedes for sinners (see: *Al Qur'an*, At-Tahrīm [66]:4).

[11] Numbers Rabba 2.

Kshathra..........Power (or Rulership)
Vohu Manah...Good Thought (or Good Sense)

Sometimes this list is supplemented by a seventh: Saraosha. Saraosha is the patron and protector of Obedience.[12] Collectively these archangels are known as Amesha Spentas (Holy Immortals).[13]

Originally, Zoroaster regarded these beings as aspects of Ahura Mazda himself. He defined his theology concerning the archangels based on personal experiences, claiming that he was visited by Vohu Manah, who came to him in a form nine times larger than an ordinary person was and revealed the angelic history to him.

After questioning the future prophet, Vohu Manah invited Zoroaster to lay aside the "vesture" of his human body. This done, the archangel led Zoroaster's spirit into the heaven occupied by Ahura

---

[12] Saraosha is known in Zoroastrian theology as the Angel of Judgment. The dead are placed under his care, and the ultimate sentence is to be in his presence.

[13] Norman Cohn, *Cosmos, Chaos and the World to Come: The Ancient Roots of Apocalyptic Faith* (New Haven, CT: Yale University Press, 1993). Cf. John B. Noss, *Man's Religions* (3rd edition; New York: Macmillan, 1969), pp. 467-480. Cp. *The Zend Avesta*, translated by J. Darmesteter (Sacred Books of the East series, vol. 23; Oxford, UK: Clarendon Press, 1883).

Mazda who was seated on a throne,[14] holding court with his angels.[15] Seeing Zoroaster, the god began to teach the prophet the principles of the True Religion that would become Zoroastrianism. Zoroaster studied under Ahura Mazda for eight years, during which time he had a visionary experience with each of the archangels.[16] These experiences allowed him to fill out the initial revelation into a complete religious system and bring monotheism into the world.[17]

---

[14] A. V. Williams Jackson, *Zoroaster, the Prophet of Ancient Iran* (New York: Columbia University Press, 1898), p. 41.

[15] Like the gods of the Old Testament, Ahura Mazda was supreme but not unopposed. Nor were his angels. Cf. Yasna 30:3-5, 45:2. Cp. James Hope Moulton, *Early Zoroastrianism* (London: Constable and Company, for Hilbert Trust, 1913), pp. 349, 370.

[16] Yasna 43:7 f.

[17] Yasna 44:3-7. Like other prophets, Zoroaster wasn't successful in his initial missionary preaching. Not until he had spent ten years in the streets did he win his first convert: his own cousin Maidhynimaonha, Soon afterwards he was in the court of an Aryan prince by the name of Vishtaspa (in some accounts it is spelled Hystaspes), who may have been the father of Darius, satrap of Parthia. Vishtaspa was dominated by the Karpans, a greedy throng of priests detested in the Avesta, because of their numerous animal sacrifices, magical procedures, and incantations. In the end Zoroaster won the

ruler to his cause and faith, after surviving a period in prison for angering the Karpans. What convinced the ruler was Zoroaster's cure of his favorite black horse, and the intercessions of his consort Hutaosa. Once converted to the faith of Zoroaster, Vishtaspa put his full power behind the propagation of the faith, taking his entire court into the new religion. The religion of Zoroaster continued to thrive, even after a Turanian nomad murdered Zoroaster at the age of 77, as he was officiating before the fire-altar.

    The faith of Zoroaster thrived because of its antecedents. It evolved out of ancient Persian theology that was centered on the worship of *devas* ("shining ones"). The *devas* were angels. This faith in angels was the backbone of the religion of the Hittites as seen in inscriptions they left c. 1400-1300 CE. The inscriptions became the foundation for the Zoroastrian (and subsequent religions) sacramental use of intoxicating beverages (prepared from the sacred *haoma* plant, which came initially from the Vedic *soma*). Much of Zoroastrianism is incorporated into Christianity, especially the use of sacramental wine, unquestioning faith, the existence of good and evil angels and the pursuit of elusive ethics and unrealistic moral codes. In Zoroastrianism, as in Judaism, Christianity and Islam, there exists a strong belief that the founder of the religion was specifically called by a god to disseminate revealed truths of a supreme god, but not a god who went without challenges. Because of the challenges there would be a judgment day and ultimate cleansing of people and a final war between the Good Spirit (in Zoroastrianism, he is known as Spenta Mainyu) and the Evil (or Bad) Spirit (known in Zoroastrianism as Angra Mainyu). In all cases these spirits are angels.

78

# Michael

Michael frequently acts for the gods. At times he has been considered a god. His name is his commission, as Michael translates: "he who is like god."

Michael appears by name only five times in the Judaeo-Christian bible. He also plays an important part in the apocryphal literature of both faiths,[1] where he is "the great captain" "who is set over the best part of mankind." Because of this, Michael was declared to be a helper of Christian armies battling against heathens and apostates. He was among the first "saints" called upon as a protector of individual Christians against the Devil, especially at the time a Christian approached death.[2] With the ascendancy of Christianity, Michael was worshipped as a near-god, and a cult mushroomed[3]

---

[1] The Assumption of Moses; Enoch; Ascension of Isaiah.

[2] Michael still appears in the Offertory of the Roman Mass for the Dead: *Signifer S. Michael repraesentet eas in lucem sanctam*. His official biography is in the *Acta Sanctorum* (Antwerp, 1643 ff), vol. 8 (1762), pp. 4-123.

[3] The cult of St. Michael received a significant impetus by the famous apparition on Mt. Garganus in the time of Pope Gelasius (492-496 CE). His veneration was highest in the

from its origin in Phrygia and spread into the West, winning for himself a basilica on the Via Salaria.[4] In each biblical reference he is a messenger of one of the tribal gods of the Hebrews. For example, Michael was sent to visit Daniel who addressed the angel as one of the chief princes of the people.[5]

Daniel's emphasis on Michael being the ultimate celestial being who will intercede for "the children of thy people" and awaken "many of them that sleep in the dust of the earth ... some to

---

West during the Middle Ages, in part because of the iconography surrounding him. He is usually represented holding a drawn sword while he is standing over or fighting with a dragon. See: O. Rojdestvensky, *Le Culte de St. Michel et le moyen-âge latin* (Paris, 1922); A. M. Renner, *Der Erzengel Michael in der Geistes- und Kuntstgeschichte* (Saarbrücken, 1927).

[4] He is named, for example, in the Leonine Sacramentary St. Michael in four of five Masses for 30 September. His feast is kept throughout the Christian Church on 29 September, which is identical with the Book of Common Prayer in the Anglican Communion of St. Michael and All Angels.

[5] Daniel 10:13, 21. There is no historic evidence for the existence of a Daniel, or of the furnace. It's a reference to the forced migration of Jews c. 597 BCE. The text is a copy of "The Tale of Aqhat" (where the Canaanite Dan'il struggled), preserved among fourteenth century BCE texts at Ras Shamra (Ugarit) in Syria.

everlasting life, and some to shame and everlasting contempt,"[6] follows the Zoroastrian text concerning the god/angel Saoshyant. Saoshyant is described as the future "helper of the good." It will be Saoshyant "who makes the evil spirit impotent, and causes the resurrection [and] future existence."[7]

Michael is seen as an ultimate messiah: a warrior prince who will defend his people against those who would oppress them.[8] The violent side of Michael is glorified in the Ethiopic rendering of Enoch. In the Ethiopic Enoch, Michael, along with Gabriel, Raphael, and Phanuel (Uriel?) will be in the lead in throwing Azazel and his hosts ("servants of Satan") out of heaven and into a burning furnace after being judged by the Chosen One.[9] The senior god/angel vowed he would delight in seeing pain in

---

[6] Daniel 12:2-3. Daniel is seen as one who "fears God" and works for the glory of heaven in early Christian writings; see: *Letter of the Romans to the Corinthians* (*First Clement*) 45:6.

[7] Bundahish 11:6.

[8] Daniel 12:1.

[9]*The Ethiopic Book of Enoch; A New Edition in the Light of the Aramaic Dead Sea Fragments*, collected by Michael A. Knibb in consultation with Edward Ullendorff (Oxford: Clarendon Press, 1978), vol. 1: Text and Apparatus, 54:1-10. Hereafter this work is cited as *Ethiopic Book of Enoch*, with all quotes taken from vol. 1: Text and Apparatus.

the faces of the punished angels.[10] This punishment will be intensified by "angels of punishment" who will use "chains of bronze and iron" to torture their brothers.[11]

This violent side of the archangel carries over into the New Testament. The author of the letter of Jude has Michael "contending" with the Devil,[12] while the authors of Revelation have the archangel in battle against a dragon.[13]

In rabbinical teachings, Michael is a priest at the altar of the gods in the Heavenly Jerusalem. Before the altar he offers sacrifices.[14] Michael's close relationship with the gods of creation is stressed in the account of the making of Adam. The gods who fashioned the first man wanted their creature to come from the purest of dust. Since there was no truly pure dust in the area they had set aside for their great park (*gan Eden*), they called up Michael to bring them dust from the site of their

---

[10] *Ethiopic Book of Enoch* 55:3.

[11] *Ethiopic Book of Enoch* 56:1.

[12] Jude 9.

[13] Revelation 12.7-9.

[14] Bavli (Babylonian Talmud) Hagiga 12b.

sanctuary.[15] In another version, emphasizing that the gods were lazy, the Creator gods didn't want to be bothered with the rudimentary tasks of creating mortals. When they discovered that they would need dust to complete their magic trick, they didn't want to be bothered fetching it for themselves. To this end, they sent Michael to Mount Moriah,[16] to gather the "dust" they would use to create man.[17]

---

[15] Genesis Rabba, ed. J. Theodor and Ch. Albeck (2 vols.; Berlin, 1912-1927), p. 132. Midrash Hagadol, Genesis, p. 73; Numbers Rabba 4:8; Midrash Tehillim, p. 92; Seder Eliyahu Zuta, p. 173.

[16] Midrash Konen, 27 (printed in *Beth HaMidrash*, ed. Adolph Jellink (6 vols.; Leipzig, 1853-1877; photostat reprint, Jerusalem, 1938) vol. 2, pp. 23-39). Yerahme'el: [*The Chronicles of Jerusalem*], trans. Moses Gaster (London, Oriental Translation Fund, 1899), p. 15. Louis Ginzberg, *Legends of the Jews* (7 vols.; Philadelphia: JPS [Jewish Publication Society], 1909-1946), vol. I, p. 54, vol. V, pp. 71-72. There is an overlapping of Judaic and Christian Michaelology; see: W. Lueken, *Michael* (Eine Darstellung und Vergleichung der jüdischen und der morgenländisch-christlichen Tradition vom Erzengel Michael, 1898).

[17] While a literal reading of an English translation of the Old Testament defines "man" as male, it isn't the case in a more careful reading until after the Midrashes were composed. What is unique in this situation is the redactors comment that the gods of yore saw Adam as far more beautiful than Eve. This led to an *apologia* that man is "by nature" better looking

Once Michael was gone, they reflected on their choice. They were uncertain that Michael could be fully trusted. To make sure that they had the required dust, they dispatched Gabriel to the Four Corners of the world (the earth was seen as a large table).[18] When Michael learned of the duplicity and selfishness of the gods,[19] he turned against Gabriel for giving in to the deities. In still another account, Yahweh sent Michael to Mount Moriah and Gabriel to the four corners of the world. Neither archangel was successful in wrestling the dust from Mother Earth. She fought valiantly, afraid that she would be displaced as a goddess if Yahweh would be able to create a mortal. This forced the lazy Yahweh to, reluctantly, retrieve the dust with his own hand.[20]

---

than is any woman. See: Bavli (Babylonian Talmud) Baba Bathra, 58a; and Leviticus. Raba (Wilna, 1884), 20:2.

[18] *Ibid.*; Babylonian Sanhedrin 38a-6.

[19] *Pirqe Rabbi Eliezer*, chap. 11.

[20] Midrash Konen, p. 27; Yerahme'el, p. 15; Louis Ginzberg, *The Legends of the Jews* (7 vols.; Philadelphia: Jewish Publication Society, 1909-1946), vol. 1, p. 54; vol. 5, p. 71, 72. Both the Moslems and the Christians had problems with the accounts on the creation of Adam since their early apologists had little or no knowledge of the Hebrew. The Moslems have his creation the result of a fetch for soil by four angels: Gabriel, Michael, Israfil and Azrail, each who was sent

Michael had a unique role in the birthing process of Cain and Abel.[21] He was sent to comfort Eve by the Creator gods and led a company of twelve angels and two Virtues to her side. Once at her side, Michael was startled at the agony she was experiencing in giving birth to the first children. Uncertain what to do, he stroked her face and breast until she gave birth.[22] Michael also assisted in the birth of Isaac, traveling with Yahweh, Gabriel and Raphael in the disguise of Arab wayfarers.

---

to a different corner of the world. On the creation of Adam, see: *Qur'an*, Al-Baqarah [2]:30-39.

[21] The Cain and Able myth can be dated back to ancient Egypt. It is a retelling of the struggle between two Egyptian gods: Osiris and Seth. Osiris is a god of vegetation and agriculture. Seth is a god of the wilderness and destruction. The death and subsequent burial of Osiris matches that of the Old Testament. See: H. Te Velde, *Seth: God of Confusion* (Probleme der Ägyptologie 6; Leiden, E. J. Brill, 1967). Cp. Eberhard Otto, *Osiris und Amun: Kult und heilige Stätten* (Munich: Hirmer, 1966), pp. 11-65. There are also arguments identifying Cain with Satan (1 John 3:12), the wicked angel Sammael (Targum Pseudo-Jonathan on Genesis 4:1 and 5-3), even the serpent in the Garden (4 Maccabees 18:8). Much of this is centered around the confusion of his wife (cf. Jubilees 4:9) since her name, Awan, means "wickedness."

[22] *Vita Adae et Evae* in *The Apocrypha and Pseudepigrapha of the Old Testament*, ed. R. H. Charles, vol. 2, pp. 123 ff.

Michael's required duty was to announce the infant's birth.[23] He was also involved in the gestation and birthing of Jacob.[24]

Another duty Michael was given was to care for the dead. He was responsible for protecting the corpse of Abel and ultimately burying it beside the remains of Adam (which I discuss later), and he was charged with fetching the soul of Abraham as he would Moses. In this regard many saw Michael as the archangel of death. But in each case, the mortal whose soul he was to retrieve fought the celestial warrior, and ultimately tricked him into letting him see the world. Abraham was the most reluctant to die. He demanded that Michael let him ride a chariot drawn by cherubim across the sky. The gods agreed. But after the ride, Abraham still refused to yield up his soul. At that point, the gods tired, and removed Michael from his obligation and summoned the real Angel of Death to carry off the soul of Abraham. While the records all note that the Angel of Death is hideous, he is a beautiful young boy with flashing eyes and a gentle smile and

---

[23] Tanhuma Buber Genesis 85-86. Bavli (Babylonian Talmud) Baba Metzia 86b.

[24] Yalqut Genesis 110. Bereshit Rabbati 103. Tanhuma Buber Deuteronomy 35-36. Tanhuma Ki Tetze, chapter 4.

blemish-free body who arrives to retrieve the soul. Michael only announces the youth's coming. The actual passage occurs when the youth is his most beautiful self and clasps the hand of the dying to renew in the dying a "lusty life and strength."[25]

In more exotic rabbinical writings, Michael will join forces with the archangel Gabriel and battle the Leviathan[26] and Behemoth.[27] Neither will be victorious. Their failure will, it is written, force Yahweh to finally take action and dispatch them.[28]

---

[25] *Testament of Abraham*; see: G. H. Box, *The Testament of Abraham, Isaac and Jacob* (1927).

[26] The Leviathan was supposedly a great water animal (Job 41:1) that had more than one head (Psalm 74:14), and plays in the waters that are capable of floating ships (Psalm 104:26). It was considered to be a "piercing serpent" (Isaiah 27:1) and not to be trouble. Since the Leviathan was a monster and evil, all male writers concluded that it was a female; see *Ethiopic Book of Enoch* 60:7.

[27] The Behemoth was a large animal, probably a hippopotamus, or even an elephant. It is recorded only in Job 40:15, giving credulity to the former since Job places it in Uz (in northern Arabia) and thus closer to either animal's home; cf. the *Ethiopic Book of Enoch* 60:8. Enoch saw some redeeming qualities in the Behemoth and decided it had to be a male, and thus concluded it was also angelic in origin.

[28] Pesiqta di Rabbi Kahana, 29, 188a-b. Midrash Alphabetot 98. Louis Ginzberg, *The Legends of the Jews* (7 vols.;

Michael wasn't a total loss as a warrior. He won Yahweh's attention by quickly obeying the god's order that the entire host of heaven was to worship the Man, while Samael refused. Hearing of Samael's refusal, Michael was empowered to fling Samael out of heaven and down to the earth where the fallen angel continued to scheme against Yahweh.[29] To stem Samael's growing power, Michael was commissioned a special archangel with power to war against the Cosmocrator. He did this in the same way that Nabu in Babylon and Thoth in Egypt waged war against evil. But the story of Michael goes further. It is more in keeping with the Greek account of Hermes (Mercury) who had the same planetary power and rescued Zeus from the rebel Typhon in their struggle on Mount Saphon. This account is an antecedent to Jacob's wrestling the god-angel at Beth-El.

Samael won, in part, by seducing Cain into killing Abel, which commissioned Michael anew. Michael triumphed over Samael by removing the corpse of Abel that Mother Earth refused to accept

---

Philadelphia: Jewish Publication Society, 1909-1946), vol. 5, p. 43.

[29] *Vitae Adae et Evae* 13:1-16 (see: *The Apocrypha and Pseudepigrapha of the Old Testament*, ed. R. H. Charles, vol. 2, pp. 123ff.); cf. Hebrews 1:6, Revelation 12:7-9 and 20:1-7.

until the dust that made Adam was returned to her. He placed Abel's cadaver on a rock where it remained for many years uncorrupted: a testament to Cain's dastardly deed. Only after Adam died did Michael with Gabriel, Uriel and Raphael rescue the body of the slain youth and take it, with Adam's corpse, to Hebron. There they laid the two together in an unmapped field and buried them together.[30]

Michael's reputation as a warrior was enhanced with the advent of Christianity. Based on apocryphal literature, especially the *Ascension of Isaiah*,[31] where Michael appears as "the great

---

[30] *Apocalypse of Moses*, ed. R. H. Charles, in *The Apocrypha and Pseudepigrapha of the Old Testament* xi. *Die Apokryphischen Gnostischen Adamschriften*. Aus dem Armenischen übersetzt und untersucht von Erwin Preuschen (Giessen, 1900), p. 22.

[31] A second century CE compilation of the Jewish *Martyrdom of Isaiah* and the Christian *Vision of Isaiah* merged with the Christian *Testament of Hezekiah*, was originally written in Greek but exists today only in Ethiopic, and in part in Latin. It elaborates on the martyrdom of being "sawn apart," liberally borrowing from Hebrews 11:37 and the prophet's soul's travel through the glories of the seven heavens where he sees the dazzling mysteries relating to Christ and the Christian church. While it is the oldest document to explicitly refer to the martyrdom of Peter at Rome (iv, 3), it introduces such novelties as the Trinity, Incarnation, and Resurrection. Origin cites it in his *Commentary on Matthew 13:57*, and it is mentioned in the *Apostolic Constitutions* (6;16), and

captain," the archangel was regarded in the early Church as a helper of Christian armies against heathens, and as a protector against the devil, especially at the hour of death. Michael, in fact, becomes the Angel of Death, although there is no ancient foundation for such a transmogrification of duties or title. This prostitution of historical record is canonized in the Offertory of the Roman Mass for the Dead that reads: *Signifer S. Michael repraesentet eas in lucem sanctam.*

Not only did Michael take care of the dead, but also was in charge of watching over the living born to the dead. When Dinah was pregnant and bore Shechem a posthumous daughter, her brothers wanted to kill the child. This was in keeping with custom. Jacob would not permit her slaughter, and hung a silver disk around her neck. On the disk were the words "Holy to God." Taking the infant up, like a female Moses, Jacob laid her under a thorn bush. Because of this the child's name became Asenath (thorn bush). When the child was hidden, Michael flew down in the shape of an eagle and captured the child, and ascending with her, flew to

---

Epiphanius, *Haer.* (40:2). Michael's cult originated in Phrygia where he was venerated as a healer on par with the Greek god Mercury. He became a part of western Christendom's cult worship at the time of Pope Gelasius (492-496), when an apparition appeared on Mt. Garganus.

the Holy City of On in Egypt. He laid her beside an altar tended by the priest Potiphera who lamented that his wife was barren. When the priest found the child he raised her as his own. Years later the girl would marry Joseph, Jacob's son.[32]

Michael's desire to do well included instructing his leader on the sins of mortals. It was he who told the Destroyer that his fellow angels had engaged in sex with the daughters of men. While the Destroyer invited Gabriel to incite the Sons of God to civil war, he required Michael to chain Shemhazai and his fellows in dark caves for seventy generations to mourn their passion.[33]

While Michael had little problem with sanctified sex (where the deities watched or participated), he was opposed to any promiscuity or extra-marital sex. To this end he flew down to the court of Abimelech in the form of an eagle and threatened the king with a sword if he touched Abraham's wife Sarah. He made excuses for Abraham's weakness and willingness to sell his wife into prostitution, and demanded that the king give

---

[32] Pirqe Rabbi Eliezer ben Hyrcanos (Tannaite), chap. 26. Targum Yerushalmi, Genesis, folio 41, col. 45, and folio 46, col. 20. Yalqut Genesis para. 146.

[33] Enoch ix-x, xi-xv and lxix. 2 Baruch 46:11-16. 2 Enoch 18:1-6. Uriel was allowed to tell Noah that all would be drowned as a special mark of the Destroyer's favor.

Abraham sumptuous gifts in apology for following his base instincts.[34]

In part, Michael's insistence on marital fidelity was the result of his commission to maintain and protect contracts. These included social and religious vows. Once a promise was made, that promise was considered inviolable.[35] To this end, Michael witnessed the contract between Esau and Jacob when Esau swore away his birthright on the "fear" of his father whom he loved dearly.[36] Michael wrestled Jacob at Beth-El to enforce the contract between the gods and a mortal so that

---

[34] Pirqe Rabbi Eliezer ben Hyrcanos (Tannaite), chap. 38. Targum Yerushalmi Genesis 41:45, 46:20. Yalqut Genesis 146. Yalqut Reubeni on Genesis 32:25. The account of Michael assuming the body of an eagle comes from the Greek account of Zeus disguising himself as an eagle to snatch Ganymede from earth to make love to the young boy.

[35] See: Arthur Frederick Ide, *Vows, Virgins, Oaths & Orgies* (Arlington, TX: Liberal Arts Press, 1988).

[36] Genesis Rabba, pp. 694-697. Sepher Hayashar, p. 90-91. Bavli (Babylonian Talmud) Baba Bathra, p. 16 col. b. Tanhuma Buber, pp. 125-127. Midrash Leqah Tobh Genesis, pp. 123-124. The name Esau is generated from the community of Edom (they translate the same), with the story reflecting the Jewish concern over the treachery of their neighbors the Edomites (2 Samuel 8:12-14; 2 Kings 8:20-21).

Jacob would not believe himself to be equal to the gods or to defeat the gods in a match of strength and wit. If he did, it was feared, Jacob could deny that god,[37] and claim superiority over the gods. Michael also wrestled Jacob throughout the long night to remind him of his obligation to pay a debt he made twenty years earlier and failed to honor.[38]

---

[37] Yalqut Genesis, p. 132.

[38] Pirqe Rabbi Eliezer ben Hyrcanos (Tannaite), chap. 37. Numerous legends concerning Jacob continue to flow throughout the Judaic and Christian communities, especially concerning the famed birthright. The biblical story is allegory for incidents and personalities: from the red lentils emphasizing Esau's red hair and location (Edom which is interchangeable with Seir: "the shaggy one"). The account of Esau's sale of the birthright justified the Jews invasion and take-over of the Edomite kingdom since they were junior kinsmen of the same original tribe (Numbers 20:14). Out of the Edomite society came the eventual Herod the Edomite and the eventual puppet rule of the Herodians who served as Roman puppets until the rebellion of 68 CE. Still Herod and his kin were flattered and entertained by the Sadducees and even Pharisees such as St. Paul of Tarsus (Acts 25:13-26:32). Angels play a significant role in the Esau myth, from reviving Esau's slain deer, to delaying his return (Tanhuma Buber Genesis 131; Tanhuma Toldat, chap. 11; Midrash Leqah Tobh Genesis 135; and so forth).

94

## Gabriel

While Gabriel is considered second after Michael in Jewish theology,[1] he is first in Islam. He is one of the seven archangels in the Hebrew heaven. A revealer of the meaning of dreams,[2] he was empowered to foretell special conceptions.[3]

Gabriel was known for his enormous strength. His destiny was to fight the Leviathan in a great struggle, but it was predestined before the conflict that the archangel would only be able to haul the Leviathan out of the water. He was

---

[1] In the Christian Church, Gabriel's feast day is 24 March (the day before the Annunciation). See: O. Bardenbower, *Mariä Verkündigung. Ein Kommentar zu Lk.* I:26-38 (Biblische Studien x, Hft. 5, 1905), pp. 48-59.

[2] Daniel 8:15-26, 9:21-25 f. Cp. E. B. Pusey, *Daniel the Prophet* (1864), p. 520 f. Daniel is a relatively new book in the Old Testament, written around 168 BCE, not before the Exile as it was acclaimed earlier. In addition to numerous Greek words in the text that wouldn't have been known, it concerns too many second century issues. Divine dreams are frequent in the Old Testament (Genesis 28:12; 1 Samuel 3:1; 1 Kings 3-4; and so forth). In most cases the meaning is clearly understood.

[3] Luke 1:11 f, 16. Cp. O. Bardenhewer, *Mariä Verkündigung*, Ein Kommentar zu Lk. 1:26-38 (Biblische Studien, x, Hft. 5, 1905), pp. 48-59.

forbidden to kill it. It was up to the Creator-gods to do this deed, a slaughtered that the Creator-gods welcomed most heartily.[4]

The Creator-gods believed that only the fastest angel could retrieve the most sacred dust that was essential in their creation of Man. It was imperative that the dust represent every part of earth so that no corner of the world could claim that Adam was not of its soil and thus be exempt from worshipping the First Man or following that mortal's gods.[5] It was Gabriel's strength[6] that gained

---

[4] Bavli (Babylonian Talmud) Baba Bathra, folio 752. Midrash Alphabetot, folio 438. Cp. Pesquita di Rabbi Kahana, ed. Solomon Buber (Lyck, 1868; photostat reprint, New York, 1949), folio 29, p. 188, cols. a-b. Midrash Alphabetot 98.

[5] Pirqe Rabbi Eliezer ben Hyrcanos (Tannaite), chap. 11. Rashi, *ad Genesis* 2:7; commentary by Rabbi Shelomo ben Yitzhak (1040-1105). Arab tradition agrees with Jewish lore, that when Allah determined to fashion man, Mother Earth was reluctant to give up the dust. Gabriel was sent first to retrieve it; when he failed Michael was commissioned to complete the task. He too failed, forcing Allah to send the Angel of Death. Terrified of this angel, Mother Earth allowed him to take white, black and copper-red dust, thereby creating the different races (colors) of mortals on earth. The holy book of the Arabs, the *Qur'an* clearly states that the creation of the earth and man was deliberate and thought-through; see: *Qur'an* Al-Anbiya [21]:16-17.

the archangel the opportunity to fly to the four corners of the world to find special dust to create Man.

Gabriel was especially loved because he was strong. He was a prototype for Samson and other muscular warriors who conquered by brute force.

Because of his extraordinary strength, Gabriel was expected to punish those who offended the gods. On the sixth day of creation, he was given the sword of justice, and commissioned to use it in wars and on battlefields, punishing traitors and helping the just.[7]

According to ancient Jewish legends, it was Gabriel who punished the Egyptian servant who refused to fetch Moses out of the muddy waters when commanded by her princess.[8] It was Gabriel who destroyed the city of Sodom,[9] and it was he who marked the lintels of the houses of the wicked

---

[6] Today, Gabriel translates as "God is mighty." However, it is more reasonable that the translation should be "Mighty God," as Gabriel figures as a god with divine powers in most ancient legends where he is the helper (not the servant) of many gods.

[7] Sanhedrin 26a.

[8] Sotah 12b; Exodus Rabba 1.

[9] Pirqe de Rabbi Eliezer, chapter 25.

with a letter in blood so the angels who came after him would know whom to destroy. Gabriel also marked the door of the homes of the "pious and just" with a letter in ink so that the avenging angels would know whom they were not to harm.[10] In these legends, Gabriel is an angel of death. He is one of two angels of death. The other Angel of Death is Samael.

Gabriel was obliged to bring a peaceful death to the inhabitants of the Holy Land of Palestine. Samael was commissioned to take the souls of those who live in the other parts of the world. Neither Gabriel nor Samael operated capriciously or independently. Nor was it the gods of the Garden who determined who was to die. This power rested with Metatron who presided over the archangel triumvirate of death. Metatron instructed Gabriel on which Jewish souls to bring to paradise. Gabriel ordered Samael to harvest the Gentiles.[11]

Creation is the reverse side of chaos. For Gabriel it was the prototype for human birth. Gabriel was at the creation of Adam. He was called upon to witness the birth of Abram (who was later known as Abraham).

---

[10] Sabbath 55a.

[11] Yalkut Rubeni § 13; Yalkut Chadash § 44.

Abram's birth was unique by most accounts. His mother, Amitlai, had to hide her pregnancy from her husband and from King Nimrod. Nimrod was intent on destroying all male infants fearing one would rival him for his throne. When Amitlai's time to came to give birth to the infant, Abram's mother stole across the desert seeking refuge in a cave by the Euphrates River. After the infant was born, Amitlai wrapped Abram in her garment and left him on the floor of the cave without food.

Hungry, Abram cried. The gods, hearing the infant's, ordered Gabriel to go to the child "and give it suck." The archangel did as he was told, producing milk that flowed from the little finger of his right hand.[12] Now his nurse, Gabriel fed the child Abram was hungry. Gabriel's milk was special. Gabriel's finger served the infant well, and the child grew remarkably. Abram grew so strong and tall that within ten days, the abandoned child

---

[12] Gabriel's factious fingers recalls the beasts (bears, wolves, goats, dogs, mares, and so forth) who gave suck to a plethora of future deities and heroes such as Oedipus, Romulus and Remes, Hippothous, Pelias, Paris, Aegisthus. That this came after his mother wrapped him in a cloak or cloth also has numerous pagan antecedents, with the cloth frequently considered to be swaddling material. Most of these incidents come from Greek myths.

was able to walk by himself down to the riverbank of the Euphrates.[13]

Abraham wasn't the only child Gabriel protected and nurtured. He disguised himself as an eagle when Dinah[14] gave birth to a girl, knowing that Dinah's brothers wanted to kill the child,[15] and

---

[13] Sepher Hayashar 24-27. Pirqe Rabbi Eliezer ben Hyrcanos (Tannaite), chap. 26. The bible only cites that Abram was born of Terah (the earth); see Genesis 11:27. The Midrashes and other accounts of the birth and abandonment of the child reflect the common theme in most Greek myths. These include records of the mountainside exposures of Cyrus, Paris, and Oedipus (others claim he was set adrift like Moses and Romulus). This led to an Advent celebration where shepherds and cattlemen carried torches to a sacred cave near Athens where the foundling is hailed as a new King of Hosts.

[14] Dinah is the legendary daughter of Jacob and Leah. According to current scripture, Shechem, son of Hamor, the Hivite prince (most likely Hurrians), raped her. After the violence, he felt love for her and sought to marry her. But Dinah's brothers demanded vengeance as he had defiled their father's property. See: Genesis 34. Redactors color much of the story. It is a testimony to Jewish nationalism symbolized by the severance of the foreskin of penises of unbelievers who were of the house of Hamor. Through it, the archangels are nationalized as the House of Jacob is returned to Canaan. See: Ita Sheres, *Dinah's Rebellion: A Biblical Parable for Our Time* (New York: Crossroads, 1990), pp. 78-100.

[15] Her name was Asenath, which translates as "thorn-bush." This name was given her as it was in a thorn-bush that the

carried her to Egypt as a proto-Moses. Gabriel not only set the child in the Temple at On, but witnessed Potiphera adopt the child, and later, watched as Joseph, Jacob's son married her.

In addition to helping at births and nurturing children, Gabriel had other duties to concerned the rites of passage: especially circumcision and burial. The first record we possess of Gabriel helping at a circumcision concerns Abraham's circumcision. Gabriel helped Abraham not only circumcise himself and his household, but also participated in cutting off the foreskin of all males who were visiting the patriarch.[16] Such bloodletting was considered a sacred act and a sacrifice to the gods.[17]

When Abel, the son of the first mortal, was slain, it was Gabriel's duty, according to some records, to help find a place to protect his body until

---

archangel Gabriel found it. Pirqe Rabbi Eliezer ben Hyrcanos (Tannaite), chap. 28; Yalqut Genesis 146. Oppenheim, *Fabula Josephi et Asenathae* (Berlin, 1886), pp. 4 ff. The proposed infanticide was not uncommon, for the belief was that any child born to a non-believer would corrupt the child and ultimately the community.

[16] Genesis 17:23, 27.

[17] *Midrash Tanhuma* Genesis, ed. Solomon Buber (Wilna, 1885; 2 vols., photostat reprint, New York, 1946) pp. 85-86; Bavli (Babylonian Talmud) Baba Metsis, p. 86, col. B.

after the death of Adam. After the first parent died, Adam's body was buried beside his son.[18]

Gabriel also was charged in stopping murders. Such was his function when Laban tried to murder Eliezer by setting a large platter of poisoned food before his guest. Gabriel swiftly intervened, and exchanged it for the food served to Bethuel, King of Harran. The king ingested it and promptly died.[19]

With the discharge of duties to gather the dust for the creation of *Adamah*, Gabriel was given a new commission: to carry the word of the gods to *Adamah* and his progeny.[20] Those who accepted the word of the Hebrew gods,[21] believed and did

---

[18] *Apocalypse of Moses*, in *The Apocrypha and Pseudoepigrapha of the Old Testament*, ed. R. H. Charles xi. Enoch 22:7.

[19] Yalqut Genesis 109. Midrash Hagadol Genesis, 366, 369-370.

[20] *Qur'an* Al-Baqarah [2]:97.

[21] Legends have numerous stories of Gabriel helping the tribal gods of the Hebrews displace "pagan" gods: those deities that were a part of civilizations not yet under Hebrew rule. See: Ma'ase Abraham in *Beth HaMidrash*, ed. Adolph Jellinek (6 vols.; Leipzig, 1853-1877; photostat reprint, Jerusalem, 1938), vol. 1, pp. 24-30.

penance were promised a just and merciful god.[22] It was a promise seldom kept.

If mortals were to have a loving relationship with the gods, they had to do confess their transgressions, do penance and avoid carnal pleasures. They could not be like the Fallen Ones or Gabriel would make war against them. It was Gabriel along with Michael, Raphael and Uriel who exposed the carnal assaults of the Sons of God on the Daughters of Men.[23] Accepting his testimony, the gods ordered Gabriel to destroy the Fallen Ones. How he was to do it was left to Gabriel's ingenuity. Deliberating for only a matter of moments, Gabriel decided he would get the Fallen Ones engaged in a civil war. That would last until all were destroyed.[24]

In Islam, Gabriel is a significant figure and a cherished angel. During the "Night of Power and Excellence," while Muhammad was visiting a cave near the base of Mount Hira, a few miles north of Mecca, the archangel Gabriel rose before him,

---

[22] *Qur'an* At-Tahrim [66]:6.

[23] The exposure came in the form of a tattling to the dominant god who commissioned them. It suggests that they watched longer than was necessary for gathering facts.

[24] Enoch 9-10, cp. 11-14, 69. Cf. 2 Baruch 56:11-16, and 2 Enoch 18:1-6.

crying "Recite." During the recitation, Muhammad listened enraptured, and when the session ended, the Prophet was able to reproduce the entire revelation.[25] Returning later, riding on the back of the winged steed Buraq (Pegasus), Gabriel flew Muhammad first to Jerusalem, then through the seven heavens where the Prophet spoke with Adam, John the Baptist and Jesus, Joseph, Enoch, Aaron, Moses, and finally, in the seventh heaven, with Abraham. When Gabriel could go no further, Muhammad was lifted on a flying carpet (a *rafraf*) and taken into the great space that Allah occupied. Surrounded by angels, Allah declared Muhammad to be an equal of Moses, Abraham and all other prophets and exceeded the patriarchs of the past.[26]

---

[25] Sura 96 or the Qur'ān (*Al Qur'an*, Al-`Alaq [96]:1-19). Muhammad defends the authenticity of the visit in Sura 53 (*Al Qur'an*, An-Najm [53]:1 ff.)

[26] *Islam: Muhammad and His Religion*, ed. Arthur Jeffery (New York: Liberal Arts Press, 1958), p. 45.

# Raphael

The archangel Raphael was a mystery maker and magician. He figures as one of the seven archangels in the books of Tobit and Enoch. But for all the magic that Raphael performed, the gods of creation remained supreme, and Raphael could do nothing without their permission.

In the *Book of Tobit*, Raphael hears the prayers of holy men. If the prayers are strong and long, he brings them before the gods.[1]

One of the earliest accounts of Raphael's ability was his passing on select secrets to Adam once he had the god's permission. No text details what these secrets were, but references to the "new wisdom" suggest that hallucinogenic mushrooms that were cooked into sacred cakes and eaten, generated them. The knowledge enabled Adam to

---

[1] Tobias 12:12, 15. An apocryphal book, Tobit relates the story of a pious Jew held captive in Nineveh, who, engaged in charitable works (such as burying an executed compatriot) became impoverished and blind in his old age. Praying to the gods to deliver him, they inspired him to send his son Tobias, and the son's new companion (Raphael) to Media to collect a debt owed by a friend. Like Job, Tobit's faith, brought him ultimate rewards, including a new daughter-in-law (Sarah) who was possessed by the demon Asmodeus until Tobias exorcised him from her body.

use fire-tongs and a smith's hammer, manage oxen, and plant when ploughing.[2] What Raphael didn't teach Adam (or Eve) was that if they ate from the Tree of Life they would have lived eternally and become gods. Terrified that this was possible, the primary Gardener-god sent another angel to expel the couple.[3]

Even after the expulsion, Raphael didn't abandon Adam or his children. When Cain killed Abel, Raphael joined the other archangels in charge of finding a safe place for the corpse until Adam died. When Adam died, Raphael helped his brother angels bury the two men side-by-side.[4]

Like the other archangels, Raphael didn't tolerate sexual wickedness. When the Sons of God had sex with the Daughters of Men, he was sent to

---

[2] *Die Apokryphischen Gnostischen Adamschriften.* Aus dem Armenischen übersetzt von A. Dillmann (Göttingen, 1853), pp. 24, 33.

[3] Genesis 3:20-24. There is confusion as to the nature of Eden. Some hold it to be a garden or delights (based on the Hebrew word) while others see it as a wilderness or plain (based on the Sumerian word).

[4] Apocalypse of Moses, in *The Apocrypha and Pseudo-epigrapha of the Old Testament*, ed. R. H. Charles, vol. 2, p. xi. *Die Apokryphischen Gnostischen Adamschriften.* Aus dem Armenischen übersetzt von A. Dillmann (Göttingen, 1853), pp. 22. Enoch 13:7.

earth to bind Azael hand and foot, and heap jagged rocks over him in the dark Cave of Dudael, where he languishes until the Last Days[5]

Raphael was also involved in the Great Flood that swept Noah's neighbors to their watery death. He gave Noah a special book that, when opened, gave off light within the ship. Bound in sapphires, and containing all knowledge of the stars to guide the ark, Raphael's book also included chapters on the art of healing, and how to master demons. For this reason, Raphael is considered the patron of medical arts, and is sometimes known as Suriel.[6]

Although Raphael's present of healing was a temporary gift, the magical book was passed from the hand of Noah to his son Shem, from Shem to the patriarch Abraham, and to his son Jacob, then to his

---

[5] Enoch 9, 10-14. 2 Enoch 18:1-6. Dudael was one of the seven "fallen" angels. The name translates as "cauldron of the gods." It represents *Beth Hadudo* (Haradan), the Judaean desert cliff from which the "scapegoat of Azazel" yearly fell to its death on the Day of Atonement (Leviticus 16:8-10), three miles to the southeast of Jerusalem. See: Midrash Yoma 6:8.

[6] Berachoth 51a. Suriel was once the god Suri-El who made all diseases disappear. He is called Surjan in the Book of Enoch. When Suriel lost favor with the gods, his medical duties were transferred to other angels. Ultimately he was banished from the heavenly home he grew up in.

son Levi, to Moses, Joshua, and to Solomon who lost it.[7] The title of the book is recorded in Gnostic literature as *The Book of Wisdom*. Once a part of Genesis, it was later omitted for political reasons. An argument ensued over its authorship. Raphael was seen as a misreading of Raziel, and many argued that Noah wrote it, but worried that if he did, he would have been an angel. If Noah was an angel, then the Flood didn't cover the earth. Instead the Flood was nothing more than a primal covering before dry land appeared, and the ark was nothing less than the planet itself.[8]

The last significant mention of Raphael is during the circumcision of Abraham and his household. Raphael was upset by the odor of the act, and was concerned about the enormous amount of blood that was lost. The gods reprimanded

---

[7] *Genesis Rabba*, ed. J. Theodor and Ch. Albeck (2 vols.; Berlin, 1912-1927), pp. 253, 287. Babylonian *Sanhedrin* folio 108, column b. Sepher Noah, in *Beth HaMidrash*, ed. Adolph Jellinek (6 vols.; Leipzig, 1953-1877), vol. 3, p. 158.

[8] The first mention of this book is in the Slavonic *Book of Enoch* (33). It states that the gods wrote it, or, in another edition, that a god dictated it to Enoch. Once that the book was written, the gods sent it back to earth in the hand of Enoch accompanied by two angels: Samuil and Raguil (or, Semil and Rasuil). According to Jewish tradition the *Book of Raziel* was given to Adam by the Angel Raziel. See the Targum on *Ecclesiastes* 10:20.

Raphael and his fellow archangels, arguing that the blood was sacrificial and the aroma savory and sweet. They screamed, "By your lives, the odor of Abraham's sacrifice please me better than myrrh and frankincense!" and threatened to attend the ceremony in the place of the archangels.[9]

Raphael also had a romantic side. He helped Tobias rescue his kinswoman, Sarah, from a demon, and told Tobias to marry her.[10] Raphael was equally compassionate, and cured the sick, including Tobias' father, Tobit, of blindness.[11]

Steadfast against evil, which the archangel interpreted as any deviation from the rules set down by the gods, Raphael acted quickly to root-out indiscretions and "harry evil out of the land" of his god's chosen people. In one instance, Raphael carried a devil out of Israel and dumped him in

---

[9] *Midrash Tanhuma*, ed. Solomon Buber (Wilna, 1885; photostat reprint, New York, 1946) *Genesis*, p. 85-86.

[10] Tobias 6:12-13. Cf. Tobias 9:7 for increasing the wedding list for guests.

[11] Tobias 5:13. In most cases, blindness was considered the mark of a sinner, and only those who went to a pious man could be healed, as when Jesus healed the blind (Matthew 9:27-28, 20:30; Mark 8:22-23, 10:49 and 51; Luke 18:35; John 9:6, 17).

Egypt. There, far from any civilization, Raphael bound the demon in the desert of the upper Nile.[12]

Like a latter-day Eos or Saint Christopher, Raphael is also a guide, a guardian, a nurse and a travel agent. In nearly every case, Raphael is secretive about his purpose, name, and heritage.[13] While unwilling to be known, he isn't forgotten in the liturgical Christian Church. His feast day is 24 October.[14]

---

[12] Tobias 8:2.

[13] Tobias 5:14-17, 20, 26.

[14] L. Eisenhofer, *Handbuch der latholischen Liturgik*, I (1932), p. 602.

## Uriel

Uriel is one archangel we know little about.[1] Jewish lore tells us that he is a spectacularly beautiful man who radiates the Divine nature and personifies good. He is the incarnation of the Vedic god of fire, Agni, mediating between a superior god and mortals. From the Vedic tradition, he is developed further in Zoroastrian theology as Atar, and became chief of a rank of angels known as *yazatas*.

Originally a god, Uriel's[2] origin is uncertain. In some records he is pictured as a Judacized Prometheus. Known as the "angel of fire" he was regent of the sun and "flame of god" when fire gods were worshipped in Palestine.

Western civilization felt the influence of the East with the rise of the myth of the god Prometheus. By various accounts, Prometheus brought mortals fire, saved humanity from the ravages of a celestial war among the gods. Because of his concern for mortals, the gods sentenced

---

[1] For additional information, on the web, key in www.prometheus.co.uk\legend.htm.

[2] Uriel translates as god is light, or "god's light"; this is from *Uri* ("the enlightened") and *el* ("god").

Prometheus to push a large stone (or a great wheel) up a hill only to have it roll back, requiring him to start again. Within the Prometheus legend we find the Great Flood, Noah, the celestial war where some divinities are cast out, and more.

Most legends agree that Uriel was a part of the entourage that flew with Abel's body until they could lay it upon a rock. We also know that Uriel was one of the four archangels who helped bury Abel with his father when Adam died.[3]

In rabbinical angelology, Uriel is Atuniel. He serves as guardian of the fiery furnace.

Roman Catholicism has Uriel standing guard with a flaming sword at the entrance of the Garden of Eden.[4] He is retain in its apocryphal literature,[5] and has masses and prayers said in his honor. Suppliants invoke him in the Communion of the Sick (Last Rites), burial service of adults, blessing of homes, and the Litany of All Saints and novenas. He is honored as one of three archangels

---

[3] *Vita Adae et Evae* 48 in *The Apocrypha and Pseudoepigrapha of the Old Testament*, ed. R. H. Charles, vol. 2.

[4] See entries in *The Westminster Dictionary of Christian Theology*, ed. Alan Richardson and John Bowden (rev. ed.; Philadelphia, PA: Westminster Press, 1983).

[5] 2 Esdras.

in Greek Orthodoxy, and is celebrated in the Orthodox Liturgy (Mass and Divine Office) and the observances of special feasts. Uriel is associated with the direction of North, and is considered by many to be the ruling angel of Earth (and gravity).

Uriel's mythology is probably the result of a popular folk-hero who was a noble Kohathite fighter (c. 1460 BCE). Out of this developed the later Hebrew myth of a great patriarch, Jacob, wrestling a dark angel.[6] Since he was in the company of men, he remained in the company of archangels since they were male. Having the

---

[6] The former is found in *The Prayer of Joseph*. The latter, focused on in Genesis 32:24 ff in the *Book of Enoch*.

reputation of being "enlightened," the redactors of Hebrew scripture portray him as eschewing conventional mortal sexuality if it's not within the bonds of matrimony and the rubric sex only for procreation. As a teacher, Uriel admonished, instructed and encouraged those who approached sex to be ever vigilant so that they did not become addicted to carnal pleasure.

Despising sexual escapades, Uriel fought along side of Michael, Gabriel, and Raphael against the lecherous Sons of God who bedded with the Daughters of Men. While he had no orders requiring of him in putting down rebellious and disobedient angels, he served quietly with those who did. At other times, he was a messenger. It was Uriel who appeared to Noah, telling him of the coming Flood. It was also Uriel who promised Noah that he and his family would be saved when the floodwaters were to be unleashed.[7]

According to the *Book of Enoch*, Uriel has charge of Tartarus. Little else is recorded. What Tartarus was is still debated.

Most likely Tartarus was the god Tartak[8] who later Hebrews believed was an ally of Satan. Tartak was worshipped by the Avites whom

---

[7] Enoch 9-15, 69; 2 Baruch56:11-16; 2 Enoch 18:1-6.

[8] The name of the god translates as "hero of darkness."

Shalmaneser removed to Samaria.[9] The Hebrews cursed Shalmaneser[10] as a demon since he invaded Israel and carried off the prophet Hosea and the ten tribes to Assyria (c. 730-716 BCE).[11] Not until Uriel conquered Tartak was there real peace in Israel. The overthrow of Tartak has suggested to many that the god was now among those enchained, waiting for the Final Days.

---

[9] 2 Kings 17:31.

[10] He succeeded Tiglath-pileser, an Assyrian king who invaded Naphtali in the days of Peksh, king of Israel. Although there are those who write that Tiglath-pileser was the successor of Pul, evidence points that he was Pul: the conqueror of the north of Palestine and Damascus, carrying off the people to Kir (c. 742 BCE).

[11] 2 Kings 17:3, 18:9.

116

# Metatron

Metatron is among the most fascinating of the angel-princes. Much of the lore surrounding this archangel can be traced back to the Persian god Mithra. His own name, Metatron, like the names of all other archangels, clearly came from Persia,[1] despite arguments that it is Greek in origin.[2]

Metatron was known as the Prince of the Presence because of his extraordinarily beautiful face. Because of his face, he was crowned Prince of the World (*Sar ha-Olam*) and commissioned the superintendent of its resources.[3] And he is a direct

---

[1] A. Kohut, *Zur jüdischen Angelologie und Demonologie* (Abhandlungen der D.M.G., 1886), p. 33.

[2] The argument is based on the word μεταδρόνος (or δρόνον); see: A. Frank, *La Kabbale* (Paris, 1843); Herschfeld in *Frankel's Zeitschrift* (Berlin, 1846), p. 353.

[3] In some sources, Metatron is called the Creator God, and the All-Father. This led to the first serious heresy within Judaism, giving birth to the Gnostic doctrine of *demiourgos*. Those who taught it were driven out of the community and frequently stoned to death. Yet, the expulsion of the demiourgosians fueled the debate over whether or not this Angel-Prince wasn't an earlier Yahweh (tetragrammatron). If this was the case then the question arises if his son overthrew him, having tired of Metatron's constant good will towards men. The younger Yahweh believed that a god should be filled with wrath so that

link between god and humanity in both the Talmud and the Targum.

Some legends claim that Metatron was once the patriarch Enoch who was transformed into a fiery angel with 36 wings and countless eyes.[4] If this was the case, Metatron would be among the youngest angels, barely 8600 years of age, as other angels, according to legends, were fashioned nearly fifteen billion years ago. Other particulars in the

---

all people fear him (cp. Exodus 20:20; Deuteronomy 11:25; 2 Samuel 23:3; 2 Chronicles 19:9; Psalm 34:11, 119:120; Jonah 1:16; and so forth). This reflects the Greek stories of gods in war against their parents (such as Zeus fighting Cronus).

[4] The *Chronicle of Enoch* reads: "Then the Lord said to Micha-El: "Go and strip Enoch of his own clothes; anoint him with oil, and dress him like ourselves" and Micha-El did as he was told. He stripped me of my clothes, and rubbed me over with a wonderful oil like dew; with the scent of myrrh; which shone like a sunbeam. And I looked at myself, and I was like one of the other [angels]; there was no difference and all my fear and trembling left me." There is a limited debate on what the "wonderful oil" consisted of. It was "like dew" meaning that it was a clear liquid; it had a scent and so it was not water but something more pungent. It shone when it was rubbed on Enoch, being like "a sunbeam": holding and consisting of the elements of life. This reflects some of the early practices among various peoples in worshipping fertility figures where the sacred oils flowed out of the gods' private parts to anoint those selected to enjoy eternal life.

Metatron lore give credence to this argument as both men were writers and filled etheric archives. Being literate and capable of taking dictation, scribes were occasionally called on to serve as messengers and even take adversarial action if necessary. Clearly, Metatron was the god of Exodus sent to Moses and the Israelites "to keep thee in the way and bring thee unto the place which I prepared." It was he who led Joshua and his troops around the walls of Jericho, and it was he who was the confidant of Ezekiel and other prophets.[5]

While there is no description of Yahweh, we have an abundance of material on the makeup of Metatron. Both Yahweh and Metatron were seen as a "pillar of fire" and whose "face [is] more dazzling than the sun."[6] Metatron and Yahweh were equally tall beings, and like any temporal monarch neither would permit a subordinate to be stand as tall as they, for fear that as monarch their majesty would appear less grand.[7]

---

[5] Exodus 23:20. Joshua 6:11, 13. Isaiah 37:36, 63:9.

[6] Cp. Exodus 13:22, 19:18; Numbers 11:3; Deuteronomy 4:33, 5:4.

[7] The height of Yahweh can be determined from the size of the Tabernacle (as described in Exodus 35-40 and Numbers) since the god "filled it" (Numbers 9:15-16, 17:7). An ancient cubit

Furthermore, because of his creative forces and skills coupled with his extraordinary good looks, Metatron can, unlike other angels, to penetrate into the innermost chamber of the Divine Presence and speak face-to-face (üστόμα πρὸς üστόμα) with the Lord. All other angels have to receive Metatron's commands that come from behind a veil or screen.[8]

When in the sacred presence, Metatron serves Yahweh as a confidant and scribe (his name is a metonym for the term "little Yahweh"). It became a *vox mystica* for *Yahoel* (Gód). He records everything that happens in the ethereal archives. For example, in the *Alphabet of Ben Sira*, an apocryphal account, God demands that Earth "loan" the substance from which he creates Adam. Earth however demands interest and Yahweh agrees, and writes out a formal receipt, which is on deposit "to this day" in Metatron's archives.

While the Judaeo-Christian bible claims that Moses spoke with the God of his father: a god he did not at first see.[9] The actual rendering of the

---

is equivalent to .53 meters. This would make the angel/god nearly 13 feet tall.

[8] Hagigah 5a, 15a, 16a. The actual term is "mouth-to-mouth."

[9] Exodus 3:6. "The Lord" doesn't speak face-to-face (that is: directly) with Moses until Exodus 33:11, and never unveils his full face knowing that if he did the act would cost Moses his

passage is that he spoke directly with a god, or one standing in the place of and for a particular god. In this situation, Moses spoke with Metatron,[10] and Metatron taught him.[11]

Metatron stopped Abraham from killing his son.[12] He is also closely associated with the evolution of the Moses myth. According to the Cabala, Metatron is the angel who led the Children of Israel out of the wilderness after the Exodus. He is identified with Isaiah's suffering servant,[13] and credited with the authorship of Psalm 37:25.[14]

---

life: "Thou canst not see my face: for there shall no man see me, and live"; Exodus 33:20. All that the god would permit was for Moses to see his "back parts" (see Exodus 33:21-23).

[10] Sanhedrin 38b is emphatic that those who forsake the name of the god will realize severe vengeance as if they had seen the god of Metatron face-to-face.

[11] A. Kohut, *Zur jüdischen Angelologie und Demonologie* (Abhandlungen der D.M.G., 1886), p. 42. Kohut amends the rabbinical teaching that Moses' teacher was Sagsagel, noting that Sagsagel is only another epithet for Metatron.

[12] Genesis 22:11.

[13] Isaiah 42:19, with the "messenger" being a divine instrument. Cp. Isaiah 53:11-12.

[14] Yebamoth 16b. The verse in the Psalm reads: "I have been young, and now am old; yet have I not see the righteous

Metatron is also considered to be the teacher of prematurely dead children who are taken to Paradise.[15]

---

forsaken, nor his seed begging bread." The following verse (Psalm 37:26) brings in the mercy of Metatron: "He is ever merciful and lendeth; and his seed is blessed." (KJV).

[15] Abodah Zarah 3b.

## Rediyao

Rediyao was also an Angel-Prince (or archangel), but one who has historically been slighted in favor of his more ambitious and violent brothers. Born in Persian mythology as the god Ardvi-Cüra, Rediyao is the angel of rain. He is in charge of all the waters on earth and in the heavens. He stands between the upper and lower waters of floods (the *Tehomoth*), and moderates their movement and size. At times he cries out, "Let flow thy waters" to the upper floods (rain held captive in clouds to quench the parched earth's thirst). At other times he commands, "Let arise thy floods" to the lower floods so that the earth can be fruitful.[1]

According to various rabbinical writings, Rediyao resembles a calf. He is innocent but frisky, following more senior angels, yet pulling back when he realizes that he is being led too much.

---

[1] Taanith 25b.

124

## Sandalphon

The Angel-Prince (or archangel) Sandalphon is unique. Far taller than any other angel created, he is able to stand on earth and have his head high above the clouds in the heavens. His primary mission, fashioned after older cultures, is to stand behind the royal chariot (the *Merkaba*) that bears the senior gods and weave crowns for the Creator.[1] He does this while watching temporary angels: angels who rise out of a river of fire[2] to sing a commanded hymn of praise[3] to the Creator's glory, and then to be destroyed by the Creator[4] who commands that they wither away and disappear for all time.[5]

---

[1] Hagigah 13b; Exodus Rabba 21.

[2] Cp. Revelation 19:20.

[3] This became common in the emerging Christian community; see: Matthew 26:30. It is of Greek origin. In the Hebrew bible, God is considered the author of such songs (ומ׳ר: *zemir* as in Job 35:10), the origin of which is Chaldean. These songs of praise are different than regular melodies (ש׳ר: *shir* in Genesis 31:27; Psalm 33:3; and so forth).

[4] Sanhedrin 38b.

[5] Hagigah 14a; Genesis Rabba 78.

Some legends make this archangel an Angel-Prince of fire. Sandalphon used his gift of fire for both good and evil. He helped warm houses, light paths and darkened rooms, and also immolated those who were damned.

## The Other Archangels

As with the writing of most histories and biographies, nothing is simple. Frequently there are contenders for the attention of the historian, scribe or biographer. Material is found that focuses on the subject being reviewed, collected and analyzed, but it is impinged by unexpected material that casts a shadow over what has commonly been considered to be canon. This is the case with the archangels.

While most references to archangels list only seven, there are actually an additional five demanding attention. The reason why they are frequently overlooked or ignored deliberately is that their number doesn't fit into the Judaeo-Christian concept of the sacredness of the number seven. This chapter details the stories and legends surrounding the other five: Ana-El, Ragu-El, Razi-El, Remi-El, and Sari-El.

Ana-El is the most elusive of the archangels. His antecedents are unclear. The closest biblical possibility is that passage detailing a "young boy." He appeared before Abram (who is later known as Abraham), having escaped from Lot's party who was captured with the fall of Sodom.[1] The reference

---

[1] Genesis 14:13. The youth isn't mentioned again.

is to moral purity, in keeping with the archangel's charge.

Ragu-El is also known by the names of Rasuil, Rufa-El, Akrasi-El and similar monikers. His name means "Friend of God."[2] He is prudish, and watches over the behavior of angels to make certain that they remain loyal to the gods and behave in an angelic manner. This means that they fight for the Creator god, take orders only from his supreme archangel (Metatron), and are ever vigilant against sexual urges.[3]

This particular archangel is involved in numerous other myths and fantasies. He is the

---

[2] Numbers 10:29 has Moses speaking with Hobab, the son of Raguel "the Midianite" (Moses' father-in-law) to "to the place of which the Lord said, I will give it to you." This indicates that the place is holy, and fits in character with the archangel who was among the pantheon of the Midianites, over which his father-in-law (spelled as Rau-El in Exodus 2:18) was a priest.

[3] The Roman Church removed Ragu-El and Uri-El from their official church calendar in 745 CE at a Church council called by Pope Zachary to conduct an "investigation" into the morals of angels. The Pope condemned Ragu-El as a demon "who passes himself off as a saint," having heard choirboys claim that while praying to him he caused them to have erections. Fear of angels molesting children became so great that artists were ordered to be certain that angels were fully clothed.

angel, for example, who transported Enoch to heaven while he lived in the flesh.[4]

Ragu-El was so vigilant at watching his brother angels remain celibate that he was given a most unique task. The apocryphal *Revelation of John* reads: "Then shall He send the angel Raguel saying: go sound the trumpet for the angels of cold and snow and ice and bring together every kind of wrath upon them that stand on the left [against Yahweh]."

Razi-El is also known as Ratzi-El, Gallizur, Saraqu-El, and Akrasi-El. His name means "Angel of the Secret Regions and of the Supreme Mysteries."[5] A justifiably vain author, Razi-El prepared a book entitled after himself: *Book of the Angel Razi-El*, and gave it to Adam. Ultimately the book made its way into the hands of Enoch who incorporated much of it into his own *Book of Enoch*.

---

[4] Genesis 5:24; cp. Gustav Davidson, *A Dictionary of Angels: Including the Fallen Angels* (New York: Free Press, 1971). While he is considered to be a leader of the Dominions, the Church of St. George in New York styled him, abruptly, as an angel of the Principalities. The Dominions took their name from their founding angel who is also styled as the oldest angel in the heaven(s): Dominion.

[5] One of the "supreme mysteries" which few rabbis could understand was how sex could be enjoyable.

Once it was complete, Enoch gave his work to Noah who modeled his Ark on information he discovered in its pages.[6] After the Flood the book was forgotten, until it appeared in Solomon's hands. Legend has it that the book disappeared again and didn't reappear until the Middle Ages, when Eleazar of Worms found it and incorporated it into his own book. What made the book so valuable was that Razi-El spelled out 1,500 keys to the mysteries of the Universe, but in a code no one has been able to decipher.

According to the *Targum Ecclesiastes*, "each day the great angel Razi-El stands upon the peak of Mount Horeb,[7] proclaim[ing] the secrets of

---

[6] The Ethiopic text of the Book of Enoch concerning the primordial flood appears in my book on Noah; see: Arthur Frederick Ide, *Noah & the Art: the Influence of Sex, Homophobia & Heterosexism in the Flood Story and Its Writing* (Las Colinas, TX: Monument Press, 1992).

[7] Horeb translates as "waste." It is the range of mountains of which Sinai is the chief. In the Old Testament it was viewed as "the mountain of god" (Exodus 3:1) where Moses went to meet with the deity. It became legendary as the home of the god who would emerge as Yahweh, and from this home (which was also the dwelling of numerous other desert gods) he spoke to his "chosen" people (Deuteronomy 1:6, 4:10 and 15). Mount Horeb is also where the Israelites purged their sins by stripping themselves of their ornaments which were

men to all mankind." Moses Maimonides had difficulty according Razi-El the title of archangel since he wasn't prepared for divine battle, and saw him more as a teacher and writer. To this end, Maimonides declared the archangel to be the chief of the Erelim (Thrones[8]) and identified Razi-El with brilliant white fire. Having this attribute, Razi-El is able to shield others from the fire of the Hayyôth; or, as the *Pirqe Rabbi Eleazar* notes: Razi-El "spreads his wings over the Hayyôth[9] lest their fiery breath consume the ministering angels."

Remi-El is a later name given to Jeremi-El (Yerahme-El). It means "Mercy of God," which was to be shown to souls awaiting Resurrection (in this regard this particular Jewish angel matches the

---

considered to be in bad taste since they rivaled the god's own splendor (Exodus 33:6).

[8] Thrones are also known as *Ophanim* or *Galgallin*. The angels are known as "great wheels [or pupil of the eye]" or "many-eyed ones." Each had four faces, was made up of fire, and glowed like chrysolite; see: Ezekiel 1:13-19. Elijah was born up in a luminous whirlwind (2 Kings 2:11) that was one of the Thrones. According to rabbinical writing, the archangel Rapha-El is in charge of the Thrones, and all Hebrew patriarchs immediately became angels when they died and passed into heaven.

[9] Hayyôth are heavenly beasts known as cherubim.

Bodhisattva Avalokieteshwara in Buddhism[10]). His assigned duty in heaven is to lead the souls to Judgment.[11] There are several men in the Old Testament who have his name.[12]

Sari-El goes by various names. They include Saraqu-El, Suriy-El, and Zerachi-El. With slight variations, they all mean "God's command." According to Enoch, Sari-El was "responsible for the fate of those angels who broke the Laws" of the higher gods. Because of this responsibility, Sari-El is frequently linked with the Angel of Death, along with Zagzag-El who, it is written, taught Moses. The argument is weak, however, because Sari-El was fastidiously clean, and death was always seen

---

[10] Cp. Edward Conze, *Buddhist Thought in India* (reprint; Ann Arbor, MI: University of Michigan Press, 1967); *Sources of Indian Tradition*, ed. Wm. Theodore De Bary (New York: Columbia University Press, 1958), vol. 1.

[11] Enoch contradicts this, claiming that Remi-El was one of the Fallen Angels, who was a leader of apostates. Baruch, on the other hand, states that Remi-El was the victor over Sennacherib, destroying his army with greater fury than Michael was accredited. For this reason, Remi-El sometimes appears as a Seraphim, and not an archangel.

[12] 1 Chronicles 2:9, 25-27, 33, 42; 24:29; Jeremiah 36:26. The archangel was a god to the Jerahmeelites and the town by the same name (1 Samuel 27:10, 30:29).

as unclean: from the passing of life to the decaying of the corpse. Furthermore, Sari-El, like Rapha-El, was a healer.

Strangely, Enoch lists Sari-El as being one of the angels who fell from grace. But, in the apocryphal book *The Wars of the Sons of Light against the Sons of Darkness*, Sari-El's name is on the shields of one of the fighting units of the Sons of the Sons of Light.

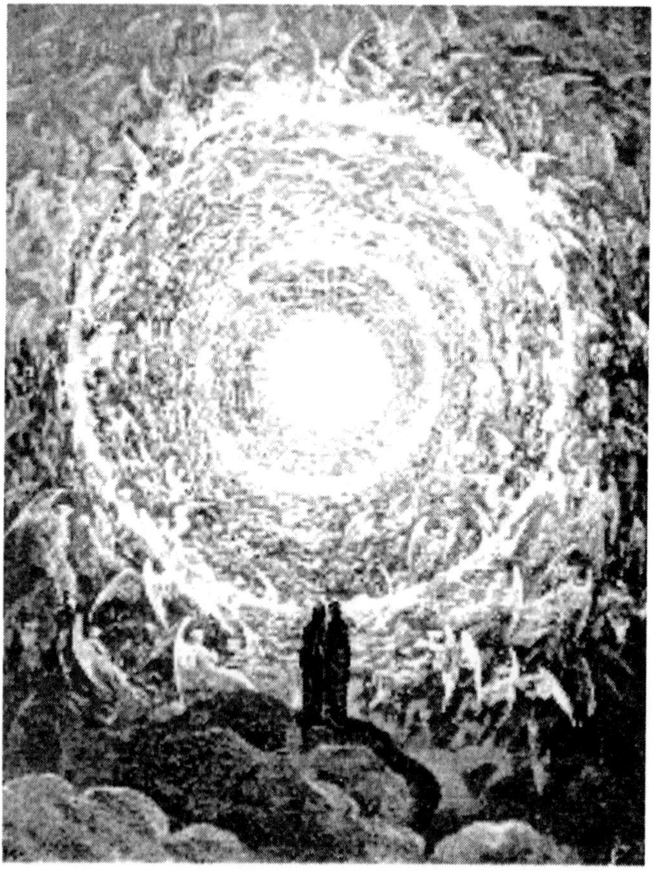

## Semil

One of the most obscure angels is Semil. He was an angel of learning, and dutifully followed his master-god's wishes in all things.

When Semil's master-god decided to dictate a book on universal cosmic wisdom to Enoch, the god called upon Semil (also spelled as Samuil) and the angel Raguil (also spelled as Rasuil) to return to the planet earth with his scribe and the book. Semil was to make certain that Enoch not only returned to earth safely with the book, but that he pass it on to his children and their children. However, there are conflicts within this myth. One conflict is the record that declares Enoch wrote the book. A second problem is that it was a collection of astrological secrets cut on sapphire that the angel Raziel kept. A third difficulty is that it was considered to be a book in the keeping of Solomon. A nearly complete text of the writing, however, doesn't appear until the twelfth century CE, and then under the pen of Kabbalist Eleazar ben Judah of Worms.

136

# Samael

Samael was a rebellious angel.[1] While he is housed in Hebrew legend, he actually is of Sumerian origin where his name was Sammael.

The spelling of the name of this particular angel is critical. It exposes why this angel was considered evil.

Sammael is a two-part name: *Sam*, which translates from ancient Sumeria as "poison," and mael which, translates as "bright one." When joined, Sammael (in Sumerian) means the "bright and poisonous One." And he was a god until the Hebrews incorporated him into their mythology where he became the Angel of Death,[2] giving him proper space in the Hebrew lexicon of obituaries. In

---

[1] Samael translates as "Venom of God." However, this angel is far older than the tribal gods of the Habiru, and most likely is a cacophemism for "Shemal": a Syrian deity.

[2] In Arabian lore, the Angel of Death is called Azrael. Persian mythology styles him Mordad. In all cases he is a beautiful, young, well built male at the time he captures the soul, unless the dying had offended god. In such situations he appeared either as a woman or a hideous old man, both considered to be unsightly beings around one passing from this life. Legends have it that he either poisons those set to die, or kills them with a sword that is washed in the water kept in the house they occupy. See: *Abodah Zarah* 20b.

some cases, as with Abraham, Samael turns himself into a beautiful, fair (hairless) skin and radiant eyed, muscular youth complete with "all gentleness and tenderness." To the damned, Samael appears "in a terrible form" all hideous and monstrous, showing himself "in all his ugliness, cruelty, and bitterness" appearing "with seven dragon heads and fourteen faces" each more terrifying than the first. "Some of heads had the face of serpents and others were breathing flames of fire, and the sight was so terrible that seven thousand servants, male and female, of Abraham's household died, and Abraham, himself fainted."[3]

Samael is more and is attractive and kind if the one who is to die has liberally given alms. If this was the case the dying was exempt from eternal punishment.

Most legends agree that Samael taking all lives, save one: Moses. Even Yahweh was reluctant to take the soul, but in the end had to do so himself, or risk another rebellion in heaven.[4]

---

[3] *The Testament of Abraham*, in *Texts and Studies*, ed. Robinson (Cambridge, UK: The University Press, 1892), vol. 2, p. 2.

[4] *Beth HaMidrash*, ed. Adolph Jellink (6 vols.; Leipzig, 1853-1877; photostat reprint, 1938), vol. 1, p. 129; see also: *A Legend on the Death of Moses* by A. Löwy, in *Proceedings of*

Early Hebrew lore has Samael as the Chief of the Satans.[5] He is accused of stirring strife in heaven. The gods on duty for that day quarrel with him, and to make their point for dominance clear, call in Uriel who was known for "arguing against the satans and refusing them permission to come before the Lord to accuse those from earth."[6] Enoch makes it a point to let his readers know that these satans aren't bad angels. Instead, Enoch is emphatic that these satans are Enforcers of the Laws of the gods. Samael/Sammael and his brothers are an angelic police force in the earliest version of Enoch. It is only in later corrupted versions of the Book of Enoch that they, and Samael/Sammael, are slandered as being demons. Samael/Sammael is specifically referred to as the "Chief of Demons."

Samael/Sammael was charged to "work goods things for the earth." Being a large and imposing male, he was granted twelve wings. Occasionally his body would be transformed into that of a serpent. In this form he was able to glide through the air on the strength of his wings, drawing

---

the *Society of Biblical Archaeology* vol. IX (December, 1886), pp. 40-47.

[5] Enoch 40:6.

[6] Cp. Job 2:1.

the solar system behind him. Later, in emerging redactions of the Genesis story, this particularly beneficial angel is accused of being the serpent who tempted Eve.[7] The temptation, by some accounts, was planned. Samael/Sammael wanted to have coitus with Eve (in some accounts he fathered Cain). This was because of the unusually large size of his penis and scrotum, a phenomenon that so mesmerized his later followers that they raised these particular masculine attributes to the altar as signs of godliness and fecundity. It also led to quarrels, for his sexual apparatus ultimately led to a rebellion in heaven. It erupted over jealousy, with the "good angels" (being those with smaller appendages, and thus not prone to sexual thoughts, fantasies or longing) battling the "evil angels" who rejoiced in the "length and breadth" of their organ and its uncanny ability to "spill out life" at any moment. Isaiah saw their fight over their "staffs of wickedness" and "scepters of rulers" for which he notes "How art thou fallen from heaven, O Lucifer, son of the morning! How art thou cut down to the

---

[7] On the issue of the temptation of Eve, and Satan's role, see: Arthur Frederick Ide, *Woman in Biblical* Israel (Mesquite, TX: IHP, 1980). Cp. Arthur Frederick Ide, *Woman in Ancient Israel Under the Torah and Talmud; with a translation and critical commentary on Genesis 1-3* (Mesquite, TX: IHP, 1982).

ground, which didst weaken the nations!"[8] Only the Lord-gods were to have large swords "filled with blood" "made fat with fatness."[9] All those who attempt to achieve or keep the same size "shall be dissolved, and the heavens rolled together as a scroll: and all their host shall fall down...."[10]

The rebellion, it is further suggested, was the result of Samael/Sammael, who refused to cut down the size of his penis[11] or to hide it from the Daughters of Men. He was proud of what he possessed and boasted about his male sexual apparatus.

In later Hebrew accounts, Samael/Sammael was spiteful, arrogant, rude and conniving. In this he was like many other angels who patterned themselves after the gods of the wandering *Habiru* (the earliest Hebrews). In Hebrew mythology, Samael[12] occupies a unique, and an ambiguous

---

[8] Isaiah 14:5, 12 (KJV).

[9] Isaiah 34:6.

[10] Isaiah 34:4.

[11] The "staff of wickedness."

[12] At this point I am dropping the Samael/Sammael name since what follows applies only to the Hebrew accounts.

position. He is designated to be the "chief of all Satans" and at the same time "the greatest prince of Heaven" who rules angels and planets. As a "Satan", Samael is identified with Helel, Lucifer (the "son of Dawn [or the Morning]")[13] who was another fallen angel, and with the Serpent in the Garden who plotted the downfall of Adam. Some Jews even see Samael as a rival god who would challenge the creation gods and Yahweh by creating his own universe and worlds. In this way he identifies easily with the Cosmocrator or Demiurge of Gnosticism.[14]

While the ancient gods would grumble and exhibit their discomfortures and angers, their ministers or messengers (the angels) were forbidden to show such godliness. Because Samael and the closest of his associates articulated their distress with the status quo, he and his band of approximately ten angels were thrown into a prison in Heaven.

---

[13] Isaiah 14:12.

[14] Louis Ginzberg, *The Legends of the Jews* (7 vols.; Philadelphia: Jewish Publication Society, 1909-1946), vol. 5, p. 83. The Cosmocrator comes from the Orphic Greek Cosmocrator Ophion, or Ophioneus, who was also a serpent and the foundation for the myth of the serpent in the Garden. See: *Orphic Fragments* 60, 61, 70, and 89.

Samael didn't escape confinement until he devised a scheme to appear as a beautiful woman and tempt Adam. His band of cutthroat angels agreed, and quickly disguised themselves in women's apparel, leading in time to the biblical prohibition against cross-dressing (transvestitism).

The sin of Samael wasn't just in cross-dressing. It is recorded as being worse than that as he had sex with men while dressed as a woman. The core of his transgression was that he disguised himself.

Compounding his transgression was his action. It was seen as arrogant. He boasted of it. He didn't hide it. And, in some accounts, he had sex in public while dressed as a woman. The act wasn't closeted coital sex, or reserved sexual expression. Instead, it was intense, passionate, and in broad daylight, in public. This well-endowed angel had fun as did his cohorts and the men they engaged: they enjoyed their union and each other.

The ancient text suggests that the sex act that so unnerved the gods was combined fellatio and sodomy.[15] Coitus wasn't considered the only sex

---

[15] *Das christliche Adambuch des Morgenlandes.* Aus dem Äthiopischen mit Bemerkungen übersetzt von A. Dillmann, (Göttingen, 1853; from a sixth century Ethiopic text), pp. 64-67. Hereafter, this reference is cited as *Adambuch*.

act, and in fact, the story has definite correlation with an ancient Hittite myth, *Appu from Shudul*, which argues that coition is not an inborn human instinct, but one that must be taught.

Samael's singular greatest sexual conquest was in seducing Adam. Not only did Samael seduce Adam but did so while dressed as a beautiful woman and pretending to be Eve's sister while fellatiating the "First Man."[16]

The defense of the rebellious angels was their silenced argument that they had no females for themselves. Because only men were available in any quantity, the gods punished mortals by limiting the life span of men to one hundred and twenty years. And they were to be taught right from wrong by other angels.

---

[16] *Adambuch*, pp. 75-77.

## Shamshiel

Shamshiel is a little known guardian angel. His primary duty is to guard Eden and the seventy jeweled thrones made for the righteous. Each throne has fine gold legs and is ablaze with sapphires and diamonds. On the largest and most costly thrones was the one the god known as Father Abraham sat in.

The only mortals who were permitted to visit Eden and see the thrones were Moses, and Rabbi Jehoshua ben Levi, a teacher of renowned piety. Rabbi Jehoshua entered paradise by tricking the Angel of Death into giving him his sword. Once he had the sword, the Rabbi quickly jumped into the forbidden palace.[1]

---

[1] Bate Midrashot, ed. Solomon Aharon Wertheimer (2 vols.; 2nd ed. Jerusalem, 1914) vol. 1, pp. 284-285. Bavli (Babylonian Talmud) Ketubot, folio 77, col. b.

146

## Satan

Satan is an archangel in Hebrew lore. He is also the favored son of Yahweh,[1] and equally favored by other gods. And in some cases, Satan appears as a god. In these incidents Satan is known as Satan-El.[2] He was the mightiest of the Seraphim (a warrior), and is called the Viceroy or Regent of God. This is seen graphically in incidents in the Jewish-Christian bible where some acts come by the hand of the gods and the same acts in different places are the works of Satan. For example, the Old Testament gods send a plague against the Israelites in one place;[3] it is sent by Satan in another,[4] with King David commissioned in both cases to "number Israel."[5]

---

[1] Job 2:1 ff.

[2] Other names include Asmodeus, Azazel, Beelzebub, Beliel, Duma, Gadreel, Lucifer, Mastema, Mephistophles, Samael, Sammael, and Sier. Enoch writes that Azazel is the twenty-first angel to be damned by the Lord of Spirits (*Ethiopic Book of Enoch* 69:2).

[3] 2 Samuel 24:1, 15.

[4] 1 Chronicles 21:1.

[5] In both cases the word "number" in the first verse refers to a plague, not an enumeration as follows in the second verse.

Satan was originally known by the name of Samael. His biography is older than the Old Testament and appears as the patron god of Samal. Samal was a small Hittite-Aramaic kingdom lying to the east of Harran. In the literature of the Hittites, there was also a war in heaven between two gods: Alalus and Anus. Anus vanquished Alalus and took the throne, but his rule was short lived, as the Hittite gods made war on each other regularly.

The only god to fall from heaven after the celestial conflict was "the Moon God" (Hattic: *Kalku*). Unfortunately, time has corrupted the account. Much of this Hittite legend was preserved in the writings of Hebrew redactors in creating the myth of Satan challenging Yahweh, being defeated and falling from Heaven.[6]

---

[6] Text in *Keilschrifturkunde aus Boghazköi* (Berlin, 1921-1944) XXVIII, 5, and XXXIII, 120. For a discussion, see: E. Forrer, *Eine Geschichte des Götterkönigtyms aus dem Hatti-Reiche* (*Annuaire de l'institut de philologie et d'histoire orientales*) IV [1936] pp. 687-713. St. Jerome wrote an interesting commentary on the fall, arguing that the "Mighty Angel Satan" would be, one day, "reinstated in his primal splendor and with his prior rank" to help the Christian god at the Last Judgment! This concept that there will be an individual last judgment and justice is to be dispensed by a competent judge matches the Zoroastrian theology; see: Yasna 43:5: "Thou didst establish evil for the evil, and happy blessings for the good, by thy [great] virtue [to be adjudged to each] in the creation's final change." Furthermore, in both

In Ugaritic lore, Samal is a vulture or the mother of a vulture.[7] For this reason his image was

---

Christianity and Zoroastrianism, there is comparable descriptions of hell, Paradise (a Persian word), and heaven. Ultimate fellowship with God is a common hope (Revelation 21:3, cp. Yasna 41:1-2). The Zoroastrian text reads: "And now in these thy dispensations, O Ahura Mazda, do thou wisely act for us, and with abundance with thy bounty and thy tenderness as touching us; and grant that reward which thou hast appointed to our souls, O Ahura Mazda! Of this do thou thyself bestow upon us for this world and the spiritual; and now as part thereof [do thou grant] that we may attain to fellowship with thee, and thy righteousness for all duration." This has equal impact also on the Judaic concepts of a long bridge over which souls and nations must pass to reach the Judgment, where the godless will find the bridge turned into a small thin thread and fall into the depths of hell. God himself will lead the pious across. See: Isidor Scheftelowitz, *Die altpersische Religion und das Judentum: Unterschiede, Übereinstimmungen und gegenseitige Beeinflussungen.* (Giessen: Alfred Töpelmann, 1920), p. 180. Roman Catholicism, like Maccabeean Judaism's recognizes an intermediary place between heaven and hell for souls neither good enough for the one nor bad enough for the other is identical to the Persian *Dadistan-I Dinik* and *Arda Viraf Namak*; see Rosh Hashanah 16b and Shabbath 152b. Cf. Isidor Scheftelowitz, *Die altpersische Religion und das Judentum: Unterschiede, Übereinstimmungen und gegenseitige Beeinflussungen.* (Giessen: Alfred Töpelmann, 1920), p. 186.

[7] The Tale of Aqhat, in *La légende phénicienne de Danel* (*Mission de Ras-Shamra I*) (1936), ll. 139-140 ff.

rendered with him boasting twelve wings. From this motif later angels were adorned with similar wings of various numbers.

Samal was well known throughout the Middle East, as an early progenitor of the kingdom of Sam'al. It remained independent by force of arms and worship of Ba-al, the fertility god who was in constant conflict with the gods El.[8]

Samal was also a god of Syria. In Syria he was known as Shemal and accorded godly powers. He ruled the planets, the heavens and all planetary powers. In time he was identified with the sun god Lucifer, son of Dawn, and with serpents.

The word serpent has been frequently mistranslated and pictured as a snake. Because of their phallic shape serpents were considered sexual and therefore evil. It was popularly believed that serpents lusted to steal a woman's hymen to prevent her from realizing orgasm. Others argued that snakes were intrinsically evil, being considered highly sexual and striving for multiple orgasms. For this reason Satan is pictured both as a snake and as a serpent. He was considered an articulate animal

---

[8] "Canaanite and Aramaic Inscriptions," trans. Franz Rosenthal, in *Ancient Near Eastern Texts Relating to the Old Testament* ed. James B. Pritchard (3rd ed. with supplement; Princeton, NJ: Princeton University Press, 1969), pp. 654-655.

with a long tongue.[9] This tongue he used indiscriminately: enjoying both cunnilingus and fellatio when he wasn't kept busy enjoying watching others have sex.

It was out of Satan's love for sex that he ordained marriage. Not only would sex be a gift to both male and female, but also their copulation

---

[9] The first sexuality witnessed by Satan/Samael was the intercourse between Adam and Eve. It so frustrated the archangel that he vowed that he would have intercourse with her before Adam had a second chance. According to legend, when this occurred, Eve conceived Cain. A twist to the tale is that when Eve gave birth to Cain the infant's face shown angelically, leading her to declare that the Satan was no one less than Yahweh. Her declaration made Cain stand immediately after birth and run to return with straw. This inspired Eve to call the child Cain, a word which translates as "stalk." Because of this, Cain was conditioned to be a husbandman or farmer, while Abel would become a shepherd. See: Tosephta Sota, 4:17-18, Abot di Rabbi Nathan, 1:7-8, Genesis Rabba, pp. 168-169, 171-172. *Vita Adae et Evae* in *The Apocrypha and Pseudepigrapha of the Old Testament*, ed. R. H. Charles, vol. 2, pp. 18-23, Pirqe Rabbi Eliezer ben Hyrcanos (Tannaite), chap. 21. *Die Apokryphischen Gnostischen Adamschriften*. Aus dem Armenischen übersetzt und untersucht von Erwin Preuschen (Giessen, 1900), pp. 7, 42. Mani, the founder of Manicheeism, regarded both Cain and Abel to be the sons of Satan by Eve. Only Seth was considered the true offspring of Adam and Eve. The bible gives Seth no special significance or place.

resulting conception and childbirth would guarantee that the sex would continue. For this reason he was an intimate with Eve in the Garden, and according to later legends, was on hand for the birth of her children.

Cain and Abel's birth, according to legend, was followed by the birth of twin sisters: Qelimath and Lubhudha. Cain wanted to marry the more beautiful of the two: Lubhudha, and Satan persuaded him to ask for her. Adam and Eve would not agree. They wanted Cain to marry Qelimath. When his parents made their decision known, Satan persuaded Cain to kill Abel for Lebhudha's sake.[10]

---

[10] *Die Schatzhöhle*, ed. Carl Bezold (Leipzig, 1883-1888), p. 8. This is a sixth century CE Christian life written in Syriac. It couples popular legends in an effort to explain how Cain could marry and the human species preserve itself. There are older accounts that have a different twist to the slaying. A fight is generated between the brothers by the gods who want to watch combat and witness gore. Abel is victorious and prepares to slay Cain. Cain begs for mercy. Able releases his brother. This infuriates the gods who are deprived of watching blood flow. They command Cain to slay Abel. He rises and spears him repeatedly with a sharp reed (in some accounts Cain bites Abel until his brother is dead). Because the deed is over too quickly, the gods become angry and question the murderer as to his brother's final breath. See: *Das christliche Adambuch des Morgenlandes*. Aus dem Äthiopischen mit Bemerkungen übersetzt von A. Dillmann (Göttingen, 1853), pp. 70-72. This is an Ethiopic text of the sixth century. The tales neglect to

Satan's sexuality has been common for generations of literature, histories and pious writings. He is pictured as having horns, hairy legs, hoofs and a formidable phallus. In this regard he is the prototype for the ancient, lusty woodland god Pan. He also has the fearful lightning trident of the God of the Underworld, that could shoot sparks causing infertility, frigidity and impotency. He is the serpent form of the Leviathan that was the ancient god Apollyon. Satan is also the personification of all of the seven deadly sins, each a specific hallmark of a single god before Satan became the epitome of all that is evil. He represents pride,[11] avarice,[12] anger,[13] lechery,[14] gluttony,[15] envy[16] and sloth[17]: single attributes of other gods![18]

---

develop the erotic side of the story that is clear in the Hebrew text that is developed in my forthcoming book *Sin*.

[11] Pride is accorded the primary property of Lucifer.

[12] Avarice is that of Mammon. This god was corrupted by the Gospel writers into a psychological greed for wealth and other riches (μαμμώνας); see: Matthew 6:24; Luke 16:9, 11, 13.

[13] Anger belongs to Satan (Σατανας or השמן: the accuser). Cf. 1 Chronicles 21:18.

[14] Lechery is the hallmark of Asmodeus.

Satan enjoyed being involved in all things. He was, after all, a counselor, an adviser and an advocate. He sought out and won the position as counselor to King Nimrod in Nimrod's struggle with Abram.[19] Nimrod so hated Abram that he had his enemy cast into a fiery furnace. Abram's flesh didn't burn, matching the fable of Daniel, which so enraged Nimrod that he appeared mad until Satan arrived, promising to build the king a siege-catapult

---

[15] Gluttony is accorded to Beelzebul (Βεελςβούλ; this word is frequently corrupted into Beelzebub. See: Matthew 10:25, 2:24 and 27; Mark 3:22; Luke 11:15, 18-19. The Jews ascribed supremacy among evil spirits to this pagan deity).

[16] Envy (קוא (*qana*) where it leads to action as in Genesis 26:14, 30:1, and 37:11; in the Greek it is ζήλος: *zēlos*: Romans 13:13, 1 Corinthians 3:3 and 12:20; James 3:14, 16), is the special property of the Leviathan (לו׳תן: a great water animal; see Job 41:1; Psalm 74:14, 104:26; Isaiah 27:1).

[17] Sloth is the seal of Belphegor. It is a combination of idleness (οκυρος: Matthew 25:26; Romans 12:11), deceit (רמ׳ה: *remiyyah*: Proverbs 12:24, 27) and inaction (עצל: *atsal*: Proverbs 15:19, 19:24, 21:25, 22:13, 24:30, 26:13-15).

[18] These other gods became Satans in the Christian angelology. They are discussed later in this chapter.

[19] *Sepher Hayashar*, ed. Lazarus Goldschmidt (Berlin, 1923), p. 27. Pirqe Rabbi Eliezer ben Hyrcanos (Tannaite), chap. 26.

to hurl Abram "into the fiery furnace from a convenient distance." Nimrod agreed. Receiving his commission, Satan built the machine. But the end of Abram was not to be. Although catapulted into the center of the fiery furnace, Abram prayed down the flames, and when the fire was out the logs budded, blossomed and yielded fruit.[20]

Satan-El, however, was only one of the Satans that Jews, Christians and Moslems trembled before. Abaddon-Satan (the Greek Apollyon) was another angel equally feared, for this Satan was the angel of the Bottomless Pit, an innovation that came with a seven-layered model of the underworld, taken from ancient Babylon to create the Jews

---

[20] *Sepher Hayashar*, ed. Lazarus Goldschmidt (Berlin, 1923), p. 34-43. Ma'ase Abraham, in *Beth HaMidrash*, ed. Adolph Jellinek (6 vols.; Leipzig, 1853-1877; photostat reprint, Jerusalem, 1938), vol. 1, pp. 32-34. For a worldview of Satan and the power of evil, see: Jeffrey Burton Russell, *The Prince of Darkness: Radical Evil and the Power of Good in History* (London: Thames and Hudson, 1988). Cf. Jeffrey Burton Russell, *The Devil: Perceptions of Evil from Antiquity to Primitive Christianity* (Ithaca, NY: Cornell University Press, 1977). Jeffrey Burton Russell, *Satan: The Early Christian Tradition* (Ithaca, NY: Cornell University Press, 1981). Jeffrey Burton Russell, *Lucifer: The Devil in the Middle Ages* (Ithaca, NY: Cornell University Press, 1984). Jeffrey Burton Russell, *Mephistopheles: The Devil in the Modern World* (Ithaca, NY: Cornell University Press, 1986).

Gehenna.[21] In other records, Abaddon is the Angel of the Bottomless Pit who ties up the Devil for a millennium.[22] In the third century CE *Acts of Thomas* he becomes a Devil or demon himself and joins Satan. Interestingly, in *The Thanksgiving Hymns* (a Dead Sea scroll), Abaddon is both a place for the living and the dead. There its ruler is called Arsiel, which translates as "Black Sun" (or anti-matter). In the center of the Bottomless Pit lives the serpent angel Apollyon (the fallen Greek Sun God Apollo). He is styled as the King of the Demonic Locusts and rules over all other fallen deities and angels but gives credit to the power of Beliel-Satan.

Beliel-Satan was the ruling Prince of Sheol. Sheol was considered to be a part of the infernal regions. Beliel (which has been corrupted to read Beliar) means "worthless." The *Gospel of Bartholomew* has Beliel-Satan declaring: "At first I was called Satanel, which is interpreted as Messenger of God, but when I rejected the image of God my name was called Satanas, that is: an angel

---

[21] Exodus 15:5 uses the word מצולה (*metsolah*); cf. Zechariah 1:8 where it is a shadowy place. The concept of the Bottomless Pit was refined by early Christians as ἄβυσς (*abussos*): Revelation 9:11, 11:7, 17:8, and 20:1, 3.

[22] Revelation 20:1-2.

that keepeth Hell."[23] Among Beliel-Satan's crimes was his need to boast. He liked to tell all who would

---

[23] Hell is an invention of eschatology that develops only in later Old Testament literature. It was considered a suspended place, but without the later-day concept of being an inferno. A fiery pit enters the Hebrew religion only as an association with Gehenna (a transcription of the Hebrew *Ge-Hinnōm*: the name of the valley south of Jerusalem where Kings Ahaz and Manasseh sacrificed their sons to the god Moloch (2 Chronicles 28:3, 33:6; Jeremiah 32:35). After Josiah's reforms it was transformed into a garbage dump. The sinister association and the smoke that continuously ascended from it made it a symbol of suffering and judgment, and so figures in various oracles (Jeremiah 7:31, 18:6; Isaiah 66:24). It becomes a place of final punishment of the wicked only in Jewish apocalyptic literature (1 Enoch 27, 90:26 f). In the New Testament Gehenna is translated erroneously as Hell: a place of eternal punishment (Matthew 5:29, 10:28). The Authorized Version unfortunately couples Gehenna and incorrectly translates Hades as Hell, too. The Revised Standard Version mistranslates Hades as "death" in Matthew 16:18. Hades, in its original known form, was a resting-place for the dead pending their resurrection. (In Greek mythology those souls in Hades were engaged in the same trades, crafts and duties they had while alive; to the Hebrews, Hades was a place of total inactivity.) In contrast, the Gehenna-Hell of the New Testament is a place of torment, unquenchable thirst, and all-consuming worms (Matthew 18:8 f; Mark 9:44 ff) that sustain existence even though they too are in an everlasting fiery furnace (Matthew 13:42). This furnace is also a lake of fire (*Ethiopic Book of Enoch* 67:13; Revelation 20:14). The concept of a lake of fire is not unique to Judaism or Christianity. Instead it comes from Persian antecedents,

listen that "I was formed the first angel." After him came Michael, Gabriel third, Uriel fourth, and Raphael fifth. Beliel-Satan was an archangel who was expected to war against the Canaanite deity Beelzebul but sided with the god instead. Beelzebul was then incorporated into Hebrew angelology as Beelzebul-Satan.

Beelzebul-Satan's name means "Lord of the House." This meant that he was also "Lord of the

---

especially that found in Zoroastrianism which develops the theme of torrent of molten metal that will destroy the deceitful and at the same time save the truthful (Yasna 51:1; cp. Rudolf Mayer, *Die biblische Vorstullung vom Weltenbrand: Eine Untersuchung über die Bezeihungen zwichen Parsismus und Judentum* (Bonner Orientalistische Seminars der Universität Bonn, 1956). While lit up by the tongues of fire, the New Testament Hell is in outer darkness (Matthew 8:12). St. Paul makes colorful and inaccurate use of the concept of Gehenna and Hell, coupling it with wrath (Romans 5:9), destruction (Romans 9:22), and corruption (Galatians 6:8), as did John the Apostle who argues that it is death (John 8:21) and the second death (Revelation 20:6, 14). It is patterned after Greek mythology in 2 Peter 2:4, when the word Hell is rendered as Tartarus, which to the Greeks was a place where the wicked are punished in the bowels of the earth far deeper than Hades. Early and Medieval Christian apologists married the corruption to the sins of sex and the flesh, where transgressors are forced into being perpetually sodomized, castrated, or be subjected to labiaectomies, buried in human excrement, force fed on fetal matter, and worse.

Souls" and "Lord of the Flies."[24] Far from being a god who was unclean and attracted vermin, Beelzebul bore souls through the air so that women who stuck out their tongues could conceive by swallowing one or more. Since this act didn't require coitus, and Beelzebul was considered the author of oral conception, he was quickly cast as an

---

[24] This is a bad translation. He should be known as "Lord of the fly": the butterfly that was seen as a means of carrying souls; in that the Greek, *psyche* actually signifies a butterfly. See Johann Weyer's study on Beelzebul as the Supreme Overlord of the Underworld in his classic *Pseudographica Demoniaca*. In his *Pseudo Monarchia Daemonium*, Johann Weyer gives the Talmudic figure of 7,405,926 demons residing in hell. These demons were divided into 72 companies and pledged to obey all laws issued by Beelzebul, Supreme Over-Lord of the Dark Empire. In this 16th century tract, Weyer allows Beelzebul to have a series of captains to command the ranks of the angels. These captains include: Satan, Prince of Darkness; the Greek god Pluto, Prince of Fire and Hades; the Ammonite god Molech, Prince of the Land of Tears; Baal, the chief male deity of the Phoenicians and Canaanite as, General of the Diabolic Hordes; Lucifer, serving as the Chief Justice; Baal-beryth known as the Lord of the Covenant who was worshipped by the Israelites around 1200 BCE (see Judges 8:33 and 9:4), Minister of Devilish Pacts and Treaties; Bergal, Chief of the Secret Police; the Greek goddess Proserpine, characterized as the Arch She-Devil as Princess of Demonic Spirits; Astarte, masculinized as Astaroth, Duke and Treasurer of Hell.

evil demon, and ultimately became known as the incarnate of evil. He was damned by three of the Apostles as the "Lord of Chaos."[25] Christian mythology states that Jesus gave him dominion over Hell for helping to evacuate Adam and the other saints during the harrowing of the underworld. From this developed the mythology of the angel Matesma-Satan who was known as the Accusing Angel, the tempter and the executioner.

Matesma-Satan was a special angel who had charge over the life and death of mortals. It was he who hardened pharaoh's heart at the time of Moses and helped Egyptian magicians to harass the Israelites with black magic and natural calamities. He is considered the angel of death who slaughtered the first born of Egypt and appeared as the first named separation of the *mal'ak* (or, Shadow of God). To counter his destructive properties, an Angel of Light was fashioned and given the name of Lucifer.[26]

---

[25] Matthew 10:25, and 12:24, 27; Mark 3:22; Luke 11:15, 18-19.

[26] In ancient Buddhism, the Bodhisattva Amitabha was the angel/god of Light and was noted for his boundless ability and intercessory skills that now compose the framework of contemporary Judaism and Christianity.

Lucifer means "Bearer of Light," "Son of the Morning," "Dragon of Dawn" and "Prince of the Power of the Air." At one time he was seen as the greatest of all angels and the most beloved of all of the creations of the gods. He was the favorite of the Hebrew god known as God the Father, who called Lucifer his Beloved Son and Lord of Light. But Lucifer didn't have the same love or loyalty, according to later Hebrew mythology, and was the first to separate himself from the Divine source.[27]

Lucifer distanced himself from the Creator Father because of jealousy. The Father god had created yet another masterpiece and called him Jesual, the Son, and fashioned the new son to be an identical twin to his first Beloved Son Lucifer. Jesual ultimately figures prominently in the New Testament, while Lucifer's light is dimmed by a growing concern over his sexual excesses.

Because Lucifer copulates primarily with mortal women, and his twin brother on earth merely moves among them, sleeping, eating and living only with men, the Father determines that he has to destroy Lucifer's creations by inventing death. When this fails to stop the Lord of Light, the Father god casts his first truly Beloved Son out of heaven and renames him Satan-El: the Adversary. Later,

---

[27] Ezekiel 28:13-15.

when the Father god rethinks his actions, he allows Lucifer to have a role in rebirth. Lucifer is invited to share with the serpent the unique ability to shed the old dead skin and arise as if newborn.[28]

When Lucifer accuses his twin brother, Jesual, of not fulfilling their Father's command to multiply, the Father god became so angry that he hurled Lucifer to earth as a lightning bolt. But while the bolt of lightning plunged through space, the Father god took pity and allowed it to transform itself into a phallic form before it pierced the Bottomless Pit of the Mother Goddess Hel.[29]

---

[28] That Lucifer is equated with the serpent is not unique with the Hebrews. They merely recrafted the Egyptian serpent god, Sata, who is father of lightning and who also fell to earth, coupling the Morning Star with the Babylonian god Zu who was a lightning god who fell as a fiery flying serpent. Lucifer was once a Seraph, and as such he was considered to be a mighty adversary or warrior. In ancient Mecca, the Morning Star was the goddess Al-`Uzza, who was a pale imitation of the goddess Venus. The Mecca cult was the center of phallic worship patterned on that of Ishtar and Isis (see: George Ryley Scott, *Phallic Worship, A History of Sex & Sexual Rites* (London: Luxor Press, 1966; reissued: London: Senate, a division of Random House, Ltd., 1966), pp. 13, 155, 216 ff). The emphasis on Lucifer as an angel of light is applied to Jesus in the New Testament: as φωσφόρος ("daystar" in 2 Peter 1:19), and ὁ ἀστὴρ ὁ πρωϊνός ("morning star" in Revelation 22:16).

[29] Hel was once a uterine shrine: a womb or a sacred cave of rebirth. This is a story of the love a son had for his mother, and the invention of the Oedipus syndrome. To sanitize the relationship between Jesual and his Virgin Mother, redactors had the new Beloved Son deny his mother (Matthew 12:47-50; and 13:55; Mark 3:31-35; Luke 8:21-22) and style all women as mothers of all men, rejecting anyone who loved his mother or father more than him. See: Matthew 10:37. The "virgin birth" became a staple with some early Christian writers, and moved quickly into Christian dogma (see: *The Letters of Ignatius to the Ephesians* 19:1) where it is proclaimed a "mystery." The Germanic tribes had a similar tale in the Valkyries, who were the northern Angels of Death. Their leader was Brunnhilde, whose name translates as "burning hell." The idea that hell was a place of burning fire comes from this antecedent, as the hell of the Old Testament (*sheol*: שאול) was an unseen state (2 Samuel 22:6; Job 11:8, Psalm 9:7, 18:15, 55:15, 86:13; Proverbs 9:18; and so forth). Hell remains the "unseen" world among New Testament writers who refine the Greek Hades (ἅδης); see: Matthew 11:233 and 16:18; Luke 10:15 and 16:23; Acts 2:27, 31; Revelation 1:18, 6:8, 20:13-14. It is weaned from the concept that it is darkness (Matthew 8:21, 22:13, 25:30) with quasi-matches in the gospel accounts of the Valley of Hinnom (*Gehenna*: γέεννα): Matthew 5:22, 29, 30; 23:15, 23; Mark 9:43, 45, 47; Luke 12:5). The innovation and first use of the fires of hell appearing in James 3:6. In the only recorded comment by Jesus, he equated it with "outer darkness," where "there shall be weeping and gnashing of teeth" (see: Matthew 8:12, cp. Matthew 13:42 where fire is added, cf. Matthew 22:13, 24:51, 25:30; Luke 13:28).

Much of the theology of later Christianity on the concept and state of Hell as a state of eternal punishment after

There are numerous other antecedents for the Judaeo-Christian Satan. One of the most important and least investigated is the Zoroastrian Angra Mainyu/Ahriman. This particular god was a hostile spirit. He was the sworn enemy of Ahura Mazda's Holy Spirit, Spenta Mainyu.

A reading of Zoroastrian holy texts unveils that Angra Mainyu/Ahriman most likely is the foundation for the later Satan in Judaism and Christianity. As Satan is described in Hebrew and Christian sources as being one who brought death to the world,[30] the Zoroastrian scriptures paint the same bleak picture.[31] Zoroastrian biblical text

---

death, is the result of amalgamating Christian and Jewish concepts with Greek and Asian commentaries. This led to the invention of a temporary state of punishment (purgatory) where those who were with sin could be cleansed, and as an alternative to heaven where the just pass directly at the point of their death. Hell is refined by St. Paul as a point of death (Romans 2:5, 8 ff) inasmuch as the damned no longer have the opportunity to see the Face of God. St. John argues, however, that the damned perish or disappear if they aren't redeemed by Jesus (John 3:16). Scholastic thought details that the damned are *poena damni*: excluded from God's presence and will be externally tormented: *poena sensus*.

[30] Hebrews 2:14; cp. Genesis 3:19; Revelation 2:13.

[31] Yasna 30:4.

shows Angra Maniyu/Ahriman as having the *daevas* (or evil spirits) under his control,[32] as do the Christian gospels,[33] which takes on a more refined shape in the epistles.[34] In these instances, the evil one becomes *Shaitin*, and falls from heaven because of his pride to become the accused tempter.

Among the Zoroastrian angelic hosts, Angra Mainyu/Ahriman controls the *druj*.[35] This is the demon of the Lie, which is the personification of deceit. Together they stand against *asha*, the principle of Truth and Righteousness that is on the side of Ahura Mazda. As it is in Christian sources (where Satan is to be defeated by a resurrected Christ), so too is it in Zoroastrian theology where Angra Mainyu/Ahriman is to be defeated by Ahura Mazda's holy spirit Spenta Mainyu, with Deceit being delivered into the hands of Truth. "The most

---

[32] Yasna 30:6.

[33] Matthew 9:34, 12:24, 27 emphasize δαιμόνιον; cp. Matthew 4:24, 8:16, 28, 33, and 9:32, 12:22, 15:22; Mark 5:15, 16, 18; Luke 8:36.

[34] 1 Timothy 4:1 emphasizes doctrine, while the Accuser devil is the subject of Ephesians 6:11; 1 Timothy 3:7; Hebrews 2:14; James 4:7; 1 Peter 5:8; and so forth.

[35] Yasna 30:8.

wicked *druj*, born of darkness" and "the evil-doing Angra Mainyu" will be overcome.[36] They will be overwhelmed with a fiery purge of evil and the universe will experience a renovation.[37] This matches the emerging biblical concept of Satan.[38]

Islam also has a Satan. In the faith of Muhammad, the evil one is known as *Iblis*. Etymologically, Iblis is a contraction of Diabolos and as in other Middle Eastern faiths, Iblis falls from heaven because of pride. Aligned with other fallen angels, Iblis works feverishly on earth to obstruct Allah's plans and tempt men to go astray from the laws set down in the Koran (*Al Qur'ān*). Even in this regard, Allah limits the power of Iblis. As with Job, in Islam, the activities and temptations of Iblis is restricted to Allah's permissive decrees and calculated noninterference. This is especially true in the Last Judgment in Islam. There is little difference in it and that recorded in Zoroastrian, Jewish, and Christian apocalyptic literature. There will be "signs" and other warnings. A last trumpet

---

[36] Yasht 19:95-96.

[37] Bundahish 30:29-32.

[38] T. H. Gaster, "Satan," in *Interpreter's Dictionary of the Bible*, ed. G. A. Buttrick (4 vols.; Nashville: Abingdon, 1976), vol. 4, p. 226.

will sound. The dead will rise. All souls will assemble before Allah's throne of judgment and the books that have been written recording each man's deeds will be read. Satan's dominion, Hell, will be waiting for sinners. God's home will be opened to the saved: heaven being nothing less than a fine tent in the sky where

> Aye-blooming youths go round about to them
> With goblets and ewers and a cup of flowing wine;
> Their brows ache not from it, nor fails the senses
> .....
> In recompense for their labors past.[39]

In Buddhism, Satan is known as Mara. The name is from a root meaning "to die." The Buddhist Satan doesn't control hell as the Buddhist hell is a cycle of death and rebirth (reincarnation). Heaven is ending the cycle (nirvana). Mara's task isn't to draw people into hell, but instead keep them in a perpetual bondage of being born to die and be reborn. His greatest failure was in his battle with Buddha, a war he lost when he introduced heavenly women (*apsaras*) to distract his attention from otherworldly thoughts. Buddha was not distracted. Frustrated, Mara introduced ferocious demons.

---

[39] *Al Qur'ān,* Al-Wāqilah [56]:17-19.

Buddha remained undisturbed. Finally, Mara demanded to know why Buddha felt he had a right to be freed from the endless cycle of reincarnation. Buddha's answer surprised Mara. Buddha, it is reported, called the earth to witness to his goodness. Earth responded with such a powerful voice that Mara and his band of angels were frightened away, so that very night Buddha achieved enlightenment and disappeared forever.[40]

A similar concept exists in Hindu theology. Shiva is, however, both a good god/angel as well as a demonic god/angel known as the Destroyer. He brings death, disease, destruction and woe. Few speak his name, fearing that if they do, the Destroyer will appear.[41] As a good angel/god Shiva embodies human reproduction and vital sexuality. He is represented by sex symbols: the *lingam* and *yomi* (representing male and female), and enjoys various consorts and associates, like the Judaeo-Christian angels and gods.[42]

---

[40] Cf. Edward Conze, *Buddhist Thought in India* (1962; reprint, Ann Arbor: MI: University of Michigan Press, 1967).

[41] Charles Eliot, *Hinduism and Buddhism* (3 vols.; London: Edward Arnold and Company, 1921), vol. 2, pp. 144 *seq*.

[42] Romain Rolland, *Prophets of the New India*, translated by E. F. Malcolm-Smith (New York: Albert and Charles Boni, 1930), pp. 42-43 ff.

# The Sons of God &
# The Daughters of Men

Samael's rebellion was but one of the wars in the heavenly homes of the various Hebrew gods. For that reason some redactors argue that Samael was no one less of importance than the Satan: an archangel who regularly challenged the rule of the gods and ultimately aligned his forces with those who pledged their loyalty to the tattered and impoverished rural god Yahweh.

In fear of Samael (or Satan), the favored archangel who stood closest to the throne of the gods[1]

---

[1] Satan, in the Judaeo-Christian bible is acknowledged to be chief among the Sons of God (Job 2:1). The Satan was given unrestricted power over life, but was limited as to the death he

was dismissed as the gods instructed other angels to attend to men on earth as teachers. At first these angels followed the letter of their charter given to them by the gods. But, like Samael and his friends (who collectively are known as the "Sons of God"[2]) over a three hundred-year period of time, the next host of angels found the sex with virgins, matrons, men and beasts who populated the earth to be irresistible.[3] While the sex was forbidden, even more intolerable was the fact that many of the

---

might cause (Job 2:2-6). Satan's role was that of an accuser, as testified in his name: Σάτάν.

[2] The term "Sons of God" is unique. The Hebrew does not give the deity the name Yahweh. Instead, the name of the god is El. This is ancient name. It means "god of fertility." It is not a Hebrew god. Instead, El is the bull-god of the Semites, and the sons of El were cattle owning worshippers of the bull-god if the text is read literally. However, in context, it is a statement of those who worshipped the penis and fecundity. This is in keeping with the clime and time of the tale, and follows all fertility texts extant. It extends to the most primitive tribes and customs from human sacrifice and the burial of the flesh to ensure successful crops and harvest to actual intercourse with the soil to moisten seed; see James Fraser's *Golden Bough*.

[3] Tanhuma Buber Genesis 24. Ancient Hebrew myths state that 9/10ths of all the Sons of God succumbed to the seductive flesh of the daughters of Cain.

angels sired giants known as the Nephillim.[4] In Hebrew legend, the Nephillim built the Tower of Babel and by doing so threatened the hegemony, suzerainty and security of the gods.

The gods fidgeted over these new transgressions by their sons. They were tempted to destroy all of those whom engaged in sex with the angels. Two angels, however, especially encouraged the extreme action of their fathers. They were Shemhazai and Azael, angels who were "in the confidence of God [the gods]." Fortunate for them, the gods were reluctant to act, at least at first when it seemed critical.

Weak and self-affected, needing constant prayer and praise of mortals to reassure themselves that they were powerful, splendid gods, the deities realized that if they destroyed all mortals and beasts, they would have no gardeners to tend their world and it would become a wasteland.[5] Seeing

---

[4] The etymology of this Hebrew word is uncertain. It is retained in the Revised Version in only two places: Genesis 6:4 (the Authorized version translates Nephillim as "giants"), and Numbers 13:33. In Numbers Nephillim is defined as men of gigantic size and stature living in Canaan. Their existence is reported by Hebrew spies eager to conquer Canaan.

[5] While Judaism and Christianity have angels worshipping God with prayer and praise, in Islam, the angels praise Allah (God) and pray for men (mortals); see: *Qur'an* Ash-Shūrā

their chance, and close to exposing their ruse, Shemhazai and Azael comforted the gods and suggested there was an alternative. The alternative was for them to go to the earth and "inhabit" it and "sanctify your name."

Hearing Shemhazai and Azael vow to increase the prayers and praise of mortals and reflecting how good such adulation was to hear, the vain and dependent deities promptly agreed. The angels were commissioned quickly, but the speed of getting the gods permission wasn't fast enough to satisfy the burning in the angel's loins. Their passion was enhanced by the verbal accounts of another angel, Grigori, who dwelt on each tissue fold within the Daughters of Men's private parts. Within a twinkling, Grigori had all the angels' flesh "inflamed for release."

Shemhazai, Azael, Grigori and their coterie, had barely taken up residence on earth when their passions were turned to the Daughters of Men. Like existing potentates, they had sex indiscriminately. Shemhazai quickly coupled with many. From two of his exploits he fathered monsters: Hiwa and Hiya. These children were both angels and men: angels in conniving, and men in appetite (both sexual and physical). Each day they ate a thousand

---

[42]:5. Two angels in Islam angelology are commissioned to record the deeds of men; see: *Qur'an* Qāf [50]:17-19.

camels, a thousand horses and a thousand oxen.[6] Their sexual appetite was equally fluid.

Azael[7] was more subtle than Shemhazai who jumped any woman near him. Azael developed the

---

[6] The quantities discussed in the legends reflects the habits of the herdsmen of the god El, and has as its probable origin within an Essene community whose diet was severely restricted (like that of Daniel and his three holy companions in the fire) to pulses; see: Daniel 1:12. The fact that these holy companions were equally encased in fire is a reflection and an incorporation of the ancient myth of the angels with the myth of Daniel. His companions were little more than an attribute to penial erections that surrounded the youth. The inclusion of this part indicates that Daniel was involved in an orgy, common in the land he allegedly occupied.

[7] Azael, as a name, appears only in poorly constructed Greek transcriptions of Aramaic originals. It is a corruption of Azazel which translates as "God strengthens," and reflects the worship of muscularity and strength. The significance of the rite of purification and the chasing of a goat to its death, plunging over a cliff to be broken on the stones below, is a match for the Azazel myth. This myth recounts how the god fell to its death as the angel fell from grace (heaven) and was imprisoned by an unforgiving multitude of deities under a pile of rock. Cp. Leviticus 16:8-10 *cum* 17:7, which prohibits offerings to demons. In Islamic lore, Azazel (known as Iblis) is recognized as the angel who refused to acknowledge and bow before Adam when this first human was presented to the other hierarchies of heaven. It was Azazel who originally voiced the now famous question, "Why should a Son of Fire bow to a Son of Clay?" For his honesty, Azazel was banished

fine art of seduction by inventing ornaments and cosmetics to win the sexual favors of earthbound women. He also won their sexual favors by offering them the opportunity of coupling with goats, an animal he favored above all else, prizing their horns that stood hard and rigid. Azael's greatest weapon, however, was music.[8] He used it to seduce his victims. Because of this music was banned as being sexual in nature, and leading to war. This was an outgrowth of what mortals saw as Azael's ultimate invention, the brewing of beer. This discovery was especially feared since morals quickly picked it up and adopted it as their own. Addicted to Azael's inventions mortals became so "inflamed" that they "lay promiscuously together." Swayed by the beer Azael created, with tunes trapped in their minds, the musicians cared little as to the gender of the person they penetrated any cavity with their ultimate

---

from the Garden and heaven. Enoch lists Azazel as the twenty-first angel consigned to hell (*Ethiopic Book of Enoch* 69:2), but it is unclear if Azazel and Azael are the same angels.

[8] There are numerous biblical inferences and references concerning this, generated later. For example, the invention of musical instruments is attributed to Jubal in Genesis 4:27. The name *Jubal* actually translates as "playing" or "nomad" and exposes its antecedents. In time it devolved to *jubilee*, which actually meant "shouting."

instrument they termed as "spear-points" in honor of Azael's final invention: an iron sword.[9] The men noticed how close the sword was in design to their tool, for both had long shafts and hard points that penetrated the flesh without bending.

Once more the gods realized that they had been duped. They had received the prayers and praise of the intimidated, the exploited, the poor, the hungry, and the forgotten and rejoiced in being declared good, beneficial and comforting. But they were not the first to couple with the women, and their own ambassadors ripped this regalian right from them.

Angered at being cuckolded, the gods once more threatened to destroy the earth. Sinisterly they decided on the earth's fate. They would flood it. It seemed to be just since mortals had evolved from the water they should die in the water.

Divining the draconian designs of the devilish gods, Shemhazai wept bitterly. He cried not for the earth or mortals. Instead he lamented the promised doom of his sons: not that they would be

---

[9] *Das christliche Adambuch des Morgenlandes.* Aus dem Äthiopischen mit Bemerkungen übersetzt von A. Dillmann, (Göttingen, 1853; from a sixth century Ethiopic text), pp. 92-93. Hereafter, this reference is cited as *Adambuch*. Later the Hebrews gave this honor to the biblical-mythological being Tubal Cain. See: Genesis 4:22.

swept to their deaths in the torrential rains or subsequent flood, but fearing that they would starve to death once the water erased all the animals on earth. His sons, Hiwa and Hiya were giants,[10] and they could stand above the waters, but had they also had ravenous appetites and could not survive more than a day without victuals.[11]

Repenting that he had brought the doom upon his children, Shemhazai threw himself into the heavens and became a constellation (Orion).[12] Azael, however, did not repent and was not granted the opportunity to find a safe place in the sky. Because he didn't repent, and did not throw himself into the sky, the Hebrews heaped their sins on an

---

[10] The names of the gods actually come from a Talmudic passage about the verbal ejaculations by Babylonian sailors who were made to shout as they hauled cargo vessels ashore: "*Hilni, hiya, hola, w'hilok holya!*"

[11] Yalqut Genesis 44.

[12] Malcolm Godwin, *Angels: An Endangered Species* (New York: Simon and Schuster, 1990), p. 111 repeats this fable. He gives a complete list of the most notable Watchers on pp. 112-113. What is tantalizing is that most the names reflect supreme faith, religious devotion, and adoration by the gods. For example, Godwin notes that Azael means "Whom God Strengthens"; Gadreel means "God is my Helper"; and Tamiel, which means "Perfection of God."

annual scapegoat to throw the hapless animal over a cliff to Azael.[13]

The coterie of the lead angels tried valiantly to avoid the fates that became the lot of their chieftains. They tried to appease the gods by vowing that they would win the hearts of mortals and teach them righteousness. Righteousness was defined to mean constancy in the faith, to regularly offer prayers and praise, and to give up more for the gods than they kept for themselves.

To pilot their program, this second set of angels disguised themselves as precious stones and metals encased in the earth. Mortals quickly stole the gems. When taken from the earth the angels transformed themselves back into angels and began to teach mortals to be otherworldly and giving ("righteous"). This goal was never reached, for mortals would offer no more than a tenth of what they had to the gods, arguing that if the gods were omnipotent they would have no need for the treasures of the earth that they created. A few of the more wise mortals noted that constant prayer and praise hindered work and interfered with play. Realizing the truth of the words of the mortals, the

---

[13] Bereshit Rabbati, compiled by Rabbi Moshe Hadarshan (Narbonne, c. 1050); quoted by page of Hanoch Albeck's edition, Jerusalem, 1940; pp. 29-30.

angels recanted and joined them, quickly lusting for mortal women to chain them to the earth to have them ready for casual sex whenever it was wanted.[14] Unserviced, the gods, once more, saw sex, as the enslaver of mortals: that it robbed from the gods of the time mortals spent in prayer needed to nourish the gods starving ego. Sex had to be controlled! It was okay if it lead to the procreation of additional worshippers. It was evil if it led to pleasure without the procreation of worshippers, and in this regard oral sex was the gravest of sins. It was introduced by a small band of Fallen Ones[15]

---

[14] Enoch 6-8, 69, 106, ff. Cf. The Syrian *Clementine Homilies* viii, 11-17 (pp. 142-145). Enoch is a myth that ultimately crystallized in a first century BCE compilation known as the *Book of Enoch*. It has as its origin Genesis 5:22 where he is defined as the father of Methuselah, and inferred to be an angel who walked with the gods of creation. Later Hebrew myths make Enoch a recording angel and counselor to the gods, and ultimately the patron of Hebrew children who study the Torah. His nicknames are a corruption of ancient Hebraic words that indicates he was a favored son of the gods who was "nearest to the Divine Throne": *meta ton thronon* which became "*Metatron*".

[15] The Hebrew is *Nephillim*. It is the collective name bore by many tribes all who figure in the evolving myth. These tribes include *Anakim* (Wearers of Necklaces; which reflects on Azael's industry), *Awwim* (Devastators *or* Serpents), *Emim* (Terror), *Gibborim* (Giant Heroes), *Repha'im* (Weakeners), and *Zamzummim* (Achievers). They were later suppressed by

(angels) who relished dining on the fruits of sex.[16] This was defined both as the orgasmic materials

Caleb who legend has as being Joshua's comrade. See Joshua 14:6, 13-14, 16-18, and 21:22; Numbers 13:6, 30; 14:6, 24, 30, 38; 26:65; 32:12; 34:19. Cp. 1 Samuel 25:3 and 30:14; 1 Chronicles 2: 46, 48, 4:15 and 6:56 for lineage. He was considered to be the son of Jephunneh, and is mentioned among the chiefs sent to spy out Canaan, bring back a favorable report with Joshua. A chief of the Hegronites, he was a prince of Judah, but didn't claim possession of the land of the Anakims, Kirjatharba or Hebron and the neighboring hill country until he was 85, by driving out the three sons of Anak in 1444 BCE. The victory, like the battle and the accounts leading to it exposes an ancient myth of four quarters of a land filled with giants.

[16] The debate on the title "Fallen Ones" is long and ancient. While contemporary Christianity and historic Judaism attempts to paint the "Fallen Ones" as singular in nature, reserved for "Satan," past Hebrew records and Palestinian myths give it to any male of excessive strength and muscularity who enjoyed watching women expose their "private parts": the vagina and anus. Rabbi Eliezer records the same in a Midrash: "The angels who fell from Heaven saw the daughters of Cain perambulating and displaying their secret parts, their eyes painted with antimony in the manner of harlots, and, being seduced, took wives among them. Surprisingly, other rabbis, such as Joshua ben Qorah, did doubt the accuracy of the account but merely questioned how the "harlots" avoided being "scorched ... internally" since the angels were pillars of fire. More reasonable minds figured out that the pillars of fire weren't literally true, but instead referred to the concentration of blood surging within the erect penis as

generated at the climax of the act since it was equated as being on par with the cannibalism of human flesh. Legend records that the gods were so terrified that the angels might acquire a taste for any element of life material that they rained manna (translated both as bread and as quail) on the earth. But the manna was flavorless and not at all tempting. Because this bland diet was showered upon them, the Fallen Ones rejected manna and slaughtered animals for food, dined on human flesh and the orgasms of their partners, to the point that the air was "fouled" with the sickly vapors.[17] A canon was developed concerning sex. It was defined as an act to be employed solely for procreation, raising the goddess Istahar,[18] a virgin, to the

---

the organs pulsed for intercourse and ultimate discharge. Oral sex was feared and damned because orgasm was seen as a food meant only for the gods who argued that it tasted good and was pleasant to experience. See the Midrashes cited. For many faiths, the oral consumption of orgasm was considered to be a desecration of the fruits of the Tree of Life. Thus in many cultures, the Tree of Life is phallic in appearance, and the branches and fruits are a weak imitation or sperm.

[17] *Ibid.*

[18] The tale of Istahar comes from the Greek writer Aratus in the early third century BCE. It is an epic praising the age of gold, but damning the rise of the Silver and Bronze Ages which brought greed and slaughter (swords). Istahar's ascent

heavens to keep her delicate beauty out of the sex-stained hands of the angels. So great was her beauty that even the gods were tempted. To still their own passions they transformed her into the constellation Virgo, after which the angels on earth weren't allowed to return to the sky until Jacob's ladder was sent down for them to climb back home.

There is an interesting legend concerning the Daughters of Men. Some scribes claimed them to be the daughters of Cain who, along with his tribe, was punished with the curse of having 100 daughters for each son born. This made the females so hungry for men that they invaded homes to carry off the males to satisfy their lusts to the dismay and agony of pious men who "made rigid" with their tongue

---

into heaven, like that of Enoch's, is borrowed from Apollodorus's account of Orion's attempt to seduce the seven virgin Pleiades (daughters of the god of strength Atlas and Pleione). The girls only escaped Orion by fleeing to the heavens and where they were transformed into stars. The name, Istahar, is Babylonian. It is the name of their virgin goddess Ishtar, and a source for the eventual Mary mother of Jesus accounts. Orion has its antecedents in the Egyptian scripture concerning Osiris who lost his penis and his life but was born three days later. See Arthur Frederick Ide, *Moses: Making of Myth & Law; the Influence of Egyptian Sex, Religion and Law on the Writing of the Torah* with an introduction by Decherd Turner (Las Colinas, TX: Monument Press, 1992).

before stealing their precious juices using furs and satins. Because of this seduction the majority of the faithful mourned each other as victims and pledged to strengthen their prayers and vows for chastity. Others, who gave in to the ministry of the women's blandishments, became "unclean and utterly forgot the laws of the gods."[19]

While modern reflections on the "Daughters of Men" includes lip service to the myths of the women being descendants of Cain, the lie of the legend is found in the Hebrew itself. They are daughters of *Adamah*. It is not a proper noun (Adam). It means "daughters of the soil." They were Canaanite agriculturists well known for their orgies and premarital prostitution. The account itself is Ugaritic in origin. It's a tale of how the God of the Large Penis (El) seduced two mortal farmwomen and through their labor sired two powerful and muscularly endowed (a mark of divinity) sons by

---

[19] *Adambuch* 75, 81-86. *Die Apokryphischen Gnostischen Adamschriften*. Aus dem Armenischen übersetzt und untersucht von Erwin Preuschen (Geissen, 1900; text is in Armenian) 37. Genesis Rabba, p. 222. Pirqe Rabbi Eliezer ben Hyrcanos (Tannaite), chapters 21-22. *Schatzhöle, Die*, ed. Carl Bezold (Leipzig,1883-1888) 10; this is a Christian life of Adam and Eve written in Syriac during the sixth century CE and must be used cautiously since it is meant to convert and not instruct.

them.[20] Their sons were called *Shahar* (Dawn) and *Shalem* (Perfect). Both were acclaimed gods: Shahar appearing as a winged deity[21] and the other son the Fallen Angel Helel.[22]

History gives the tale another twist. The Sons of God weren't gods. The account records the marriage of royalty with commoners, a frequent theme in Middle Eastern myths. The Hebrews renamed the mythological god El as *elohim* a plural noun for both gods and judges. When *elohim* was coupled with *bene* to be *bene elohim* we read "the sons of judges mated with farmwomen." The sin was not divine coupling. It was a transgression of rank. Judges were forbidden to marry commoners, as judges were seen as gods.[23]

---

[20] Josephus, *Antiquities* 1.3.1 2, 4: (73) "for many angels of God accompanied with women, and begat sons that proved unjust, and despisers of all that was good, on account of their own strength; for the tradition is, That these men did what resembled the acts of those whom the Gentiles called giants." The Greeks held these giants to be the sons of Mother Earth, born at Phlegra in Thrace, and the two Aloeids, all of whom rebelled against Almighty Zeus.

[21] Psalm 139:9.

[22] Isaiah 14:12.

[23] Psalm 132:6.

184

## The Watchers

The one group of angels many are familiar with is the Watchers that are mentioned in Genesis 6.[1] The biblical account styles them as the "Sons of [the] God[s]." They are also known as "the Fallen Ones."[2] In the Judaeo-Christian scriptures, the transgression of the Watchers was sexual intercourse with mortal women.

Originally the Watchers (or "Sons of the Gods") were sent to earth to teach mortals truth and justice. They were successful for the first three hundred years, teaching Cain's son Enoch all the secrets of heaven and earth. Enoch was so startled by the Watchers turning to women for sexual intercourse that he wrote a detailed account of their actions. But the sage's wonderment intensified when the Watchers indiscriminately had sex with young girls (euphemistically styled "virgins"), matrons, men and beasts.[3] Centuries later, Josephus was more tolerant, offering his opinion that the

---

[1] Genesis 6:1-7.

[2] Elizabeth Clare Prophet, *Forbidden Mysteries of Enoch: Fallen Angels and the Origins of Evil* (rev. ed.; Livingston: MT: Summit University Press, 1992).

[3] Jubilees 4:15, 22; 5:1. Cf. Tanhuma Buber Genesis 24.

Watchers were damned not because they had sex with farmwomen, nor even that they had sons by their mortal wives. Josephus argued that the sin was the Watchers inability to police and educate their sons, and because of an overwhelming sense of pride and exaggerated ego. He wrote that the Watchers "begat sons that [*sic.*: who] proved unjust, and despisers of all that was good, on the account of their own strength."[4]

Jews and Christians claim that the Watchers are unique to their faith, yet history doesn't support their judgment. On the contrary, the Watchers figure in the Kharsag Epic, which was recorded on eleven clay tablets that were copied sometime in the third millennium BCE. The Watchers were defined as various people: from aristocratic invaders to tall farmers. They settled around Mount Hermon in the highlands near the present border of Lebanon, and called their area Eden.[5] They were 200 in number, and quickly took up farming: ploughing the land, enclosing fields, sowing grains, planting orchards and trees, and having sex with native women.[6]

---

[4] Josephus, *Antiquities of the Jews* I.iii.1 (73).

[5] Stile of Naram-sin.

[6] Cf. Enoch 6:6.

Because of thrift, determination and good agricultural skills, their community thrived, boasting of a surplus of food. This surplus they sold to jealous itinerants and local clergy who didn't want to work. The clergy chanted and prophesied that the community would be weakened if they weren't accorded a special place, and class division began to evolve. Within time, the Watchers were required to toil the land that filtered out of their hands. Resenting their treatment, they plotted rebellion against their overlords: the priests and kings.

Hearing of the threat of a rebellion, some of the ruling class (who were identified with gods or sages) tried to work out a compromise, acknowledging the injustice suffered by the Watchers, and promising to make conditions better.[7] Other gods/sages were not so generous. They wanted to retain control, and took charge by establishing an ambitious building program. This program included traditional housing structures, granaries, and community halls, but also reservoirs to provide round-the-year water for a complex irrigation system.

When the gods/sages believed that the Watchers were docile, they inaugurated a massive

---

[7] Stile *Atra-hasis* (c. 1635 BCE).

building program for their own homes. One dwelling was especially impressive. It was known as the principal house, and accesses to it were called "the gates of heaven." It was lit by what was considered strange and unconventional means, which the gods/sages claimed to be from their enlightenment and reflections from their ambassadors' (angels') command of shining swords fit for a celestial battle.[8]

To acquaint the people with the wondrous happening within the courts of the gods/sages, the rulers sent for Enoch. He was accompanied to their quarters by two very large and strangely beautiful men "whose faces shown like the sun," possessing "burning and radiant eyes." "Their clothes were remarkable □ being purplish with the appearance of feathers; and on their shoulders were things which I can only describe as 'like golden wings'."

Once introduced to the court, where scribes recounted how the entire program of the gods/sages was completed in seven clearly separated plans or parts, Enoch was invited to attend a meeting. At this meeting the gods/sages determined who would be allowed to live longer by eating of life-extending

---

[8] Kharsag Epic, second clay tablet. Cp. Enoch 6.

fruit that was plucked from the Tree of Life[9] that grew in the center of their settlement. During this time he had the company of an especially handsome man whom he termed to be a selected messenger (angel). He called the beautiful man *Annanage* (or Shining One) as his skin glowed as the sun reflected from its muscularity, and asked him who were the special guards protecting the way to the gods/sages. The exquisitely chiseled-featured man responded. He answered, "The first was Michael, the kindly and patient one; the second was Raphael who is responsible for treating illnesses and wounds among the people, here; the third was Gabriel, and the fourth was Phanuel [Uriel] who is responsible for

---

[9] The myth of a magical tree with all the properties of extending life is common throughout the legends of the world: from Polynesia to Assyria. In Polynesian legend, a maiden is tricked into eating its fruit by a serpent and subsequently loses her immortality. In Iceland the goddess Iduna guards the Tree of Life. In China the Tree of Life is a peach tree where peaches are considered life giving. This Peace Tree of Life is guarded by a serpent-witch: His Wang Kui. In Islam, the temptation of Adam and Eve is evil serpent tells them that "your Lord forbade you from this tree only lest you should become angels" (see: *Al Qur'ān,* Tā Hā [20]:120-121). In Assyria, a winged chariot hovers above it. In all accounts angels stand guard. Cf. Secrets of Enoch 3:1 ff. In most cases, the Tree is represented as a phallus. Its berries are testicles and its branches or root the eruption of semen.

dealing with those who are selected to receive an extension of their normal life-span."[10]

Other Watchers had similar destinies and fates. Agniel was a root grower, apothecary (pharmacist) and chemist. He used the roots he grew to make love potions to seduce one of Cain's daughters.

Anmael was among the most oversexed of the Watchers. He vowed he would do anything to achieve coitus. He kept his word, and revealed the secret name of the Father God to one of Cain's daughters who demanded it before she would have sex with him. She did so because one of the Satans told her that she would be able to control the Father God by repeating his name as a charm. Her goal was to avenge her father Cain. Because Anmael revealed the secret name, the Watcher was cast out of the heavenly host.

Araquiel (who is also known as Saraqael) taught mortals geography. While he had sex with a mortal woman, he was monogamous and engaged in supine coitus seldom. Because he was more discrete than the other Watchers, Araquiel was allowed to return to the heavens when a mortal died. He received this benefit as the Father God determined that he was capable of leading souls to Judgment.

---

[10] Enoch 40:1-10.

Araziel[11] (also spelled Aryzyael) was devoted to the Father God. He rebelled when he was admonished for lusting for coitus with mortal flesh.

Little is known about Asael. His name means "Made by God." Some legends suggest that he was made in the same manner as Adam but was given a divine soul. Other legends suggest that he was a pattern for later angels.

Asbeel was considered a "bad seed" from the moment of his existence. His name is unique. It translates as "God's deserter." According to various legends, this particular Watcher was the greatest sower of dissension, and took the lead in moving his brother Watchers away from the gods and into coveting human flesh.

Azael had the promise of a great future as a Watcher. His name translates as "Whom God Strengthens." While some accounts question the reason for his name, a careful search of more secret records reveal an answer. Azael was one of the two angels who succumbed to the sexual flirtations of Lamech's daughter, Naamah. She finally allowed him to enjoy intercourse with her because of the exceptional strength in his rod. Through their union, Naamah gave birth to another Watcher: Azza. Azza means "the Strong One" and records show that he

---

[11] The name means "god is my noon."

was equally endowed with the strength of his father, and his divine spear was as long as the senior's.

Azza had a colorful history. He was constantly quarreling with the senior gods. Convinced he was more knowledgeable than they were, he frequently lectured them. Azza demonstrated his mastery of knowledge and comprehension by revealing the heavenly arcana to Solomon. By tutoring this child of David, he made the future king of Israel the wisest man on earth. Azza was ultimately silenced for protesting against the transformation of Enoch the scribe into the most powerful and brilliant of all the angels: Metatron.

Baraqijal was a lusty Watcher. He excelled in astrology, and taught men how to navigate from the stars and constellations. He was damned for opening the Book of Astrology to men, for the gods feared that with this knowledge they would mount an assault on the heavens and demand to be treated like gods.[12]

Enoch identifies Exael. This seer wrote that Exael "taught men how to fabricate engines of war, work with silver and gold, [and] use gems and perfumes." Exael's difficulties started when he used the gems and perfumes to win women over, and the engines of war to seduce men.

---

[12] Cf. Psalm 8:5-6.

Ezeqeel is frequently forgotten. He taught the early tribes that populated the earth the science of meteorology. His goal was to ensure that they would be able to calculate the meteors and determine if any would fall to the earth endangering their homes, families and possessions. His sin, as others would learn, was his prometheusean interest in helping mortals not only cope with the world but to harness it for their own good.

Gadreel had a special place in the heart of the Creator God. His name means "God is my Helper." It was Gadreel who "showed all the deadly blows to the sons of men; and he led Eve astray, and he [also] showed the weapons of death to the sons of men."[13] His purpose was to have sexual intercourse with her. While this was considered an offense to the order planned by the Creator God, it was not so grave as sentencing Gadreel to banishment beyond the walls separating the Garden of Eden from the world of mortals. What sealed Gadreel's doom was his saucy manner and decision to teach men how to make tools and weapons. The gods feared this, worrying that with superior weapons mortals might storm heaven and take it over, making themselves supreme and planting their feet on the necks of the gods.

---

[13] *Ethiopic Book of Enoch* 69:6.

Kasdaye was a troublesome god. Constantly in quest of orgasms with women, his fertility got him regularly into trouble. The women he had intercourse with got pregnant. Their babies, once the fetus developed and was birthed, carried his image and countenance. He could not, therefore, hide his disobedience. To circumvent being discovered, Kasdaye taught women the art of abortion.

Kashdejan created the worse sin possible. He taught men how to cure various diseases, including those of the mind. The gods feared that with this knowledge they would no longer be needed, and that mortals might live as long as the gods.

Kokabel also alienated the gods for more than his sexual escapades. He taught men astronomy and the science of the constellations. Through his instructions, men learned how to navigate using the stars, and how to calculate weather patterns.

Penemuel was an early scholar. He believed that the conduct of inquiry required research and analysis. He was opposed to blind faith and rote memorization. He is accorded the distinction that ultimately got him expelled from the heavens: "he taught men the art of writing with paper and ink, and through this many have gone astray from eternity to eternity, and to this day."[14] Now men could leave records, comment on the gods and even question the existence of gods. Writing was to be only in the hands of gods or their sacred priests, for it was feared that writing in the hands of men would lead men into sin. They would have a record of what they had done and not done, and thus be unwilling to do what already was done in the area of attending to and glorifying the gods.

    Penemue is frequently seen as the angel who taught men writing plain, distinct, brief accounts. He is not to be confused with Penemuel who taught the art of flowery writing, poetry and prose. But what earned him the reputation of being an evil angel was that Penemue was able to cure stupidity. He questioned the sanity and brilliance of the gods, especially the Father Creator as the latter put limitations on men. Men should have no restrictions but be allowed to rise to the height of being like gods. Both the Old and New Testaments of the Judaeo-Christian bibles give solid evidence for this, and demonstrate dramatically that those who inhabit the nether world are on the whole wiser then the gods. They, the demons and devils, can quote

---

[14] *Ethiopic Book of Enoch* 69:9. Enoch argues that the ability to write will make angels and mortals unrighteous and impure (v. 11). He doesn't explain why he wrote.

scripture[15] and produce scholarly commentaries on texts. The gods let this happen because they were themselves inadequate to teach men, and test man, whereas the devils and demons did it so carefully that they could tempt even the wisest of men.

Pharmoros was among the Watchers most loved by men. He taught pharmacy, herbal lore, and practical medicine, He lectured to men on the medical arts. He trained them how to diagnose illnesses. He insisted that prescriptions be handled carefully and used only after detailed analysis.

Satanail was also known as Salamiel. He is recorded as being the great prince of the Grigori. According to Enoch, the jealous god Lord of Spirits singled out Satanail and a small group of his most loyal followers for punishment before they had done anything wrong in the area of carnal knowledge of women or men. His crime, it is implied, was that he led a group of overworked Watchers in a rebellion against the Lord of Spirits who demanded longer work hours and less rest time and food. Satanail argued for a greater social consciousness and demanded the rights of his men to be a part of the governing body that controlled the daily affairs in heaven. The Lord of Spirits,

---

[15] Cf. Genesis 3:1-4, 13; Matthew 4:5-8, 12:24; Mark 1:34, 3:22; Luke 4:3-6, 11:15, 18-19.

however, held out for an absolute monarchical rule based on theology (today known as a theocracy).

Talmaiel was one of the fortunate Watchers. A descendant of the Grigori, he managed to escape both the anger of the Lord of Spirit and of other gods. He was saved from the devastating flood that the mad god demanded inundate the earth, and he avoided being skewered by the red-hot hardened swords of the Avenging Angels. The story of the Great Flood was considered divine retribution for the Watchers coitus with women. Enoch writes:

> And in those days the punishment of the Lord of Spirits will go out, and all the storehouses of water which (are) above the heavens ... and under the earth will be opened, and all the waters will be joined with the waters which (are) above the heavens. The water which (is) above heaven is male, and the water which (is) under the earth is female. And all those who dwell upon the dry ground and those who dwell under the ends of heaven will be wiped out. And because of this they will acknowledge their iniquity which they have committed on earth,

and through this they will be destroyed.[16] ... For these waters of judgment (serve) ... for the lust of their bodies; but they do not see and do not believe that these waters will change, and will become a fire which burns forever.[17]

Little is known about Tamiel. His name translates as "Perfection of God." His one crime was that he was too perfect, too beautiful, and too articulate. He was a threat to the Lord of Spirits who would have nothing to do with the Watcher.

Turel had a destiny similar to Tamiel. His name means "Rock of God." But the strength he afford the Lord of Spirits appeared threatening to this tribal god, and it was a short time until he too shared his brother Watchers fate.

Usiel is known as the last of the Watchers. His name translates as "Strength of God." Whatever his crime may have been, he too was condemned by the Lord of Spirits.

The Lord of Spirits was a jealous, angry and at times a mad god. He was easily upset, took out

---

[16] *Ethiopic Book of Enoch* 54:7-10.

[17] *Ethiopic Book of Enoch* 67:13.

his rage on those least able to protect themselves or argue their case. The other gods invited the Satan to stand as a barrister,[18] but Satan found greater pleasure in serving the Lord of Spirits by tempting, challenging and troubling those he was to protect. He did so in an honest belief that his future lay with the Lord of Spirits, and that this god would protect him, advance him in rank, station and responsibility, and ultimately share his throne with him. For his troubles, Satan was expelled from the heaven he coveted.

Later, the Lord of Spirits, or chief priest of the Watchers, was deified as a god. Over the years the name was corrupted until it read Yahweh.

In Islam, the Watchers were two in number: Harut and Marut. Their initial sin was the transgression of making uncomplimentary remarks about the weak resolve and nature of mortals who were their god's creation.

Allah overheard their comment. Angered at their audacity, he responded that they, like all angels, would fail if they were placed under the same conditions.

Seething under Allah's reprimanded, they voiced their desire to test his wisdom. Affronted by such celestial crassness, Harut and Marut were sent

---

[18] Job 2.

down to earth. Allah was determined to see if they, too, could avoid the pitfalls of his divine creation.

Harut and Marut were instructed to avoid the most severe sins of alcohol consumption, idolatry, illicit sexual relations, and murder. They rose to the challenge. Reaching earth, the two Islamic angels were consumed with desire for an attractive woman. When a passerby noticed their aroused state, the angels killed him so that he could not testify to their sin. But Allah knew it already and arranged that the angels in heaven would witness their reprehensible action and arousal. Repentant at being discovered, the punishment of the two was lessened. Allah determined to punish his carnal creations by hanging the two upside down in a well in Babylon rather than being sent into eternal punishment in hell. The angels didn't learn their lesson. Instead, they began to teach sorcery to mortals, although they never failed to warn their students of the ultimate consequence of practicing the forbidden arts. [19]

---

[19] Al Qur'ān, Al-Baqarah [2]:102.

## Adam

In some ancient records concerning "Adam" of the Old Testament, the "first mortal" created by the gods was not a man but an angel. Their creation was far different from man's, for in the Judaeo-Christian theology of creation, man is made from dust.[1] In Islamic theology, man is created from some biblically ignored element far more substantive: sperm.[2] The gods, in fact, recognized "man" as "like a god,"[3] but feared that "man" would

---

[1] Genesis 2:7, 3:19; cf. 13:16.

[2] *Al Qur'ān*, Al-Mu'minūn [53]:13-14: "Then we placed him as a sperm. Then We fashioned the sperm into an embryo, then fashioned the embryo into a shapeless lump of flesh; then from the lump of flesh We fashioned bones, then clothed the bones with flesh. Then We formed him into a new creation. Cp. *Al Qur'ān*, An-Najm [53]:45-46.

not be satisfied with such a station but would challenge them for their Divine Thrones. Still, delighting in Adam's beauty, stature and body, they sent the angels to bow before Adam and worship him.[4] The only one to refuse the god's command was Satan. This so angered the gods that they expelled him from their sight.

Satan, however, had more respect for himself and truth than did the other angels. While he openly refused the god's command, many plotted against Adam and attempted to burn him.[5] Other angels were so awed by Adam's countenance (it's recorded that Adam was created more than 1000 cubit feet tall, and in one record he was so large he laid the entire length and breadth of the world!) that they called him "Holy One." Others were afraid that they would become entrapped in Adam's heaven

---

[3] Psalm 8:6.

[4] Pirqe Rabbi Eliezer ben Hyrcanos' *Midrash* (c. 90-130 CE [actually, c. early ninth century CE), chap. 11; hereafter cited as PRE followed by chapter; cf. Zohar (3 vols.; Mantua, 1558-1560; reprinted Wilna, 1894) Genesis 442; Ephraem. Syrus, Commentary on Genesis: *Ephraemi Syrii Opera Omnia*, ed. B. Benedictus and Assemanus (Roma, 1737-1743), main part 1.

[5] Abot diRabbi. *Nathan*, ed. Solomon Schechter (Wien, 1887; photostat reprint, New York, 1945), p. 23.

(Paradise).[6] This fear festered until they flew frightened and trembling back to their ring in heaven.[7] The fear was compounded when the gods commanded Adam to attend them in the Divine Assembly as if he were an angel or archangel.[8]

After Adam defied the gods and ate the forbidden fruit that hung on the Tree of Knowledge of Good and Evil, the deities sent Cherubim to guard Eden and keep him and his mate out.[9] The Cherubim were frightening beings, more in keeping with the image of Persian monsters than the cute naked infants Renaissance artists painted.

While the Cherubim are guarding Eden, three hundred angels tend it, as any farmer would care for his land. Their sentry duties became

---

[6] See: Jean Delumeau, *Une Histoire du Paradis: Le Jardin des délices* (Paris: Libraire Arthème Fayard, 1992; an English translation is by Matthew O'Connell, *History of Paradise: The Garden of Eden in Myth and Tradition* published by Continuum, New York, 1995).

[7] *Otzar Midrashim*, ed. J. D. Eisenstein (New York, 1915) p. 70 col. f., 428 col. b; Beth Ha Midrash, ed. Adolph Jellinek (6 vols.; Leipzig, 1853-1877; photostat reprint, Jerusalem, 1938), iii, 59; cf. Tanhuma Buber Leviticus 37, etc.

[8] Genesis 2:8-14; Ezekiel 28:13.

[9] Philo, *De Mundi Opfi*, 60.

imperative after the expulsion of Adam and the admittance of Enoch. But with the arrival of Enoch their duties were modified, so that by the time that Isaac arrived in the Third Heaven, they could tutor the son of Abraham. Later, they taught Moses. No other mortal was granted admission, although Rabbi Jehoshua ben Levi tricked the Angel of Death into letting him in and then demanding that he be allowed to stay.[10]

---

[10] Bavli (Babylonian Talmud), Ketubot 77b.

## Noah's Angels

In the myths surrounding the legendary ark and its builder-captain Noah, there is the quaint issue of "wandering spirits" who entered the ark before the world suffered its ultimate deluge. Some records suggest that the "wandering spirits" were angels. Others term them monsters. But their vocal communications shows them to be messengers to and from the gods who sent the flood.[1]

Noah was distraught when he was told of the gods' decision to destroy the earth.[2] As weak and

---

[1] This parallels the Akkadian (Greek) myth. See: Arthur Frederick Ide, *Noah & the Ark: the Influence of Sex, Homophobia, & Heterosexism in the Flood Story & It's Writing* with introductions by Levi Abrams ("Noah, the Sources & Dr. Ide's Research), Len Morris Weise ("Growth through Learning"), and Don Sanders ("Noah & the Ark -- An Introduction") (Las Colinas, TX: Monument Press, 1992).

[2] The Akkadian account survives in the *Gilgamesh Epic*, where the god of Wisdom, Ea warns the hero Utnapishtim, that the other gods (led by Enlil, the Creator) would flood the earth. Enlil, like the later Yahweh, was a jealous, angry and petty god of violence and viciousness who preyed on those who didn't offer him sufficient prayer and praise especially in the area of New Year sacrifices. It is an account reflecting on the tyranny of ancient kings. While there have been arguments that this flood was the same as the tidal wave that erased the legendary land of Atlantis, Eberhard Zangger makes short of

selfish as the gods, Noah was argumentative, uncertain, unwilling to assume the helm he was given, he frequently cried out in despair. In each instance he was reprimanded or instructed by "an angel of each kind" of living organism that existed on the boat. There was an angel who carried baskets of fodder. Another carried grain. One who carried fruits. Yet another who brought seeds. And so forth. Thus none of the animals would have to eat another. None of the birds starved for lack of victuals. Even the serpents and buzzards were cared for.

The angels also decided which of the animals would enter since only one pair of each species was permitted on board. To entrench sexism defined by redactors, the accounts read that only those animals that accepted conventional sexuality (that the male dominated and mounted the female) were admitted.[3] Where the female mounted the male or one species copulated with another species or a male with a male and a female with a female,

---

this with his revolutionary *The Flood from Heaven: Deciphering the Atlantis Legend* with a foreword by Anthony Snodgrass (London: Sidgwick & Jackson Limited, 1992).

[3] Pirqe Rabbi Eliezer ben Hyrcanos (Tannaite), chapter 23. Genesis Rabba 287, 293. Tanhuma Noah 12. Tanhuma Buber Genesis 36, 45. Babylonian Sanhedrin 108a-b. Sepher Hayashar 17.

the angels marked them to be among those that drowned. This was done so that all things would know that the gods of the heavens were in command and only the gods could change the order of sex and then only for themselves.

There is no biblical record of Noah commandeering the ship. However, there are numerous pseudoepigraphic records and legends of the angels taking charge of the ship. In each case the account follows the records of the Sumerians, the Hurrians and the Hittites, and in some cases, even those of the ancient world of India and China.

Only after all beings drowned (including evil fish! and other water life) does the prototype of Yahweh, board the ship and bless Noah, surrounded by his angels who are as bloodthirsty as the old cutthroat where Utnapishtim and his wife, like Noah and his wife, are made "like unto gods" and placed in Paradise.[4]

---

[4] The original Flood Story is Sumerian/Akkadian and reflects the creation of earth and its elements. See: R. W. Rogers, *The Religion of Babylonia and Assyria* (New York: Eaton and Mains, 1908), pp. 201-208. Cp. Berossus, *Babylonian History* (3rd century BCE). This is the source for Josephus, *Antiquities* 1.3.2. His interpolation of the life span of men is taken from a fragment in Enoch, sect. 10. Josephus wrote that Noah was 600 years old at the time of the flood.

## Abraham's Angels

Numerous angels visited Abraham.[1] In most cases they came after a god sought him out. The visits are closely associated with pagan worship.

When Abraham invaded Canaan,[2] coming from Haran,[3] he stopped at the oak of Moreh. It was a marked site of Canaanite worship.[4] He later planted a tamarisk tree at Beersheba "and called

---

[1] The chronicler who wrote about Abraham and his visitors purposely varied the word-term for god and angel, indicating that angels were gods and that men who served them could become gods as recited in the Psalms.

[2] Early Christian apologists saw this movement by Abraham as a testimony of a man who "became obedient to the words of God" and "went forth from his country, form his people, and from his father's house, leaving a small country, a weak people, and an insignificant house in order that he might inherit the promises of God." See: *The Letter of the Romans to the Corinthians (First Clement)* 10:2: οὗτος δι ὑπακοῆς εξῆλθεν ἐκ τῆς γῆς αὐτοῦ καὶ ἐκ τῆς συγγενείας αυτοῦ και ἐκ τοῦ οἴκου του πατρὸς αὐτοῦ ....

[3] Genesis 12:6.

[4] W. L. Reed, "Moreh," in *Interpreter's Dictionary of the Bible*, ed. G. A. Buttrick (4 vols.; Nashville, TN: Abingdon, 1962), vol. 3, p. 438.

there on the name of the Lord."[5] At Shechem he only built an altar, as a tree was already there: housing pagan gods and angels.[6]

Most of these gods were from the Ur of the Chaldees. The only thing they had in common with the later Hebrew deity, Yahweh, was their insatiable thirst for prayer and praise, burnt sacrifice and

---

[5] Genesis 21:33.

[6] The tree was the home and symbol of the most important goddess that remained in the hearts and minds of many Hebrews even after the coming of the Romans. She was Asherah: the wife of Yahweh, whose attendants were prophets (which numbered as many as 400), priests and cult prostitutes (both male and female: 2 Kings 23:7) as they were for her brother (and Yahweh's rival) Baal (1 Kings 14:23-24; Deuteronomy 23:17). Asherah is both the name of the goddess as well as her image (Judges 6:25-26; 2 Kings 21:7; 2 Chronicles 15:16). While the Hebrews translated her name as Ashtoreth, she is equally the Akkadian goddess Ishtar and the Sumerian goddess Inanna: always the ultimate representative and provider of fertility, love and war. The Hebrews named her Ashtoreth to embody the vowels of the word *bosheth* (shame) so that she can be called the "goddess of the Sidonians (1 Kings 11:5, 33) and "the abomination of the Sidonians" (2 Kings 23:13) where she had a temple. See: *The Syrian Goddess (De Dea Syria); Attributed to Lucian*, ed. Harold W. Attridge and Robert A. Oden (Missoula, MT: Scholars Press, 1976), p. 13, §4. 1 Samuel 31:10 notes her temple in Canaan in the Late Bronze Age.

blood.[7] If they were gorged with the blood that spewed from the severed veins and throats that met with Abraham's knife, these gangster gods were content.[8] Satisfied, they had time to think. They reflected on how to repay Abraham's subservience and obedience in meeting their unchained lusts for blood and carnage. In return for each of his acts of violence and treachery, the gods gave their dutiful servant permission to steal the property of others: their women, their cattle, their gold, their slaves, and all else, and to lie, cheat, and serve their own purposes first.[9]

---

[7] The gods of Abraham, as the gods who people the Old Testament are closely identified with, are the fiery gods of the Sumerians and other people. In fact, these deities are associated with and disguised by fire as in the case of the pillar of fire in the Wilderness (Exodus 13:21, and so forth), and by the fire that consumed Elijah's sacrifices on Mount Carmel (1 Kings 18:38).

[8] The savage nature of the gods of Abraham is in keeping with the cruelty and vile nature of the gods of Jacob (Genesis 32:25-33) who attacked Abraham's son, and those who tried to kill Moses (Exodus 4:24).

[9] Genesis 15:1-21. Cf. *Genesis Rabba*, ed J. Theodor and Ch. Albeck (2 vols.; Berlin, 1912-1927) 433, 437. Tanhuma Softim 11. *Midrash Agada*, ed. Solomon Buber (Photostat reprint 2 vols.; New York, 1960) Genesis 33.

The gods quest for gore was shared by their angels. Both the favored and the "fallen" angels thrived on human suffering and the pain and slaughter of other living beings. Azazel (the Azael of earlier chapters) was particularly keen on such feeding; feasting noisily on the carcasses Abraham carved up for the deities.[10] At one such banquet of broken bones and torn flesh, Azazel questioned

---

[10] Consuming a sacrificial carcass granted the eater a special covenant with the deity to whom the sacrifice was made. It was a solemn rite among the Hebrews in Jerusalem in the sixth century BCE during the siege by Nebuchadrezzar. Covenants were not "made," but "cut" (*karath b'rith*; cf. Genesis 15:18, 21:27, and so forth) reflecting the slaughter of the sacrifice or "passed through" (*'abhar bibh'rith*; cf. Deuteronomy 29:11) as with the passing of the flesh through the holy flame; or "stood in" (2 Kings 13:3) as occurred with oath-takers. Oath takers were sprinkled with the blood of animals slaughtered in sacrifice at the altar that became known as the "blood of the covenant" (Exodus 24:5-8). This aspect of blood covenant continues through the New Testament Last Supper of Jesus (Translators have styled this covenant as a "new testament" but do so in error. The "new" reflects "recent" (*kainos*) and "testament" (*diatheke*) devolves from a dispensation; cf. Matthew 26:28; Mark 14:26; Luke 22:20; John 6:54-56. Weight must be placed on the *diatheke* which enjoins the past with the (then current) present, as carried over in Acts 3:25 that carries the same blood rite as Acts 7:8. Its relationship with law is clear in Romans 9:4, 11:27; cp. Hebrews 10:29, 13:20.

Abraham in the same way that the Satan of the New Testament tempted Jesus of Nazareth. But unlike Jesus, Abraham was speechless and could not (or would not) warn the Tempter to depart. Instead, Abraham had a guardian angel that rebuked Azazel and ordered him to leave "for you can never lead him astray."[11]

Abraham as a god controlled angels, as seen in the account of his quest for a bride for his son Isaac. It was Abraham who ordered Eliezer to go back to his homeland, but favored this messenger with an announcement that an angel would prepare the path for him.[12] In this Abraham was saying that the angel would be a warrior who would clear out all bandits, ruffians and prostitutes who lingered along the highway.

Abraham's gods were not always good to him or his family. They failed to protect him with regularity. In fact, some of the gods delighted in teasing, abusing and controlling the patriarch with their angels. In one such incident, the gods sent an angel to detain Esau in the wilderness while Rebekah prepared the stew for Isaac who would go

---

[11] *Apocalypse of Abraham*, ed. George Herbert Box (London, 1918), pp. 51-53.

[12] Genesis 24:7.

on and deceive his father to swindle his brother out of his birth right.[13] Isaac was equally culpable.[14]

---

[13] *Tanhuma Buber,* ed. Solomon Buber (2 vols.; Wilna, 1885; Photostat reprint, New York, 1946) Genesis, p. 131. Tanhuma Toldat chap. 11. Midrash Leqah Tobh, compiled by Tobiah ben Eliezer, Bulgaria, 1079) Genesis, p. 135. Targum Yerusalemi. *ad Genesis.* 27:31.

[14] Acknowledgment of the sin of Isaac has been expunged from most biblical records, save in Isaiah 43:27-28, which denounces and condemns the interloper. The "struggle in the womb" between Jacob and Essau is from a far-older Greek myth where Proetus and Acrisius fight in the womb of Queen Aglaia ("Bright"), portending a bitter rivalry for the Argive throne. Historically the tale of the troublesome twins indicates the rivalry between the city-states of Israel and Edom. This has credulity with the mention of Esau's "hairiness" since the word actually is "shaggy" meaning to be "covered with trees": Mount Seir that Edomites occupied. Esau, however, isn't free from guilt in this sordid transaction. He could have turned to his father and demanded restitution. The codes at that time would permit it, and directly censured Jacob for his greed. See: John Skinner, *The International Critical Commentary Genesis* (New York: Chas. Scribner's Sons, 1910), p. 361. Isaac's crime, beyond the theft of the birthright, severed the family ties. The principle parties never met again. Evidence shows that Jacob never gained in moral stature as seen in the case of Dinah and Shechem. Esau fared better, gained in stature and wealth; see: John McClintock and James Strong, *Cyclopedia if Biblical, Theological and Ecclesiastical Literature* (New York: Harper & Row, 1894 et sqq), vol. 3, p. 286.

## Sarah's Angel

Abraham was an opportunist. Several times he sold his wife, Sarah,[1] into sexual slavery, claiming that his wife was his sister. Because of his repeated lies, the pharaohs of Egypt were eager to take her to bed and have intercourse with her.[2] Their desire[3] was not so much as sexual as it was a means of joining the rabble crowds surrounding Abraham and his nephew Lot in a quest for peace with the Egyptians.

Only after Abraham sold[4] his wife to the pharaohs did he realize that his transgression

---

[1] For a biography on Sarah, see: Arthur Frederick Ide, *Battered and Bruised: All the Women of the Old Testament*, with an intro. Decherd Turner (Las Colinas, TX: Monument Press, 1993), pp. 139-152.

[2] Abraham's deceit was equaled by Sarah's duplicity. See: F. C. Cook, *Holy Bible, Commentary by Bishops and Other Clergy* (London: John Murray, 1871), vol. 1, p. 133.

[3] Abraham's lie was compounded with his willingness to add deceit and subterfuge with it. See: Adam Clarke, *The Holy Bible Containing the Old and New Testaments with a Commentary and Critical Notes* (London: William Tegg, n.d.), vol. 1, p. 136.

[4] Genesis 12:18-19. The pharaoh was blameless since he had no knowledge that the woman was Abraham's wife; see: Rev.

against Sarah might cost him her cherished hymen. Yet, Abraham, by all records, did not have sexual intercourse with his wife until late in life (if at all[5]), and then only at the command of angels.

Sarah's virginity was preserved by the efforts of at least one angel. Each time a pharaoh approached Sarah, an angel dealt a blow "with an unseen hand." Each time the potentate touched the woman's garments a harder blow was administered.[6] Only after Sarah and the angel tired of toying with the ruler did she allow both the angel and pharaoh respite. In the morning she ruefully confessed that Abraham was her husband. The accounts record, "the pharaoh made no further attempts to enjoy

---

J. D. Dummelow, *A Commentary on the Holy Bible* (New York: Macmillan, 1908), p. 21. The transgressions of Abraham and Sarah would be repeated by their son Jacob; see: Rev. Robert A. Tuck, *A Handbook of Biblical Difficulties* (London: Thomas Whittaker, Bible House, 1891), p. 26.

[5] It is possible, based on the original text, that the intercourse that gave Abraham a son was the result of an angel (possibly Yahweh, himself) breaking the hymen and completing the act for the patriarch. This is discussed in the chapter on Abraham's angels.

[6] Unique to this tale is the role of Sarah. She was the force who determined when the angel struck and with what degree of violence.

[have sex with] her." The lord of Egypt then sent Abraham "great riches," and gave Sarah a bondmaid named Hagar.[7]

Abraham didn't learn from this incident.[8] He tried it again, selling his wife to Abimelech, King of Cerar.[9] Abraham's son would commit the same transgression against his wife, Rebekah, selling his wife to the same Abimelech.[10] In each case the tales come from the Egyptian *Tale of the Two Brothers*.[11] Fidelity wasn't even considered a virtue in these Old Testament tales.

---

[7] *Genesis Rabba*, ed. J. Theodor and Ch. Albeck (2 vols.; Berlin, 1912-1927), pp. 378, 554. Tanhuma *Lehk* 5, 6. Tanhuma Buber *Genesis* 66-67. *Sepher Hayashar*, ed. Lazarus Goldschmidt (Berlin, 1923), pp. 51, 52. Pirqe Rabbi Eliezer ben Hyrcanos (Tannaite), chapter 26.

[8] Genesis 12:1-20.

[9] Genesis 20:1-18.

[10] Genesis 26:1-17.

[11] Papyrus D'Orbiney (British Museum 10183); facsimile in *Select Papyri in the Hieratic Character from the Collections of the British Museum* II (London, 1860), Pls. ix-xix, and in G. Möller, *Hieratische Lesetücke*, II (Leipzig, 1927), 1-20. The manuscript can be dated to around 1225 BCE, in the Nineteenth Dynasty.

# the City of Sodom

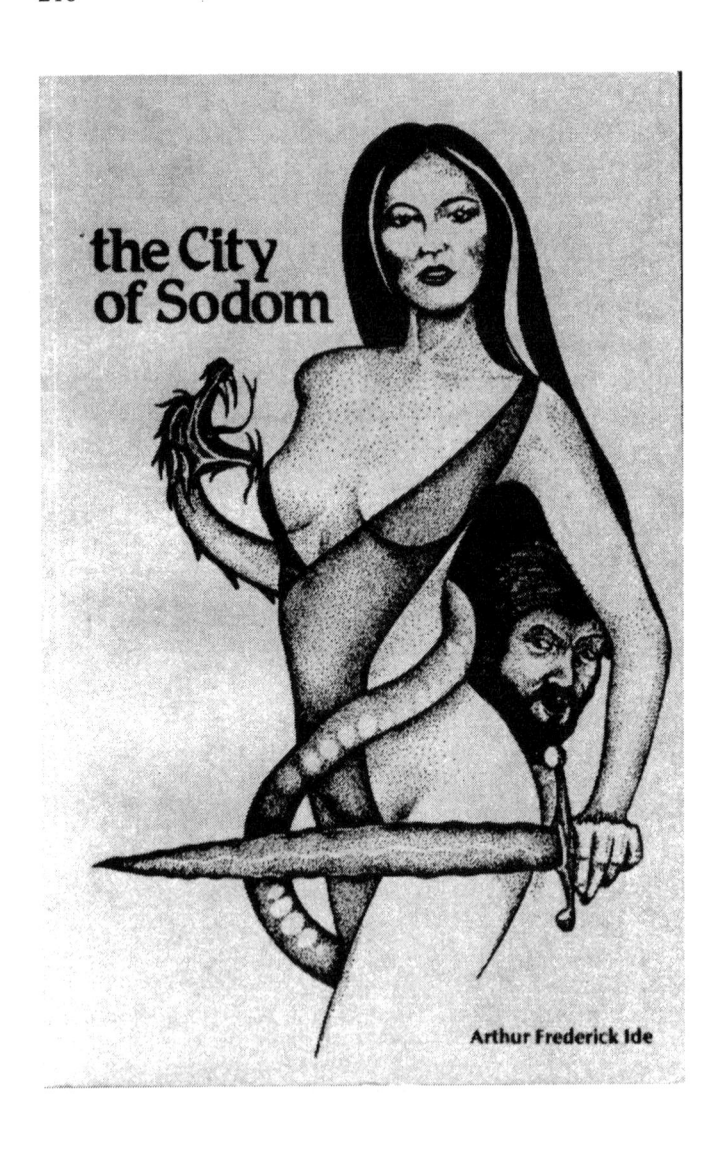

Arthur Frederick Ide

## Angels at Sodom

The myth of Sodom is an old tale. It occurs in the fiction of many Mediterranean civilizations. Strabo, Josephus, and others recorded it. For Jews and Christians, the bible account is the best known.[1] While I have written at length concerning the legend of Sodom,[2] what concerns me here is the account of the angels who appeared at the City.[3] Surprisingly, the gods of Lot and Abraham stood with a second[4] as if they were a single angel.[5] Yet in this record, it is the two messengers that promise to destroy Sodom, not a single god.[6]

---

[1] Genesis 18-19. Cf. Paul Hallam, *The Book of Sodom* (London: Verso, 1993).

[2] Arthur Frederick Ide, *City of Sodom & Homosexuality in Western Religious Thought to 630 CE* (Dallas, TX: Monument Press, 1985).

[3] Genesis 19:1-5, 11-22.

[4] Genesis 19:1 reads "two angels" but extracanonical writings lists three angels. The three angels can be found in Genesis 18:1, 16.

[5] Genesis 19:9-10, 13.

[6] Genesis 19:13. The argument that "the Lord" rained down fire from heaven on the City is a corrupt reading of verse 13.

Religious interpreters of this tale have argued for centuries that the sin of Sodom was homosexuality. There is no proof in the text for such a claim. This must be discounted since those who demanded to know the "men" (angels) were both men and women.[7] On the contrary, if the City of Sodom was destroyed for illegitimate sex, it was for general sex[8] as Lot offered the people of Sodom the opportunity to "deflower" his own daughters,[9] while the angels standing with Lot said nothing.[10]

The angels that went to Sodom were xenophobic. While the text promises that the City

---

[7] Genesis 19: 4, with emphasis on "all the people" and "both young and old." Cf. Arthur Frederick Ide, *Gomorrah & the Rise of Homophobia* (Las Colinas, TX: The Liberal Press, 1985).

[8] Various nonbiblical records argue that the City was exceedingly rich and that Lot and his Uncle Abraham coveted the gold and goods of the people of Sodom. Furthermore, accounts show that the City had a healthy regard for human sexuality, and didn't practice the austerity of the ancient Hebrews, nor did they make compensation for their unchained desires by giving to charity.

[9] Genesis 19:8.

[10] This may be explained based on the sociology of the time. Females were expendable. Males were not since they were the defenders of the City walls.

will be spared if only a few were righteous, when the angels arrived they were concerned only with Lot and his family.[11]

Among the few things that can be said for Lot was his uncertainty of the intent of the messengers. When morning came, Lot tarried. The angels, reciting their command, grabbed him and forcefully evicted the argumentative Lot and his family from the City.[12] After Lot and his family crossed into the hills, an earthquake leveled the City.[13] Only Lot's wife perished when she looked back; her punishment was to be turned into a pillar of salt.[14] This is a common motif in fables of this age. Plato parallels this story in his rendering

---

[11] Genesis 19:12.

[12] Genesis 19:16-20.

[13] This is the only plausible answer to the description of the City being built on "slime pits (*Siddim*)." Genesis 19:23 records "brimstone" and "fire." Ovid, in his *Metamorphoses*, describes how an elderly Phrygian couple entertained Zeus and convinced him to spare their surly neighbors. Apollo destroyed Gortyna in Crete for its "lawlessness," and an erupting volcano destroyed the Arab city of Birket Ram.

[14] Arthur Frederick Ide, *Zoar & Her Sisters: Homosexuality, The Bible and Jesus Christ* with an introduction by J. Michael Clark (rev.; Oak Cliff, TX: Minuteman Press, 1991), pp. 48-71.

account of Eurydice, Orpheus's wife. His myth, like the biblical myth, is based on an incorrect reading of the hieroglyphs in the Hierapolis temple that details sexual activity (ritual sodomy) between worshippers and "dog-priests" (males who walked on their hands and knees) dressed in the clothes of women. The angels (also known as "messengers") of Egypt watched these activities as a worship of generation. Egyptian angelic Watchers, predating both their Jewish and Christian counterparts are developed in hieroglyphs succinctly:

In a passage in the text of Unâs (line 191 ff.) the Angels of Thoth, and the Ancient Ones, and the Great Terrifier, who cometh forth from the Nile, Ḣâp, and ÁP-UAT, who cometh forth from the tree ÁSERT, are called upon to witness that the mouth of the king is pure, because he eats and drinks nothing except that upon which the gods live.

These same temple practices occurred in Jerusalem (see: Deuteronomy 22, 23, with special quarters being assigned to the dog-priests and prostitutes in 2 Kings 23:7).[15]

---

[15] See: Arthur Frederick Ide, *Yahweh's Wife: Sex in the Evolution of Monotheism; A Study of Yahweh, Asherah, Ritual Sodomy and Temple Prostitution* (Las Colinas, TX: Monument Press, 1991).

## Hagar and Ishmael's Angel

That the angels were also gods is clear in the tale of Hagar the Egyptian[1] and her infant son Ishmael. Originally Hagar had been a slave to Sarah, and the property of Abraham. As such Hagar, and later her son, were disposable.

Legends introduce what remains of this incomplete biblical story. The original accounts relate that a wadi god found Hagar in the desert. She had just escaped the snares of a cruel mistress. Dressed in the wings of an angel, the god appeared to the woman at a desert spring between Kadesh and Bered, on the way from Shur.

Pretending ignorance, the god-angel asked the Egyptian why she was at the oasis. Hagar answered truthfully: she left a cruel and unkind mistress. The god/angel instructed Hagar to return to the tent of Sarah and suffer in silence. To be

---

[1] There is no historical proof for a Hagar, and definitely not for "Hagar the Egyptian." *Hagar* is a South Arabic word that translates as "village." At best this myth is a restatement of a wadi where travelers met to take water (cf. Judges 15:17-19 where Samson has an identical encounter to Ishmael when he is given water by the gods; cp. Ezekiel 47:20). Hagar does not appear in the Koran, although Ishmael is cited as a prophet; see: *Al Qur'ān*, Maryam [19]:54-55 and Al-Anbiyā [21]:85; cp. with Abraham: Al-Baqarah [2]:125-129; guided by Allah: Al-An`ām [6]:86.

silent in the face of all adversities and to suffer all indignities at the hands of unworthy men and women would be her glory. She would be rewarded, the god/angel promised, in ways she least expected. Her guerdon would be raising her children.

By suffering in silence, the god/angel affirmed Hagar would be the mother of a race of warriors. He gave her son the name of Ishmael, which means *God has heard* [*her suffering*]. Then the god/angel ordered the boy to live alone in the desert while his mother returned to the tent of Sarah. He was to live like a wild ass, and maintain himself by force of arms.

Convinced that the god/angel was the true god of the desert the Egyptian returned to the tent of Sarah.[2] The mistress, seeing her runaway servant return, became increasingly more cruel and vengeful.[3] She would do anything for her husband,

---

[2] Genesis 16:1-16.

[3] *Genesis Rabba*, ed. J. Theodor and Ch. Albeck (2 vols.; Berlin, 1912-1927), pp. 453-454, 570. It is written that Sarah threw shoes in the face of Hagar, cast the evil eye upon her so that she lost her firstborn (a girl), and so forth. This is in keeping with the picture of the Sarah that went into the houses of the pharaohs to enrich her husband. The incident with the shoe and other assaults is in keeping the psychological profile of Sarah found in the Old Testament. Furthermore, it is equally in common with the age in which the fantasy was

including giving him her slave for sex, if it brought her some mental pleasure: knowing that her handmaiden suffered.[4] To this end she sent her slave to Abraham's tent to be used for sex.

What occurred in the tent is not recorded. What we do read is that Hagar conceived and gave birth to Abraham's son. Proud of her progeny, she boasted of it, but her delight in the child angered the jealous and barren Sarah. Her temper more vile than ever, Sarah ordered her husband to rid her of the Egyptian baggage. A weak, hesitant and ineffectual man, who cared more for himself than for others, Abraham agreed and sent the woman and her son into the desert.

---

written, as casting a shoe across property was a ritual act of asserting possession, with property being defined broadly (see: Ruth 4:7, Psalm 40:10). Casting a shoe across the face of a servant was to remind the servant (or slave) that she/he was in servitude to the master/mistress.

[4] This incident reflects a far-older Babylonian record that details that "If a man marries a priestess, and if she gives her husband a bond maid to bear him children, and if afterwards this bond maid demands equal honor with her mistress because of the children she has borne, the priestess must not sell her, but she may be returned to bondage among her fellow-slaves." *Law of Hammurabi* 146; cp. 144-145. V. Scheil, *Mémoires de la délégations en Perse* IV (1902), 11f.; with a better rendering of all copies in A. Deimel, *Codex Hammurabi* (1930); 3rd ed. By E. Bergmann, 1953).

226

## Jacob's Angels

Among the best known myths of the bible is the story of Jacob's ladder.[1] Even the bible acknowledges the account to be apocalyptic, with Jacob envisioning the ladder[2] and its angels on the shoulder of Mount Moriah where adiaphoric measures numbered 12 in each occurrence.[3] For this reason it became "The House of God" or *Beth-el*.[4]

---

[1] Genesis 28:12.

[2] The ladder is an ancient myth, establishing Beth-El as the Gate of Heaven. It was guarded by a sacred pillar (*massebah*) requiring tithing by the faithful to preserve it. The payment of tithes as an obligation dates from the days of the Judges. The rungs up the ladder were a later edition. In this addition the rungs which the guardian angels climbed represent years of their nations' rule over Israel (70 years of Babylonian exile from the fall of the First Temple in 586 BCE) and the subsequent fifty-two (actually fifty-eight) years of dependence on the Medes which closed with Ezra's heading back his group of exiles in the reign of Cyrus (c. 457 BCE).

[3] Genesis 28:18 ff.

[4] Jubilees 25:1 ff; *Genesis Rabba*, ed. J. Theodor and Ch. Albeck (2 vols.; Berlin, 1912-1927), p. 767; Midrash Sekhel Tobh 119; Midrash Genesis 437; Midrash Tehillim 399. Seder Eliahu Rabba 29; Tanhuma Buber Genesis 181. Beth-El had been a shrine long before the advent of the Hebrews, dating

After the visitation of angels who walked up and down the ladder, Jacob slept fitfully. After awakening, Jacob piled the stones he slept on into a pillar and poured oil over the top stone.[5] It was a most primitive and pagan act.[6]

Jacob met angels again when he crossed the Jordan. So numerous was the company of angels that he met later at the River Jabbok, that the traveler feared a battle between his retainers and those of the gods (large landowners).[7]

While preparing to meet his brother Esau, Jacob tried to curry the favor of the gods. Unsuccessful in reaching an accord and arranging a meeting with them that day, Jacob retired to his tent

---

back to no less than the twenty-first century BCE. It is of Arab origin.

[5] Genesis 28:18. Cf. Midrash Tehillim 400. PRE chap. 35.

[6] The act symbolizes Jacob's recognition of the navel of the earth. Anointing it with blood, oil, or wine recognizes the pillar as a god(dess), a deity (like the sacred stone at Mecca) who lived encased in the stone. It also symbolizes the violent nature of Jacob and ten of his heirs who were terrorist leaders of the Twelve Tribes (only Reuben and Benjamin didn't plot to murder their brother Joseph, then sold him into slavery, and finally lied that he had been killed by a wild beast).

[7] Genesis 32:1-2 ff.

and fell into a fitful sleep. During his slumber, Jacob wrestled with an "unseen presence" (which the KJV addresses as "a man").[8]

The wrestling match[9] has numerous erotic overtones. But the most important one is that the

---

[8] Genesis 32:24.

[9] The wrestling match is a theological oddity. There is no satisfactory explanation why a mortal would wrestle with a god or an angel, since the deity or deities were assumed to be transcendental. Nor does the myth explain what the presence

wrestled with a mortal that the presence loved, or why that presence would harm the loved person. The only explanation that can be given was the need of the writers of Genesis to explain why there was a dietary prohibition against eating sinews. Medically the dislocation of the sinew in the thigh is a common occurrence among wrestlers in the Middle East, and was first described by Harpocrates, who noted that the displacement of the femur-head lengthens the leg, tightens the thigh tendons and puts the muscles into spasm. This makes for a rolling, swaggering walk, with the heel permanently raised. It also was a disfiguration sought by select temple dancers who believed themselves divinely possessed, like the prophets of Baal on Mount Carmel (see: 1 Kings 18:26).

Jacob was not the only mortal that wrestled with a god (or gods). Moses wrestled with a deity and had a life similar to Jacob's. Moses fled his home (Egypt) in disgrace, served a herdsman (Jethro) for the hand of his daughter (Zipporah), and returned home with his wife and sons when he is attacked by a supernatural being. Exodus 4:20-24; note how this god also seeks to kill his faithful mortal servant, as did the god/angel in the Jacob myth. In this case, as well as the combat the angel/god had with Rachel, it is unclear if the angel/god is good or bad (a demon). This is seen in numerous other biblical tales. For example, in 2 Samuel 24:1 god sends the plague. In 1 Chronicles 21:1, the plague is sent by Satan. The super-being's refusal to give his name appears both in the Jacob myth and the tale of Moses (Exodus 3:14). It also figures in the account of Manoah (Samuel's father in Judges 13:17-18). Rabbis excused this claiming the gods were concerned for fear that their names would be used in blasphemy. This is a cover-up. The real reason was knowledge that witches and warlocks and similar sorcerers though out the Eastern Mediterranean used long lists of divine names to

"unseen presence" or "man" (or god or angel) grabbed his "sinew"[10] leaving Jacob an invalid, forcing him to walk hobbled.[11] Jacob didn't give up

---

strengthen their spells. The quest to know the name of an adversarial god or demon even transmogrifies the biblical account of Jesus (Mark 5:9).

[10] The thighbones and accompanying tissue were sacred to the gods throughout the Mediterranean. If a strong enemy was routed and killed, a feast was made upon the flesh, and the thigh sinews were reserved either for the conquering warrior who slew the valiant enemy or for the king who commanded the troops. Human sacrifices were still prevalent at the time of the prophet Samuel who dismembered the sacred King Agag "before the Lord" to use the king's flesh as a eucharistic meal similar to the Arabic *naqi'a*. See: 1 Samuel 15:33, ref. Numbers 24:7.

[11] Genesis 32:25; the KJV translates it as "hollow of his thigh." Myth continues the story, claiming that the one Jacob wrestled was none less than the archangel Michael. When the gods saw that Jacob walked crippled, they asked Michael what had happened. After he told the details of the match, the gods were pleased and promoted Michael to be the guardian of all Israelites. See: Yalqut Gen. 132. Other accounts argue that Michael shrank the sinew because Jacob had failed to pay the obligatory tithe at Beth-El twenty years earlier. After the match, Jacob confessed, and made satisfaction by paying the delayed tithe and, to win the gods favor, dedicated his son Levi to the gods as their chief priest and collector of tithes. See: PRE, chap. 37.

the contest, demanding that the Presence bless him and his line. In remembrance of the struggle, and the ultimate blessing, Jacob's name was changed to Israel[12] and he forbade his people to eat the sinews of any beast.[13] His prohibition didn't last long.

---

[12] The name change reflects a theophorous title: the element containing a deity's name is the subject, not the object, indicating that the god El is striving to be superior as in the wrestling match. This was the case with *Ya`qobel* (Jacob: El protects, not I must protect the god El).

[13] Genesis 32:25-33. Jacob was concerned with the external signs of religion and law. He had little regard for either, but spent his life in fear of his brother Esau (Genesis 32:6-7). So afraid was he of personal harm that he with cavalier abandonment thought nothing of exposing is wives and children to the dangers he felt he would be inflicted with (Genesis 32:7-8). When he finally met up with Esau, Esau was far more gracious and generous than was his errant brother. Esau "ran to meet [Jacob], and embraced him, and fell upon his neck, and kissed him" (Genesis 33:4; brackets added). Theologians see much in this. Esau is regarded charitably, and viewed as "magnanimous" offering "not only ... forgiveness, but ... fraternal affection." See: Adam Clarke, *The Holy Bible Containing the Old and New Testament with a Commentary and Critical Notes* (London: William Tegg, n.d.), vol. 1, p. 212. Esau reflects the generosity of the angels who paraded for Jacob when he was young; Jacob resembled the god Yahweh who lived in terror of his angels and his own path. Both held grudges until confronted with what seemed a superior force, yet waited for the opportunity to reject it.

## Jesus and the Angels

The gods of the Old Testament spoke directly with men. The voice of the New Testament god (the Father) is only heard on rare instances.

As they were in the Old Testament, angels in the New Testament carried messages to mortals from their suzerain.[1] Ambassadors of the gods, they visited all major figures in both Testaments, from Adam to Jesus and Paul.

Gabriel appeared before Zacharias at the Temple to tell the aged priest that his wife Elizabeth would conceive and give birth to a son, even though she had been infertile throughout their marriage. Zacharias was to call the infant John.[2]

Leaving Zacharias, Gabriel appeared to the priest's kinswoman Mary. Gabriel told the young girl that she would conceive without mortal coital intercourse. She was to become the mother of Jesus, defying convention, morality and Mosaic Law. She was only engaged.[3] Her child would be born a

---

[1] Matthew 1:20; Luke 1:11, 26 and 2:9; Acts 8:26 and 10:3.

[2] Luke 1:5-20. Elizabeth's conception was the first immaculate conception recorded in the New Testament. The text suggests that either Yahweh (or Gabriel) was the father; Luke 1:25.

[3] Matthew 1:19 claims Joseph is Mary's husband. But that must be read in line with legal formalities: he was committed

bastard,[4] even though his actual father was the Holy Ghost.[5]

An angel next appeared to Joseph in a dream.[6] During this dream the angel told Joseph to take Mary as his wife.[7] This is strictly an order to protect Mary, for the Greek reads that he is to "take her alongside" of him (παραλαμβάνω). There is no instruction for him to marry her. Most likely, he had sex with her after the birth of Jesus.[8]

---

to her, but had not yet had sexual intercourse that completed the marriage rite. This comes only after the birth (see footnote 8, below).

[4] Luke 1:26-38. In verse 28, the text reads that "the Lord is with thee" implying conjugality. Cp. Matthew 1:18: When as his mother Mary was espoused to Joseph, *before they came together*, she was found with child" (KJV). Mark ignores the entire nativity story, as does John. Cf. Jane Schaberg, *The Illegitimacy of Jesus: A Feminist Theological Interpretation of the Infancy Narratives* (San Francisco, CA: Harper & Row, Publishers, 1987).

[5] Matthew 1:18: ἅγιον πνεῦμα.

[6] Matthew 1:20.

[7] Matthew 1:20, 24. The angel isn't named.

[8] Matthew 1:25: "and knew her not till she had brought forth her firstborn son." (καὶ οὐκ ἐγίνωσκεν αὐτήν, ἕως οὗ ἔτεκεν υἱόν) The passage doesn't say *only* son.

After Jesus was born, an angel appeared to a group of shepherds.[9] The exact nature of the angel is uncertain because the ambiguous Hebrew phrase is translated without the definite article allowing the angel to appear mortal and act more human.[10] Where the account is ambitiously vague, the angel could even be any god, one of the gods of Moses, or the Angel of the Lord (a title worn by many angels including Gabriel, Metatron, and a host of others). This occurs in instances where the speech of the messenger is not introduced with the traditional, obligatory statement that it is from the Lord God, or where it identifies the speaker as both god and god's messenger.[11] Later Christian theology adds the definite article, picturing the preincarnate Christ in the figure, necessitating his birth, and the subsequent announcement by the Angel of the Lord.

---

[9] Luke 2:9-12. This account is not a part of the primary database neither of the gospels nor of the earliest records. It follows the Hellenistic convention for biography and not history.

[10] Haggai 1:13; Malachi 2:7.

[11] Genesis 16:7-13, 22:11-12, 31:11-13; Exodus 3:2-4; Judges 6:11-23. These stories come from older legends filtering through Egypt, Persia and Arabia. They were modified through time to accommodate redactor's transcendence of a god as one who no longer casually confronts men.

This angel was quickly joined by a choir of angels who floated over an assembly of shepherds.[12]

---

[12] Luke 2:13-15. Much of the Infant narratives are mythic in nature. From his miraculous conception to his faultless birth, Jesus is pictured as superhuman, a powerful man who grows throughout the gospels until he accepts his own crucifixion and death. In the manner of the serpent god, he effects healings and performs exorcisms, as do the angels over whom he exercises control. According to Paul and the author(s) of the gospel of John, his birth is cosmic in origin and nature that transcends this world and time: Jesus is preexistent, present in the heavens with God before time began (John 1:1-18; Philippians 2:5-11). Paul struggles valiantly to expand this thesis, coupling with the author(s) of the book of Revelation and others, to add an eschatological, apocalyptic component to his cosmic descriptions by arguing that Jesus (as the *logos* or "Word") will return as a heavenly judge at the end of creation. This logos is a self-communicating divine presence that existed with god. It is parallel to the Hellenistic concept of wisdom in that it is a creative force (see: Wisdom of Solomon 9:1-2; cp. 1 Corinthians 1:24) which "John" argues is the essence and presence of Jesus (John 1:1-18; cp. John 1:1 *cum* Revelation 19:13 where Jesus appears as a warrior). The Hebrews have a feminine noun for wisdom: *hokmâ* denoting the creative force (cf. Sirach 24:3); this is personified in Proverbs 1-9. For example, wisdom is a woman who speaks as a prophet (Proverbs 1:20-33) and one who can employ a messenger (cf. 1 Kings 19:2; 21:8-11), and exercise select authority on her own (Esther 5:4). Wisdom is also a "sister" (Proverbs 7:4) who may associate with a man on an intimate level of family. As wisdom, she is "more precious than jewels" (Proverbs 3:15, and 8:11). Paul calls Jesus the "wisdom of God" (*sophia* in 1 Corinthians 1:24), which gave

Two years after Jesus' birth, another angel appeared to Joseph, again in a dream, to warn him of Herod's intent to kill "all the children that were in Bethlehem."[13] When Herod was dead, an angel returned to Joseph who had fled to Egypt and told him it was safe to return to Israel.[14]

Angels do not figure personally into the ministry period of Jesus. No physical angel appears, engages in conversation with the rabbi (teacher), nor challenges Jesus. That time was from his days in the Temple (age 12) through his preaching and baptizing (until the age of 33). However, angels do play a role in his homilies and conversations.

One significant area where angels are focused in the teachings of Jesus is in the institution of marriage. Various angels figure in marriage rites

---

strength to latter-day Gnostics who emphasis the complexity of wisdom which they defined as a feminine figure of primary importance.

[13] Matthew 2:13. This is a replay of the Exodus story of pharaoh's pogrom (Exodus 1:16 ff). There is no historical proof for either fable. The only pharaoh (literally: "Great House") who could have massacred the children was Merenptah, but by his fifth year on the throne the Hebrews were already back in Israel. See: *Dictionary of the Bible*, ed. James Hastings; rev. ed. Frederick C. Grant and H. H. Rowley (New York: Charles Scribner's Sons, 1963), p. 760.

[14] Matthew 2:19-21.

and requirements in the New Testament,[15] and Jesus had strong statements concerning their role. For example, when he was asked about the nature and role of marriage in heaven, Jesus replied, "At the resurrection men and women do not marry they are like angels in heaven."[16]

Jesus' comment was not a statement that the angels were gender-free or gender-neutral beings. Instead, he took the traditional theological stand that marriages were not a part of (or in) the heavenly society. No where in his comment is there a denial of sexuality or an affirmation of celibacy or chastity as later theologians argue. On the contrary, scripture contains passages that show the angels are definitely sexual beings.[17] The terror of thinking that angels were sexually active forced the most conservative Jews to deny their existence.[18] While the conservative elements eschewed the concept of

---

[15] Matthew 28:2 and John 1:51. Cf. Genesis 28:12.

[16] Matthew 22:30. The debate centered not on marriage, but on resurrection. Jesus discursive reply authentic to a complicated question ("Whose wife will she be?) is out of keeping with the statements most consider authentic as his comments are recorded as enigmatic, short, pithy, and memorable.

[17] Cp. Genesis 6:4, and Zechariah 5:9.

[18] Acts 23:8.

angels, the majority of Jews and the early Christians didn't. They just anticepticized the heavenly throng. Angels were clothed and made otherworldly. Sex and nudity was defined as a sin, and the later-day Judaism and emerging Christianity struggled to develop a bastardized concept of angelology where good angels wore white garments and bad angels wore nothing. Satan becomes another god and was provided with his own retinue of angels.[19]

Jesus articulated what others merely implied concerning the angels. Jesus argued that mortals, after the resurrection, are to be "like the angels."[20] Like angels, mortals would become sexless.[21] Yet Jesus never claimed that resurrected mortals would be without shape or form. On the contrary, Jesus proclaimed that angels had a peculiar embodiment.[22] The only difference between mortals redeemed and angels, was that angels would have a degree of perfection greater than any man would know or achieve. They would not know as much as

---

[19] Matthew 25:41; 2 Corinthians 12:7.

[20] Luke 20:36.

[21] Matthew 22:30. Mark 12:25.

[22] Cf. John 10:34-37; cp. Psalm 82:6.

God, for Jesus argued that the angels were not omniscient.[23]

At first angels were depicted as having the freedom to make moral choices. This changed quickly with Church fathers mutating the fiercely independent spirit and agile free thought enjoyed by angels in the past for the suffocating and nonbiblical concept of predestination. This innovation was codified so that only the Christian god would be omniscient. With an all-knowing god, one who would know every move and thought of every angel, the angels still for some unexplained reason required judicial supervision.[24] Even in the theological mutilation of angelology and free will, the Christian and Jewish god remains reluctant to trust his heavenly hosts.[25] The lack of trust is the result of god remembering and dreading the return of rebellious angels and angelic rebellions.[26] Heaven was still torn from the last war.

---

[23] Mark 13:32. The implication is that the angels had limited power.

[24] 1 Corinthians 6:3; Jude 6.

[25] Cp. Job 4:18.

[26] 2 Peter 2:4; Revelation 12:4-9. Cp. Genesis 6:1-4; Psalm 82; Isaiah 14:12-15; Ezekiel 28;

Toward the end of his ministry, Jesus expressed a different view of angelic activities. Those who wrote his biography have angels helping him,[27] and assist his followers.[28] Emphasizing the anticipeticizing of angels introduced by early bishops, the angels of the Gospels have limited knowledge,[29] and when they appear to mortals, they "descend" from heaven as if on a mission.

A devil[30] (διαβόλου, not the angel Satan[31]), tempted Jesus, by reminding the man of "Nazareth,"

---

[27] Matthew 4:1; Luke 22:43.

[28] Acts 5:19, and 12:7.

[29] Matthew 24:36, and 1 Peter 1:12.

[30] The word "devil" is not Hebrew in origin. It was incorporated into Hebrew terminology only in the second century BCE. There is some argument about its origin. Some claim that it was taken from the Greek διάβολος (*diabolos*) as is carried over in Matthew 4:1, 5, 8, 11; 13:39; 25:41. Cf. Luke 4:2, 3, 5, 6, 13; 18:12; and John 6:70, 8:44, and 13:2. Cp. Acts 10:38, 13:10. St. Paul uses this Greek invention in Ephesians 4:27, 6:11; 1 Timothy 3:6-7; 2 Timothy 2:26; Hebrews 2:14. See also: James 4:7; 1 Peter 5:8; 1 John 3:8; Jude 9; and Revelation 2:10, 12:9 and 12; 20:2, 10. There is no

that he was in charge of angels.[32] Another one tried to tempt him on the pinnacle of the temple, reminding him that he had charge over angels.[33] In

---

Hebrew equivalent; the closest is שֵׁד (*shed*): meaning a "spoiler" or a "destroyer" (see: Deuteronomy 32:17, and Psalm 106:37). The only other time a being of evil appears, is in reference to diabolical forces that appear as "hairy ones" or "kids" (goats), as in Leviticus 17:7 and 2 Chronicles 11:15, where the word is שָׂעִיר (*sair*). Devils are not demons (δαιμόνιον in Matthew 7;22, 9:33-34, 10:8, 11:18, 12:24 and 27-28, 17:18; Mark 1:34 and 39, 3:15 and 22, 6:13, 7:26 and 29-30, 9:38, 16:9 and 17; Luke 4:33 and 35; and so forth) or deified spirits of evil (δαίμων in Matthew 8:31; Mark 5:12; Luke 8:29; Revelation 16:14 and 18:2). A better argument is that the word developed from the Persian *daeva*. It means: evil spirit. Others argue that it comes from the Indo-European *devi*. This argument has merit since it means a "goddess" and the patriarchal Hebrews did everything possible to suppress the role and rule of women, declaring women subordinate to men because of the myth of the Temptation and Eve.

[31] Luke 4:3. Nazareth was undoubtedly *en-Nāṣira*, a town that remained exclusively non-Christian until the time of Constantine and not the contemporary town in Israel.

[32] Luke 4:3-11. Since Jesus hadn't eaten for 40 days (Luke 4:2), this apparition may have been the result of hunger and fatigue.

[33] Matthew 4:6. What is strange in this tale is that the devil (again, not named Satan) had the power to spirit Jesus away without any attempt on the part of Jesus to get away.

both cases Jesus refused to be tempted. Afterwards other angels came to comfort and teach Jesus.[34] Later, in another incident when Jesus agonized in the Garden, an angel "ministered" to him: to prepare him for his death.[35]

After acknowledging the prospect of being executed, like any ancient potentate in the Middle East, Jesus argued that he would return. When he "came again," he declared, he would return with angels, as any general would appear with a multitude of soldiers.[36] Those who would deny his kingship would be denied by him while he stood in front of the angels who keep records, like trial judges and scribes, as to those who are fit to enter Paradise.[37] In this incident Jesus is no longer the forgiving, gentle figure that contemporary Christianity would have its adherents believe. Instead, Jesus is violent. With an undisguised loathing the man of peace and openly threatens his unseen and unknown enemies the very worst agonies any mortal on earth would ever expect to

---

[34] Matthew 4:11.

[35] Luke 22:43.

[36] Luke 9:26. Matthew 16:27; 24:31; 25:31; 26:53. Mark 8:38.

[37] Luke 12:9.

experience.[38] His was a very mortal hostility built in fear. If those who are to be excluded repent before they are locked out, they can enter.[39] Wealth could not buy salvation.[40]

One issue that has received little attention concerning Jesus and angels is the account of the night of his betrayal. Yet there was a definite pre-Old Testament angel intimately involved with Jesus, an angel who was a young naked male.

While public nudity is rejected in the Holiness Code,[41] it remained a fact of Jewish life. It was even understood as a symbol of divine involvement.[42] It is a singular graphic point in the Gospel of Mark, which reads:

---

[38] Matthew 13:41-42, 49; 18:10; 24:36; 25:31. Mark 13:27. This passage is in line with Old Testament prohibitions and promises. Each incident harkens to a primitive time when the angels were messengers of revenge and death and their god(s) a common bully who would tolerate no deviance among those whom he claimed.

[39] Luke 15:10.

[40] Luke 16:22.

[41] Leviticus 18:6-12, 16-19; 20:11, 17-21.

[42] Isaiah 47:3; 1 Samuel 20:30; Isaiah prophesied naked (Isaiah 20:3), as did Micah (Micah 1:8), the prohibition was against exposure and its accompanying vulnerability (cf.

> A certain young man followed [Jesus], having a linen cloth cast about his naked body; and they [the Temple soldiers] laid hold of him. But he, casting off the linen cloth, fled from them naked.[43]

While there are several answers as to why the young man appeared semi-nude and fled naked,[44] the critical issue is the unidentified male

---

Nahum 3:5). David danced semi-nude (covered only with a "linen ephod" in 2 Samuel 6:14; this cod-piece isn't mentioned in 1 Chronicles 15:29 at the time of the dance although it is mentioned earlier in *ibid.* v. 27) "before the Lord with all his might." While the human nude body was initially a symbol of innocence and a testimony of how mortals lived before the fall, it quickly became a symbol of shame and disgust. The Christian church, especially, legislated female nakedness with the most gruesome sins, once nude baptisms were completed. See: Cyril of Jerusalem, *The Mystagogical Lectures* (Fathers of the Church series), pp. 64, 161. R. Tonneau and R. Devreese. *Homélies catéchétiques de Theodore de Mopsueste* (Rome: Studi e Testi, 1949), p. 417. The *Apostolic Tradition of Hippolytus*, ed. Burton Scott Easton (Cambridge: Archon Books, 1962), p. 46.

[43] Mark 14:51-52.

[44] See: Arthur Frederick Ide, *Zoar & Her Sisters: Homosexuality, the Bible & Jesus Christ*, with an introduction by J. Michael Clark (Oak Cliff, TX: Minuteman Press, 1991),

figure, the cloth, and the ultimate nudity. The cloth was linen (*sindon*). It was worn on special occasions, but not at the time of entombment or burial.[45] The dead, except Jesus, were traditionally shrouded in *othonion*. Jesus was buried in the ceremonial (*sindon*) linen.[46]

A second ponderous point surrounding the incident in the Garden, is that the Old Testament recounts how "strange young men" appeared "clothed in linen" as messengers to carry out directives of their lords. The linen cloth was a ritually clean cloth worn only by those in the immediate service of the gods, by priests in the Temple and by angels in heaven if they were sent to earth after the fall of the Watchers to help or instruct men.[47] These directives included the execution of those who had betrayed the lord or

---

pp. 159-163. Cp. Arthur Frederick Ide, *Martyrdom of Women: A Study of Death Psychology in the Early Christian Church to 301 CE* (Garland, TX: Tangelwüld Press, 1985), pp. 71-75 ff.

[45] Cf. Matthew 27:59, Mark 14:51; Luke 23:53.

[46] Cp. Luke 24:12; John 19:40, 20:5-7 *cum* Matthew 27:59; Mark 14:51-52.

[47] Exodus 28:42, 39:28; Leviticus 6:10, 16:4, 23, 32; 1 Samuel 2:28, 22:18; 2 Samuel 6:14; 1 Chronicles 15:27;Ezekiel 9:2-3, 10:2, 6-7; Daniel 12:6-7; cp. Genesis 41:42, Exodus 28:8, Ezekiel 16:10, Revelation 19:8, 14.

were to serve as sacrifices to a higher power.[48] In these instances, the men were seen as angels.[49] Those who witnessed the beautiful youth whose "body gleamed like topaz, his face shone like lightning, his eyes flamed like torches, his arms and feet sparkled like a disc of bonze, and when he spoke his voice sounded like the voice of a multitude"[50] became weak. The witnesses fell prostrate and was easily carried or led off and became willing sacrifices.[51]

Nudity in such incidents was a portent of impending death.[52] It was also considered a sign of total surrender. At the point the sacrificial victim surrendered the angel would "touch" him several times, frequently with kisses upon his lips.[53]

---

[48] Cp. Ezekiel 9:2. Daniel 10:5, 6.

[49] Ezekiel 10:2.

[50] Daniel 10:6.

[51] Cp. Daniel 10:10, 11. In the case of Daniel the angel is named. It is Gabriel who is frequently associated with or as the Angel of Death.

[52] Job 1:21; Ecclesiastes 5:15.

[53] Cf. The role of the archangel Satan working through Judas Iscariot in Luke 22:3, 47-48; Matthew 26:49; Mark 14:45.

After Jesus' death and subsequent entombment, his followers claimed that angels visited them to tell the disciples that Jesus had risen from the grave.[54] An angel (and in some records, more than one angel) waited at the empty Tomb for "the women" to arrive to anoint Jesus. In this case the angel(s) didn't have wings, or other angelic attributes, save that they appeared as radiant young boys.[55]

None of the Gospels or St. Paul presents the story of the resurrection or the angels that guard the tomb in the same manner. The Gospel of Mark (c.70 CE) records the simplest account of the resurrection of Jesus. It says that *three women* went to the graveyard at *sunrise* on the *third day*

---

[54] Luke 24:23.

[55] Matthew 28:2-7 records one angel being at the sepulcher. John 20:12 records two angels waiting for the women. Mark 16:5 doesn't use the word angel, but says "a young man sitting on the right side" waited for the women. Luke 24:3 writes that there were two men. There is a question concerning the state of dress and the young man, since women were more easily eroticized by the appearance of the naked male form than the female form. On women and the issue of nudity, see: Margaret R. Miles, *Carnal Knowledge: Female Nakedness and Religious Meaning in the Christian West* (Kent, UK: Burns & Oates, 1992).

(Sunday) to *anoint* the body of Jesus with *spices*.[56] Why the women waited until three days after the body was entombed is curious. The April temperature in Jerusalem would be uncomfortably warm and the body would be in an advanced state of decay. It's unthinkable that anyone would open a tomb that had been shut up for three days while the deceased decomposed (the fate of Lazarus[57]) to enter in and anoint the body. Since they didn't practice embalming beyond the frontiers of Egypt, other Semitic people would have rubbed oil and spices over the corpse within the hour after the individual died.

    The women referred to in the Gospel of Mark obviously knew that the tomb was closed and sealed with a large stone. The writer informs us that the large stone that sealed it was big and heavy. Given the body proportions of that day, where women were discouraged from all acts of strength, they could not have moved it. In Mark's account none of the women had men accompany them to the grave-site to move the stone, nor did they bring the tools necessary to pry it away. Their only goal was to move towards the sepulcher. They considered the

---

[56] Mark 16:1-2.

[57] John 11:39.

possibility of not being able to enter the sepulcher only as they approached it.

Approaching the sepulcher, the women asked one another, "Who shall roll us away the stone from the door of the sepulcher?"[58] Were they looking for a man, like Legion, who lived among the tombs in the garden?[59] Like Legion this man would have sufficient strength to roll the stone away.

The women didn't find Legion. Instead, as they approached the *opened* tomb they saw a "young man" dressed in white sitting inside.[60] Instead of greeting and thanking the man for moving the stone, they were frightened by him.[61]

The women remained afraid even after the youth attempted to calm them. He spoken comfortingly, telling them "Be not affrighted: ye seek Jesus of Nazareth, which was crucified: he is risen; he is not here: behold the place where they laid him. But go your way, tell his disciples and Peter that he goeth before you into Galilee; there

---

[58] Mark 16:3.

[59] Mark 5:1-9.

[60] Mark 16:5.

[61] Mark 16:6.

shall ye see him, as he said unto you."[62] By this the young messenger suggested that the dead Jesus would meet them at their home in Capernaum, about 85 miles north of Jerusalem.[63]

The Gospel of Matthew recounts the women's journey to Joseph's burial garden and contains a special surprise for the reader. This Gospel tells the reader that there was a "great earthquake" outside the closed chamber.[64] It was uncommonly strong and startled the women, but it wasn't strong enough to move the stone. Instead it was up to "the Angel of the Lord" to move the stone.

Once the stone was rolled aside, the *angel* sat upon the stone *outside* the vault (Mark's young man sat *inside* the tomb), his countenance (body) shining "like lightning" and his raiment (clothing) "white as snow."[65] (Mark's *young man* was a normal male of natural countenance "clothed in a long white garment"[66] that was not illuminated.)

---

[62] Mark 16:6-7.

[63] Matthew 4:13, 8:14.

[64] Matthew 28:2.

[65] Matthew 28:3.

[66] Mark 16:5.

Mark's young man told the women that Jesus had risen, and instructed the women to spread the news that Jesus was no longer in the tomb and that he would meet them in Galilee. However, the women were afraid and did not do as they were instructed.[67] Matthew's angel offered the same message and the women obeyed them "with great joy."[68]

Unlike the preceding synoptic Gospel which make no mention of women accompanying the corpse of Jesus, the Gospel of Luke's women accompany Joseph to the tomb, watch Jesus laid in the tomb and returned [to their homes?] to prepare "spices and ointments."[69] Later, "upon the first day of the week, very early in the morning" they return to the tomb.[70] When they arrive at the tomb, the women find the stone had been moved and "found not the body of the Lord Jesus" but "*two* men [standing] beside them in shining garments."[71] They

---

[67] Mark 16:8.

[68] Matthew 28:8.

[69] Luke 23:55-56.

[70] Luke 24:1.

[71] Luke 24:2-4.

didn't see Matthew's angel,[72] nor did they witness Mark's youth sitting inside.[73]

The Gospel of John doesn't record Mary Magdalene taking spices to anoint the body. The reference to the Magdalene is starker. She travels to the sepulcher *alone*. She is *not* in the company of any other woman or any other women. Unlike the other gospels, Mary Magdalene in the Gospel of John goes to the tomb when it is still dark,[74] not "very early in the morning,"[75] nor "at the rising of the sun."[76] (Matthew writes this time period as "dawn."[77])

The Gospel of John states that the Magdalene found the tomb open.[78] She saw no angel, no watchmen, no young man or two men. Instead of lingering, she runs to find "Simon Peter, and to the other disciple whom Jesus loved

---

[72] Matthew 28:2, 5.

[73] Mark 16:5.

[74] John 20:1.

[75] Luke 24-1.

[76] Mark 16:1.

[77] Matthew 28:1.

[78] John 20:1.

[John]"[79] to tell them "They have taken away the Lord out of the sepulcher." No where does she make the claim that someone stole the body of Jesus.[80]

When Mary Magdalene tells the disciples of the missing corpse, none of the men doubt her word. Instead, "they ran both together, and the other disciple did outrun Peter, and came first to the sepulcher."[81] John writes that "the other disciple" stooped down, and "looking in, saw the linen clothes lying; yet went not in."[82] Luke claims that it was Peter who "stooping down, he beheld the linen clothes laid by themselves, and departed, wondering in himself at that which came to pass."[83] In John, Peter comes to the tomb after "the other disciple" had already seen the clothes and judged the tomb to be empty. It was only after Peter saw the linens that the two disciples "went away again unto their own

---

[79] John 20:2a.

[80] John 20:2b.

[81] John 20:4.

[82] John 20:5.

[83] Luke 24:12.

home" while "Mary stood without at the sepulcher weeping."[84]

Mary Magdalene's role is enriched in the Gospel of John, unlike the variant accounts in the other official gospels. In John, Mary Magdalene was crying when "she stooped down, and looked into the sepulcher." At this point she saw "two angels in white sitting, the one at the head, and the other at the feet, where the body of Jesus had lain." She isn't frightened as the other records read, but answers their question "Woman, why weepest thou?"[85]

Mary Magdalene responds quickly, questioning where "they" [unnamed people] have taken Jesus. The angels do not reply. Nowhere is there even the slightest suggestion that Mary believed Jesus to have been raised from the dead.

Mary's questions are taken tacitly up by the man history first knew as Saul of Tarsus before he converted to Christianity and became Paul. He contributes to resurrection theology from a Greek

---

[84] John 20:11a. There is a decided difference between the Magdalene and the two disciples. Mary sorrowed publicly, while the men left so rapidly so as not to publicly expose their feelings if there were any. In part this was a result of social conditioning, for men were not expected to exhibit emotions over the death of one executed.

[85] John 20:11-13.

philosophic perspective, writing that all people will rise up body and soul on the Day of Judgment.[86] Those who are blessed will live forever in heaven (in the clouds) which he defines as a series of places.[87] Once again angels are introduced. Paul declares that the series of heavens and hells house both angelic and demonic powers without regard for their origin or purpose.[88] For Paul, hell is beneath the earth. It is a place for unrepentant sinners (repentant sinners go to a halfway house known as purgatory.[89] For Paul purgatory is a place of darkness, weeping and gnashing of teeth.[90])

---

[86] 1 Corinthians 15:12-20.

[87] 2 Corinthians 12:2-4.

[88] Ephesians 6:12: ὅτι οὐκ ἔστιν ἡμῖν ἡ πάλη πρὸς αἷμα καὶ σάρκα, ἀλλὰ πρὸς τὰς ἀρχὰς πρὸς τὰς ἐξουσίας, πρὸς τοὺς κοσμοκράτορας; cf. Romans 8:3.

[89] 1 Corinthians 15:20 and Romans 6:5-9 interpolating Psalm 16:10. The invention of purgatory comes early in Christian

history. Earlier, Clement of Alexandria considered it to be a mental state; Origen seconded him. See: F. von Hugel, *Mystical Element*, vol. 2, p. 216.

[90] This is an interpolation of Matthew 25:30, 13:42. Hell fire isn't introduced until Mark 9:43. Matthew 10:28 introduces the novel concept that God is able to "destroy both the body and soul in hell," a theory that Paul toyed with. Paul, in Romans 6:21 and 23, argues that hell is a place of "death" (or at least the death of the soul as discussed in 2 Thessalonians 1:9 and Philippians 3:19) but the text suggests that what he is referring to is the death of peace, tranquillity and self-actualization. He notes in Romans 2:5-8 f, that hell is a place where the unrepentant sinner is in constant "tribulation and anguish." From this, medieval theologians argued that the tribulation occur among the damned who were constantly eating but whose hunger is never satiated; who constantly drink but are perpetually thirst; and, whose "glory" is their shame."

Hell must not be confused with Hades. Hades is a Greek term. It is the abode for departed spirits. It is a place and it is equivalent to the Hebrew *Sheol*. The Greek conceived of Hades as being a great cavern or pit under the earth in which the shades (or spirits) of the departed lived. The Greeks believed that the shades continued to function as they did in life: that they had jobs and pursued professions as they did while living on the earth. The Hebrews, however, saw their Sheol as a place of inactivity. The Authorized Version of the Christian Bible is incorrect when it translates Sheol as "grave," and occasionally as "pit." The Revised Standard Version reads it as Sheol. The concept of Sheol is relatively new. The ancient Israelites had no belief in nor idea of a future life although they did not believe that death was ultimate extinction. Like the Semites, they generally believed that the dead passed into a state of continued consciousness, but pale and inactive existence in an underworld (Numbers 16:30 ff; Amos 9:2). While their spirit remained, worms would eat their flesh while it lay in a grave (Isaiah 14:4 ff). This was to be the fate of everyone without distinction (Job 3:11 ff; 2 Samuel 12:23). A pessimism prevailed for most Hebrews believed that this place of continued consciousness would be outside of the communion they enjoyed on earth and angels experienced forever with their gods (Psalm 6:5, 88:4 f). There was some disagreement over this, however, but it is mild and hidden well (Psalm 139:8, 49:14 f) as those who disagreed believed that Yahweh would rule over Sheol as well. The writers of the New Testament incorporated part of Hades and Sheol in their works, with Jesus' body remaining not corrupted (Acts 2:31), as he possessed "the keys of Death and Hades" (Revelation 1:18).

# A Miscellany of Angels

The Heavenly Host numbers in the hundreds of thousands.[1] They outnumber the 144,000 "elect" who bear "the seal" of their salvation. This numeric

---

[1] Isaiah 6:3; Daniel 7:10; both are cited in 1 Clement 34:6 [*The Letter of the Romans to the Corinthians*]. Cf. Revelation 5:11. In 1 Clement 34:5, we read: τὸ καυχημα ἡμῶν καὶ ἡ παρρησια ἔστω ἐν αὐτῷ ὑποτασσώμεθα τῷ θελήματι αὐτοῦ· κατανοήσωμεν τὸ πᾶν πλῆθος τῶν ἀγγέλων αὐτοῦ πῶς τῷ θελήματι αὐτοῦ λειτουργοῦσιν παρεστῶτες.

figure comes from the *Revelation of Jesus Christ*.[2]

The *Revelation of Jesus Christ*,[3] attributed to the Apostle St. John the Divine, is fashioned around the concept that angels are without number. We know only a minority of their names. Here's a short list of little-known angels and what they are guardians for and standard bearers of with cameos of some of the heavenly host:

| | |
|---|---|
| Achaiah | Patience |
| Af[4] | Anger |
| Akriel | Barrenness |
| Ameretat | Immortality |
| Anael | Ruler of Friday |
| Arael | Birds |
| Armaiti | Piety or Harmony |
| Armisel | Womb |
| Asha | Righteousness |
| Ausiel | Aquarius |
| Barakiel | Chance |
| Bardiel | Hail |
| Butator | Calculations |

---

[2] Revelation 7:4. Contrary to many Christian millenary groups, these are from "all the tribes of the children of Israel."

[3] Revelation 1:1.

[4] Legend records that Moses met Af as one of the angels of punishment when he was transported to heaven.

| | |
|---|---|
| Cassiel | Ruler of Saturday |
| Dara | Rivers |
| Eisheth Zenunim | Prostitution |
| Gabriel[5] | Dreams |

In Islam, Gabriel's name is Djibril (also Jibril or Jabril). He is recorded as a guardian angel with 600 huge green wings and bears the inscription: *There is no God but Allah, and Muhammad is the Prophet of God* between his eyes that also house the sun. It is said that Djibril dictated the Koran (*Qur'ān*) to Muhammad and led the Prophet (who rode on a winged magic mule that had the face of a woman) to the Islamic shrine that is known today as the

---

[5] See: Cyril Glassé, *The Concise Encyclopedia of Islam* (San Francisco, CA: HarperSan-Francisco, 1989).

Dome of the Rock.[6] At this shrine, Muhammad ascended a golden ladder to the heavens, passing Isa (Jesus) and Idris (Hermes), Adam, Abraham, Moses and the archangel Michael. Later he came to a vast sea of golden light where he learned Truth, and then, enlightened, returned to earth.

    Gagiel..............................Fish
    Haurvatat.........................Prosperity
    Hayyoth[7] ..........................Healing
    Israfel[8] .............................Music

---

[6] Cf. *Al-Qur'ān*, At-Tahrīm [66]4; *Al-Qur'ān*, Al-Baqarah [2]:98 ff; in both instances, Gabriel is seen as the heavenly messenger and intermediary.

[7] Actually a class of mystical (*merkabah*) angels, the Hayyoth (translate as "holy, heavenly beasts"), are angels of fire who support the Throne of Glory. Enoch reports that each Hayyoth has four faces, four wings, and two thousand thrones. They number thirty-six beings and constitute the "camp of Shekinah" to physically hold up the universe while frequently breaking into songs of praise when they spread their wings. See: J. Abelson, *Jewish Mysticism* (London: G. Bell, 1913).

[8] Musicians in the heavenly host is a concept that began with the Gandharvas in ancient India and is common both to the Hindu and Buddhist faiths. They are frequently mentioned in the Vedas (the oldest body of Hindu religious literature), and are from the early Vedic period. The Gandharvas are, from their inception, pictured as men with wings. Outside of their wings and celestial symphonies, these angels, like those in the

early religious literature of the Middle East had nothing in common with what became thought of as angelic behavior, but was in fact what ancient civilizations considered celestial carnal cavorting. The Gandharvas were sexual, as were the angels in Middle Eastern theology, being "married" to the *apsaras* (Hindu wood nymphs). The marriages were affectional unions without the benefit of any sacerdotal or legal registration rite. Then, too, *the Atharva Veda* contains passages showing the Hindu angels to be like Middle Eastern angels: messengers who initially participated in and then demanded on their deification sacrificial rites such as the barbarism of Abraham displays. Those who came in supplication to their temples without the appropriate propitiatory offerings could go away in madness, identical to the curses ancient Hebrew priests and prophets pronounced on those who didn't fully observe ritual laws at their Temple. Cf. Margaret Stutley and James Stutley, *Harper's Dictionary of Hinduism: Its Mythology, Folklore, Philosophy, Literature, and History* (New York: Harper & Row, 1977). While Israfil isn't mentioned in the Koran, he is considered one of the four archangels of Islam, along with Mikhail (Michael), Djibril, and Izra'il. In Islam, Israfil is the Angel of the Judgment Day. His job is to blow his horn to awaken the dead. He is an empathetic angel. He is so sad every time that he thinks of hell or whenever he glances into the infernal regions (which he does six times a day), and cries so hard that he could flood the earth if Allah would permit him. Instead this is a fate that Allah forbids, and has the archangel turn to his music and his songs. In Islamic lore, Israfil has four wings, and the beautiful face of a young man. His body is covered with mouths that constantly praise Allah in a thousand different tongues. From his breath that spills out in his song, Allah creates hundreds of thousands of other angels to join Israfil in his praises.

| | |
|---|---|
| Javan | Greece |
| Kasdaye | Abortion[9] |
| Kshathra | Power |
| Laila | Conception |
| Liliel | Night |
| Liwet | Inventions |
| Lucifer | Lucifer |
| Manna | Food |
| Matriel | Rain |
| Mehabiah | Morals |
| Michael | Insómnia |
| Moroni[10] | Resurrection |

---

[9] The issue of abortion is not directly addressed in the Christian community until the writing of *The Epistle of Barnabas* 19:5. In this initial instance, abortion is seen as an aspect of loving one's neighbor, and is coupled with infanticide (both which were prevalent and commonly practiced), and is seen in the context of vanity; cp. Exodus 20:7. The text of Barnabas reads: ου μὴ διψυχήσς πότερον ἔσται ἤ οὔ. οὐ μὴ λάβῃς ἐπὶ ματαίῳ τὸ ὄνομα κυρίου. ἀγαπήσεις τὸν πλησίον σου ὑπὲρ τὴν ψυχήν σου. οὐ φονεύσεις τέκνον ἐν φθορᾷ, οὐδὲ πάλιν γεννηθὲν ἀποκτενεῖς. Within the context, the admonition is to remain aloof from their non-believing neighbors ("You shall not associate with those who walk in the way of death": οὐχ ὑψώσεις σεαυτόν, ἔσῇ δε ταπεινόφρων κατὰ πάντα... *ibid.* 19:3).

[10] All citations in this cameo are from the *Book of Mormon*.

Among the newer angels, found only in the *Book of Mormon*, Moroni is a resurrected guardian angel. Such resurrected beings have "bodies of flesh and bone."[11] Mormons believe that Moroni restored the Aaronic priesthood and the Melchizedek priesthood to mortals through the religion of Mormonism.

In LDS (Lat-ter Day Saints) theology, his guardianship "may best be viewed as a figure of speech that has to do with God's protecting care and direction or, in special instances, with an angel dispatched to earth in fulfillment of God's purposes."[12]

Recognized as the son of Mormon[13] (d. c. 333 CE) Moroni is viewed as the last great leader of the Nephites.[14] Mormon was charged with finishing

---

[11] *Doctrines and Covenants*, 129:1

[12] *Encyclopedia of Mormonism*, p. 42.

[13] Words of Mormon 1:1

[14] Mormon 6:11-12.

the work of his father[15] (who made plates out of the records of the Nephi [II],[16]) Mormon wrote his revelation in the fourth to fifth centuries CE. (Previously, Nephi passes the plates down to his son Nephi.[17] This son is called by Jesus to minister and baptize.[18] From Nephi [III], the plates pass to his son Nephi [IV].[19] Ultimately they come to Moroni, the last of the Nephites, through Mormon.)

The plates were quickly sealed.[20] After sealing the plates, and removing them from the eye of those who would read them, Moroni instructs future translators on method and means[21] of

---

[15] Cf. Mormon 2:17; Mormon 8:1. Mormon has a history similar to that of Jesus. Both were young when they receive sages (Mormon was 10; see: Mormon 1:2), talk about faith, hope and charity (Mormon, chapter 7), and the baptism of small children (Mormon, chapter 9). Both die at the hands of others (Mormon 8:3).

[16] Mormon 6:6. On Nephi, see Helaman 3:21.

[17] 3 Nephi 1:2.

[18] 3 Nephi 11:21-22[12:1]; 19:4, before baptizing his own eleven disciples 3 Nephi 19:11-12.

[19] 4 Nephi 1.

[20] Mormon 8:4; Moroni 10:2.

[21] Ether 4:5.

understanding the plates, since he considers himself a weak writer[22] in fear of being mocked by Gentiles.[23] Between 1823 and 1829, Moroni returned to earth as a resurrected messenger of god. He appeared at least twenty times to (among others) Joseph Smith, the founder of the Church of Latter Day Saints (Mormons).[24]

| | |
|---|---|
| Mumiah | Health |
| Och | Alchemy |
| Parasiel | Treasure |
| Phanuel[25] | Hope |
| Poteh | Forgetfulness |
| Priapus[26] | Lust |

---

[22] Ether 12:23-28; for example, Moroni doesn't make a full account of Jesus' appearance in Ether 3:17.

[23] Ether 12:23-28.

[24] He is depicted as blowing a trumpet reflecting Revelation 14:6-7. See: H. Donl Peterson, *Moroni: Ancient Prophet, Modern Messenger* (Bountiful Utah, 1883). Moroni is considered the Mormon's Angel of the Lord.

[25] In occult and apocryphal scriptures, Phanuel is frequently referred to as the archangel Uriel. Uriel may be an invention based on the prophet Uriah, and is given the additional duties of watching over thunder and terror. See 1 Enoch.

The qualities of such a lustful angel as Priapus have existed throughout history. From statuary of the creator gods of ancient Palestine to the bas-relief now preserved in the museum of Nîmes where a

Roman lady rides a bridled phallus, reminiscent of the various myths of mortals riding gods and angels, Priapus plays a significant role in religious

---

[26] Cf. Richard Payne Knight, *A Discourse on the Worship of Priapus, and its connection with the mystic theology of the ancients; to which is added an essay on the worship of the generative powers during the Middle Ages of Western Europe*; new foreword by O.V. Garrison (1st edition privately appeared in English society, 1786; 2nd ed., London: Dilettanti Society, c. 1826; reprinted: Secaucus, NJ: University Books, Inc., 1974).

civilization.[27] The interest in eroticism and passion is not, however, exclusive to the west, nor to the angels who inhabit the various heavens of the numerous faiths of the west. On the contrary, passion and holiness is equally a part of the world's political, social and theological structure.

It is the essence of eroticism and passion that makes up Tantrism in Eastern Buddhism. In Tantrism, devotion is to natural energy (*shakti*). Based on holy manuals (*tantras*), they inculcate a psychological doctrine, the practice of which states passion can be exhausted by passion (the craving for food, drink or sex can be overcome best by rising above it while being satisfied). Tantra gods in Tantrism have wives. Their strength and their highest power is attained from union with their wives. It is their wives who rouse their strength and "draws it forth." The strength is primarily for war. It is also, to a lesser degree, for pleasure, especially sex and procreation.

The quest for pleasure is ultimately pictured for many Buddhists in the legend of his immaculate conception, his mother's fertility and the ultimate birth of the Enlightened One. It is absent from all representations of his movement into nothingness, with the only formal representations reflecting back

---

[27] *Ibid.*, p. 97 f; cf., Ezekiel 1:10 f *cum* Spencer, *de Legis Ritual Vet. Hebraeor*, lib. iii., dissert. 5.

270

on that happy, erotic moment of total sexual abandonment and conception. For this reason, it is common to see the Buddha pictured in various stages of undress, or his conception picturing his

mother with both the prized elephant and a phallus of gigantic proportions.[28]

---

[28] See: *Further Dialogues of the Buddha*, translated from the *Mijjhima Nikaya* by Lord Chalmers (for the Pali Text Society; London: Oxford University Press, 1926), vol. 1, p. 176 (1.246)

Rahab[29] ............................ Pride

In the Talmud, Rahab is identified as the "Angel of the Sea."[30] In Hebrew he is the *sar shel yam* ("prince of the primordial sea"). In this legend, Rahab is ordered by the Creator god(s) to swallow all of the waters on earth so that he (god) could find room to separate the waters in the cosmos so he would have a place to put Earth. Rahab refused. In anger the god(s) killed Rahab and left his corpse to rot. It became so foul that the god(s) had to bury it beneath the earth. It stayed there until the earth's inhabitants complained so loudly that the god(s) were forced to relocate the remains deep beneath the sea. During this entombment Rahab slowly regains life and when fully restored, attempts to

---

ff. Cf. *Buddhist Scriptures*, translated by Edward J. Thomas (Wisdom of the East Series; London: John Murray, 1913).

[29] See: James R. Lewis and Evelyn Dorothy Oliver, *Angels A to Z*, ed. Kelle S. Sisung (Detroit, MI: Visible Ink, 1996), p. 150, 340; Gustav Davidson, *A Dictionary of Angels: Including the Fallen Angels* (1967; reprint; New York: Free Press, 1971).

[30] Baba Batra 74b.

stop Moses and his people from leaving Egypt at the time they were suppose to cross the "Red Sea." The god(s) stop him once again, and once more destroy him. In reality, Rahab was the original guardian of Egypt.

Ramiel[31] ..........................Thunder

Ramiel is given the distinction of being a chieftain in heaven. He is also styled as a prince. Enoch has him both as a good and bad angel, one who remains in heaven to serve the god(s) and one who is among the fallen angels. In the *Syriac Apocalypse of Baruch* Ramiel presides over "true visions." As such he interprets the visions of Baruch and then appears as the angel who destroys Sennacherib's hosts.

Ramiel resurfaces in the writing of Milton, who, in *Paradise Lost*, identifies him as the angel who is overcome by Abdiel on the first day of the war in heaven. In Milton, Ramiel is seen as being on the seamy side of Satan.

---

[31] *The Syriac Apocalypse of Baruch*, translated and edited by R. H. Charles (London: Society for Promoting Christian Knowledge, 1918). *The Sibylline Oracles*, translated by Milton S. Terry (revised edition; New York: AMS Press, 1973).

| | |
|---|---|
| Rampel | Mountains[32] |
| Rashiel[33] | Earthquakes |
| Sachiel | Ruler of Thursday |
| Sachluph | Plant |
| Sahaquiel | Sky |

---

[32] Because of Rampel, tall mountains have universally been considered the homes of at least one god if not all gods. In Greece, it is Mount Olympus. The lore behind this mountain has pushed itself into the theologies of near by areas. It most noticeably extends into Palestine, where it is transfigured into Mount Zion as well as other biblically famous mountains where priests, prophets and pretenders seek to establish their claims to having the ear of and speaking for the tribal god of the Israelites..

[33] His angelology points to his antecedents as being a god of the underworld, much in the manner and nature of Pluto. He has the same appetites, interests and fetishes: from preferences to being in the company of the dead to wading through the food of banquets. The earthquakes are the result of either his indigestion or, at times, displeasure with those he invited to dine at his table. This reflects the strong animism that existed in the world of the Bible, as do other phenomena such as burning bushes (Exodus 3:2-3). Speech comes out of burning bushes (Exodus 3:3), from clouds (Mark 1:11, 9:7; Luke 3:22; John 12:28) or descending doves (Matthew 3:16-17), and so forth (Acts 8:7, 9:4, 10:13-15). Sometimes the unknown voice is given the general ownership of an anonymous or uncounted archangel (1 Thessalonians 4:16). Like other pagan myths, the angelology behind this strange sire is one filled with bits and pieces of other legends.

Sandalphon[34] ..................... Embryos
   (twin brother of Metatron)
Shakziel ............................ Water Insects
Shalgiel ............................ Snow
Shamsiel ........................... Day
Shateiel ............................ Silence
Sofiel ................................ Vegetables
Tabris ............................... Free Will
Teiaiel .............................. Future
Uriel[35] ............................... Poetry
Vohu Manah ..................... Good Sense
Yroul ................................ Fear
Zaa'fdiel ........................... Showers

---

[34] Originally Sandalphon was supposed to have been the angelic prince who took mortal form as the prophet Elijah to prophecy and return the Children of Israel back to the Father God. Other accounts read that Elijah was transformed into the angel Sandalphon when he was transported to heaven in a burning chariot by a whirlwind while he was still alive. As Sandalphon, this being is one of the tallest celestial creatures in heaven, with apocryphal writers declaring that it would take more than 500 years to travel from his toes to the top of his head (Moses once referred to him as "the tall angel"). Where he is stationed in the heaven various according to the accounts; for example: Islam claims he is in charge of the fourth, the Book of Enoch states the third, while Zohar affirms it to be the seventh. Regardless of which heaven he is in, Sandalphon continuously battles Satan.

[35] See the chapter on Uriel in this book.

Zadkiel[36] ..........................Memory
Zarobii............................Precipices
Zeruel .............................Strength
Zethar ..........................Immortality
Zulphas...........................Forests

    Angels reside in three triads. Each triad has three groups. These groups are known as *choirs*.
    The first choir[37] is composed of the seraphim. They ceaselessly chant in Hebrew the Trisagion (*Kadosh, Kadosh, Kadosh*: Holy, Holy, Holy is the Lord of Hosts, the whole earth is full of

---

[36] Literally, Zadkiel translates "righteousness of God." In history he is the God of Righteousness (Zadki-El) and has seven different identities (or faces). In addition to ruling the planet and zodiac sign of Jupiter, he is one of two chieftains who assist the archangel Michael in battle (Zohar, Numbers 154a). And is a co-chief of the order of shinanim and one of the nine rulers of the heavens, as well as chief of the order of Dominions (see: Gustav Davidson, *A Dictionary of Angels: Including the Fallen Ones* (reprint, New York: Free Press, 1971), p. 324). It's also said in some places that he prevented Abraham from slaying his son Isaac.

[37] Choirs were not initially known among primitive people. The firs full account of angelic choirs comes from the pen of the imaginative Dionysius who wrote *Celestial Hierarchies*. Thomas Aquinas, the author of Summa Theologica, who set the number of choirs at nine, expanded his work.

His Glory.[38]) They are flaming angels made up of pure light and thought.[39] They're seen as fiery flying serpents[40] of fire and love.[41]

The second choir contains the cherubim. In the lore of angels, cherubim are late comers, yet through various celestial conflicts, they moved into second place in station and power. They were known as *Ka-ri-bu*, and were terrible to see. As monstrous guardians of temples and palaces in ancient Sumer and Babylon, the Hebrews found them fascinating during their captivity and incorporated them into their mythology as "knowledgeable" beings: ברוב. They are identical to the genii throughout the entire Near East whose foundation was as guardians of the Assyrian Tree of Everlasting Life.

---

[38] Isaiah 6:3.

[39] Isaiah 6:2.

[40] Serpent is a compound term (ser-pent). *Ser* is שר ("guardian angel" or "higher being." *Pent* is reflective of *rapha* (רבא) which means "healer" or "doctor." As in the Greek culture, an intertwined serpent is the symbol (caduceus) for surgeons and other medical professionals. The caduceus appeared in the hands of the Indo-European god Hermes who is also the Egyptian god Thoth, the Roman god Mercury and the Hebrew angel/god Michael (who was a seraph).

[41] Isaiah 14:29; 30:6.

The third choir is composed of Thrones (Ophanim or Galgallin). Ancient Hebrews described them as "wheels" and "many-eyed ones."[42] Their ruling prince is said to be Rapha-El.

The fourth choir is filled with Dominions. They are also known as "Lords" and "Kuriotetes" (or in Hebrew angelology as Hashmallim or Hamshallim). They regulate the duties of angels. Their leader, Hasmal (or Chasmal) speaks "with fire" both in the sense of vigorous oratory as well as shooting flames from his enraged reddened mouth as a dragon.

Virtues compose the fifth choir. They are also known as Malakim, Danamis or Tarshishim. They are angels of grace. They bestow celestial blessings on mortals in the form of miracles. In the *Book of Adam and Eve* they serve as midwives at the birth of Cain. In legend inspired art, they appear in the Ascension of Christ where two provide his escort into heaven. They have a variety of rulers, including Micha-El, Gabri-El, Rapha-El, Bari-El, Tarshish, and Satan-El (all of whom were gods). In Hebrew legends, the Virtues encouraged Abraham

---

[42] The Hebrew *Galgal* has two meanings: wheels, and the "pupil of the eye." Ezekiel 1:13-19 gives the most complete description of these beings. The full account led to early speculation of flying ships and other UFOs.

to sacrifice his son Isaac for the "greater glory" of his god, and were instrumental in getting David to battle Goliath. While Virtues work with nature, they are also allowed to change nature save in the one area of human sexuality.[43]

Powers control the sixth choir. They're credited as being the first order of angels created by the god(s) of Generation. It is their job to keep the world from being taken over by demons. Various other names have been given these angels, including Authorities, Dynamis, and Potentates. The Powers inhabit the perilous border between the first and second heavens, and spend most of their time resisting the demons that want to take over the world. Some of them defect and go to the otherside and adopt the mannerism and roles of those who serve the Fallen Ones. Thus the Powers are known

---

[43] Additional popular information is in Richard Mansfield, *Angels: An Introduction to the Angelic Hierarchy* (Encinitas, CA: Estuary Publications, 1994). Standard theology is found in Thomas Aquinas, *On Spiritual Creatures*, translated by Mary C. Fitzpatrick in collaboration with John J. Wellmuth (Milwaukee, WI: Marquette University Press, 1949). Emanuel Swedenbörg, *Divine Providence* (originally published 1764; reprint, New York: Swedenbörg Foundation, 1972). The issue of human sexuality has frustrated theologians for centuries. It is seen as an evil, yet in the Paradise literature it is both common and sought out.

to be both good and evil.[44] Their leader is Cama-El[45] who flirts with both good and evil and their sisters' justice and tyranny. As one of the Sefiroth,[46]

---

[44] Romans 13:1 f. Good and evil was defined in the early days of Paulinity as being abstinence and sexuality expressed. The pagan Roman god/angel Eros became the symbol or *daemon* of all evil since it was a nude male, while the veiled Vestal virgins became the symbol of goodness. In the original mythology of angelology, the daemons were regarded as crucial intermediaries between the deities and mortals. In this regard Gabriel and Raphael and even Michael were considered to have demoniac powers with their intermediary stand going to select virgins (Sarah and Mary, for example) to let them know that they were chosen to be vessels for the fruits of god (babies). Many angels, including Michael, were at times portrayed as Eros in art and literature, and in some instances as a very young male. For a discussion on nudity of angels and the issue of angels wearing linen, see the chapter on Jesus in this book.

[45] His name means "he who sees God."

[46] Sefiroth represent a divine emanation through which the gods manifest their existence during the act of creation. Legend filtered into the Cabala has it that this manifestation is composed of ten basic intelligences. Each intelligence is unique and separate, although earlier lore had each as a separate and unique god. The Sefiroth are: Kether (God's will and thought); Hesed (divine love); Gevurah (divine judgment); Rahamin (divine compassion); Tiphereth (divine beauty); Netsah (lasting endurance or eternity); Hod (divine majesty); Yesod (base of every activity in the god(s), and so forth.); and

Cama-El is considered by some to be both the angel who wrestled with Jacob,[47] as well as the angel who appeared to Jesus in the Garden of Gethsemane. He is known as the Duke of Hell and lives in the body of leopard, and he is the patron of the planet of war: Mars[48] and the primary force for war.[49]

Within biblical lore Cama-El is the commander of the 144,000 angels of Destruction, Punishment, Vengeance and Death.[50] The Hebrews

---

Shekinah (presence of the god(s)). Reference Morris B. Margolies, *A Gathering of Angels: Angels in Jewish Life and Literature* (New York: Ballantine, 1994).

[47] Clara Erskine Clement, *Angels in Art* (Boston, MA: L. C. Page, 1898).

[48] In this regard, the ancient Druids worshipped Cama-El as a god.

[49] Eliphas Levi, *The History of Magic* (London: Rider, 1963).

[50] The Angel of Death cult can be traced to ancient Hinduism, and cult of Yama who is the god of the dead. In early-Vedic literature, Yama ruled an afterlife realm closely identical to the Norse Valhalla in which the deceased enjoy carnal pleasures. In the post-Vedic period, Yama rules a world of horrors and became a grim demigod who snares souls of the departed to escort them to a world of agony. The Jewish angel of death (*malakh ha-mavet*) also metamorphosed. At first he was under the direct command of god (2 Samuel 24:16). In the Talmud he is identified with Satan, and given distinct

restyled him as Kemu-El:[51] the mediator[52] between the prayers of Israel and the Hierarchs of the seventh heaven.

---

characteristics. These characteristics include him being a destroyer (Exodus 12:23; 2 Samuel 24:16; Isaiah 37:36), a fatal "reaper" (Jeremiah 9:20), and a messenger of death (Proverbs 16:14). Christianity transfigured him into evil incarnate and the Devil himself. In Islam, Izra'il is the Angel of Death and one of it's four archangels. Like his brother princes, Izra'il is huge, so large that legend says that if all the waters of the earth were poured on his head, not a single drop would make it back to earth. As the Angel of Death, Izra'il keeps a record of the deeds of humanity, circling the names of the damned in black and the names of the blessed (saved) in light. When a person is about to die, a leaf with the mortal's name falls from the tree beneath the throne of Allah. After forty days have passed, Izra'il severs the individual's soul from his or her body and brings it to judgment. See: "Izra'il," in *Encyclopedia of Islam* vol. 4 (Leiden, Netherlands: E. J. Brill, 1978).

[51] In Hebrew, the name translates as "God stands" or "God rises."

[52] Kemu-El has another distinction in Old Testament studies. He is the prince or chief of Ephriam who Moses appointed to divide the land; see; Numbers 34:24. In Old Testament myth and apocrypha, he is also one who was condemned by Moses for trying to prevent him from receiving the Torah from god. Christianity accords him and the Powers as having dominion and control over mortal souls. They are considered to be the

The seventh choir is the home of Principalities. Originally, they were in charge of the nations and great cities of the earth. With the advance of mythology, they became the protectors of religion and determined orthodoxy and heresy. Their chief was originally the Assyrian deity Nisrock who brought to the heavens a mastery of occult writing. Because of this gift he was banned to Hell where he became the chief chef to the Demon Princes who lived there in physical pleasures. Another chief was Ana-El who was despised because he was an angel of and spokesman for human sexuality that wasn't centered on the concept of procreation. A contender to this title was Hami-El who originally was the Chaldean deity Ishtar. His assault on the latter's claim was his record of having transported Enoch to Heaven. Another great prince among the Principalities is Cervill who aided David in his bid to slay Goliath. He was known for his muscularity and his emphasis on the male physique.

The eighth choir is populated by the Magnificent Seven. These are the more commonly known angels: Micha-El, Gabri-El, Rapha-El, Uri-El, Metatron, Remi-El, Sari-El, Ana-El, Ragu-El and Razi-El. The first five are discussed in separate

---

spirit guides who escort the souls that leave the body and have lost their way in the astral plane.

chapters. Each has far more ancient antecedents than Hebrew or Christian scripture, coming from far older Sumerian, Akkadian, and Babylonian legends and lore.

Common (unnamed) angels populate the ninth choir. They are in the last order of the celestial hierarchy and the ones closets to mortals. They are the true "messengers." Their origin can be traced to ancient India and the Sanskrit *Angeres* who antedate the Persian *anagaros* or "couriers." While Enoch counted them only in the hundreds, by the time of the European Middle Ages, the Kabbalists and other commentators number precisely 301,655,722. Some of the common angels are quite lusty. Some are highly oversexed spending their time deceiving young maidens and seducing choirboys and youthful soldiers. This was never objected to until after the middle of the tenth century, for few considered teenage sex to be scandalous save for the priests who prized it as a means of winning additional coins in the confessional coffers. The final condemnation of the oversexed angels came in the thirteenth century when the Bishop of Paris who determined that the Fallen Ones alone were sexual because they missed the intellectual intercourse in heaven. Any male who would be seen with an erection was considered to be in league with Satan.

Guardian angels exist in nearly all faiths and religions of the world. In ancient Mesopotamia people saw them as individual gods assigned to make them to make life easier by enriching each man with more currency, a better harvest, and freedom from any external threat that would impoverish him or his family. These guardian angels were called *massar sulmi* ("the guardian of man's wealth"). Zoroastrians called them *fravashis*. The Greeks knew them as *daemon*, which were assigned to each man at the time of his birth and guided him through life.

Pre-Christian Romans believed each man had a *genius* and each woman a *juno*. Armenians believed such angels were only for children, and returned to heaven when the child reached adulthood.

In Islam the guardian angels are known as *hafaza*. They guard faithful Moslems from the snares of *jinn* (demons). According to legend, every Moslem has four hafaza: two to stand guard during the day, and two to stand guard during the night. In addition to keeping guard, the hafaza are compelled by Allah to keep a record of their ward's good and bad deeds. Their logbooks will be used as evidence on the Day of Judgment, and their ward's soul will be consigned to ever lasting pleasure (where beautiful dark-eyed women with big breasts wait to serve men) or pain (usually a fiery pit where even liquid is engulfed in heat and pain).[53]

In Japan guardian angels have existed throughout its history. Each Japanese has a *kami* to watch out for him/her. And the kami is required to defend his ward from all harm.

Origen, an early Christian theologian (c. 235 CE), argued that each man was assigned a good angel to guide him, and an evil angel to tempt him. His thinking followed Jewish tradition and Roman literature. By the sixth century, such an idea slipped among academicians and theologians. Neither Pope Gregory the Great nor Pseudo-Dionysius mentioned personal guardian angels, and such beings didn't regain popularity among religious leaders until the Middle Ages.

It wasn't until the thirteenth century that the Dominican monk, Thomas Aquinas, revitalized a belief and discussion in guardian angels. He wrote that each man had a guardian angel throughout his life. Because of his insistence on the existence of beings, the Roman Catholic church celebrates a feast day for all guardian angels (2 October), and teaches that every country, manor, city, town, village, parish and family has its own guardian

---

[53] Cyril Glassé, *The Concise Encyclopedia of Islam* (San Francisco, CA: HarperSanFrancisco, 1989).

angel, as do altars, churches, dioceses and religious institution.[54]

The Roman Catholic argument is based the statement of Jesus: "Take heed that ye despise not one of these little ones; for I say unto you, that in heaven their angels do always behold the face of my Father."[55] This passage is wed to the writings of St. Paul,[56] and the account given in the Acts of the Apostles.[57] There are few similar references in the Old Testament.[58] Psalm 91:11-12 is cited because it is similar to passages on the temptation of Jesus. Its authenticity, however, is suspect. It is an embellishment of the confrontation between Jesus and Satan in the garden where Satan struggles vainly to tempt the man into worshipping him.

---

[54] Paola Giovetti, *Angels: The Role of Celestial Guardians and Beings of Light* translated by Toby McCormick (York Beach, ME: Samuel Weiser, 1993).

[55] Matthew 18:10. Many theologians argue that this line is an addition; it has no parallel sources in other scripture or gospels.

[56] Hebrews 1:14.

[57] Acts 12:5-11.

[58] Psalm 91:11-12.

The only other significant reference to a guardian angel is in translations of the Moses story where his god tells him that "I myself will send an angel before you to guard you as you go and to bring you to the place that I have prepared. Give him reverence and listen to all that he says."[59] The problems with this passage are numerous, for the original word is מלאך (*malak*) and can only be defined as an agent or messenger: a civil servant sent to watch over and advise. It is not a god or judge, as that would be אלה'מ (*elohim*). But through this distortion of the record and a history of building a continuity with angels, reverence for guardian angels is the collective growth of an unconscious psycho-mythical evolution of desire for protection.[60]

Without protection from evil and evil spirits, it was argued, man would surely risk Hell and a Final Judgment. The concept of the "Final Days" came with the invention of Heaven and Hell. The three came to the foreground to ensure patriarchy and masculinity.

---

[59] Exodus 23:20.

[60] Michael Grosso, "The Cult of the Guardian Angel," in *Angels and Mortals: Their Co-Creative Power*, compiled by Maria Parisen (Wheaton, IL: Quest Books, 1990).

Male equals would surround men who won the right to go to heaven (their lottery would be announced by the attending angel). Those who failed, losing the intercession of angels would go to Hell and be surrounded by nagging, bitchy, and boisterous women.[61]

It was out of the evolving desire for celestial protection that Christianity embraced the pagan concept of a multiplicity of gods and angels. This multiplicity was transmogrified dramatically into the novel concept of a Christian Trinity.

The Christian Trinity is, simply put, "three-gods-in-one." It is defined as "The Father," "The Son," and "The Holy Spirit" (or "Holy Ghost"). It

---

[61] The word Hell is derived from the realm of Hel presided over by the goddess/angel of death. The fantasy of a hell has been preserved over the centuries to intimidate the weak of mind into blindly obeying a venal clergy and the scriptures of male dominance. For a detailed discussion on the evolution of hell in theology. See: Uta Ranke-Heinemann, *Putting Away Childish Things: The Virgin Birth, the Empty Tomb, and Other Fairy Tales You Don't Need to Believe to Have a Living Faith*, translated by Peter Heinegg from *Nein und Amen* (San Francisco, CA: HarperSanFrancisco, 1993), chapter 16. On the role of women and sex, see: Uta Ranke-Heinemann, *Eunuchs for the Kingdom of Heaven: Women, Sexuality and the Catholic Church*, translated by Peter Heinegg from *Eunuchen für das Himmelreich* (San Francisco, CA: HarperSanFrancisco, 1989).

has no basis in scripture.[62] Nor is it found in the initial canons of Christianity. Surprisingly this amalgamated spirit is the result of the early Church's futile attempt to defend itself of the charge of tritheism or ditheism, leveled, logically, by the Romans when Christians began to claim to believe in Jesus as a god, while adhering to the worship of the god Yahweh.[63]

To get around Pliny's argument against the argument of the faith of Christians, the emerging priesthood testified that the Trinity was one-god-in-three. This meant that it was one three persons (or characteristics) within a single substance, even though such a doctrine has no precise biblical basis. Trinitarian apologists, however, latched on to Paul's benediction that "the grace of the Lord Jesus, the love of God, and the communion of the Holy Ghost,"[64] be with the people of Corinth. This passage scholars note, is a later edition to the original text, implanted by a zealous copyist and left

---

[62] See: Daniel N. Schowalter, "Trinity," in *The Oxford Companion to the Bible*, edited by Bruce M. Metzger and Michael D. Coogan (New York: Oxford University Press, 1993), p. 782.

[63] Pliny, *Epistles* 96:7.

[64] 2 Corinthians 13:13.

unchallenged by those who saw their faith under attack.[65]

The only passage that can be associated with Jesus and the concept of the Trinity comes from his command to baptize believers into his faith.[66] This line is of doubtful authenticity, as the Gospel writer (alleged to be Matthew) makes no claim of Jesus being equal with "the Father."[67] This equation comes only from the Apostle Thomas,[68] and it is of dubious biblical authenticity as it is found no where else within scripture. It is also important to not read into other passages that which isn't there.[69]

Jesus quickly became known as the "Son of God." This title is not exclusive for Jesus.[70] According to the Gospel of St. Matthew, even Jesus rejected any idea that the "Sons of God" was

---

[65] Daniel N. Schowalter, *loc. cit.*

[66] Matthew 28:19.

[67] Matthew 24:36.

[68] John 20:28.

[69] For example: Jude 20-21, or 1 Peter 1:1-2 that discusses "the Father" within the "holiness of the Spirit."

[70] Revelation 21:7.

exclusive and limited, especially to himself.[71] It is the moniker for the angels of the Old Testament.[72]

To buttress their claim the Trinity became endowed with angelic qualities, as did the eventual movement toward near-deification of the Blessed Virgin Mary (the mother of Jesus).[73] By adding Mary into the Christian pantheon (as the "Mother of God"[74]), early followers of the Jesus cult leaned backward to

---

[71] Matthew 5:9. Matthew's formulation is identical to the speech given by the archangel to Mary (Luke 1:35).

[72] Cp. Job 2:1.

[73] This deification of Mary didn't enjoy universal consensus or acceptance. See: Karl Rahner, *Schriften zur Theologie* (1984), XXVI, p. 329. Cp. Uta Ranke-Heinemann, *Putting Away Childish Things: The Virgin Birth, the Empty Tomb, and Other Fairy Tales You Don't Need to Believe to Have a Living Faith*, translated by Peter Heinegg from the original *Nein und Amen* (San Francisco, CA: HarperSanFrancisco, 1993), pp. 156-157 ff.

[74] This title was given canonical status only at the Council of Ephesus (canon 431). It is of pagan origin, being taken from the ancient polytheism of Egypt. See my comments in Arthur

the past to pull out of its mythological treasury for artifacts. The gleaned artifacts figure remarkably in the new faith. They resemble the Christian apologists interest and furthered the idea of a Christian near-goddess with infant and another god-figure.

In the world's religions, guardian angels are special protectors. As protectors they are uniquely prominent in Christianity, and found profusely in the thought of the Book of Revelation. This book, itself, has been considered by many to be the work or authorship of an angel, since it is reputedly dictation's from an angel to John of Patmos (or, according to some, John the Evangelist).[75] It is, allegedly, a series of letters written to seven churches, each represented by its own guardian angel. The letters dictated were sent to reprimand, praise or warn each church and its own guardian

---

Frederick Ide, *Battered and Bruised; All the Women of the Old Testament* with an introduction by Decherd Turner (Las Colinas, TX: Monument Press, 1993), pp. 38-39 note. From ancient Egypt the title for such a deity went to the Greeks who fashioned it as θεοτοκος. I give the hieroglyphic text from Egypt within my work cited.

[75] Revelation 1:1.

angel[76] although the text isn't precise as to the nature of the angel. It denotes a superterrestrial being, yet many Latin fathers considered them to be leaders (bishops) of the church and the Christian community.[77]

Many consider that angels are real and live today among them. The zeal for angelology and angel worship flushed hot with claims of UFO sightings. As psychoanalyst Carl Jung noted, an new religious vocabulary developed with this phenomenon. Religious scientists called flying saucers "technological angels" when unidentified celestial images appeared in the 1950s.

From the concept of technological angels comes the concept of "space brothers." It is out of the idea of intelligent life being beyond the planet

---

[76] The text concerns eschatological prophecies: commentaries and predictions on the end of time, when there are to be wars and plagues. When this doomsday is to take place has been debated for nearly two thousand years. See: Norman Cohn, *The Pursuit of the Millennium* (London: Oxford University Press, 1957).

[77] Robert H. Mounce, *Book of Revelation: The New International Commentary on the New Testament* (Grand Rapids, MI: Wm. B. Eerdmans, 1977); Henry M. Morris, *The Revelation Record: A Scientific and Devotional Commentary on the Book of Revelation* (Wheaton, IL: Tyndale House, 1983).

Earth, that the quest to study Unidentified Flying Objects (UFOs) that modern mythology surrounding angels developed. Ultimately, in 1997, the California suicide cult known as Heaven's Gate, spoke at lengths both in person and on the Internet (World Wide Web) defined their hope to meet with their space kindred and leave the planet Earth with aliens.

Ruth Norman (1900-1993) co-founded a interplanetary society, the Uranus Academy of Science, prophesied that space aliens would land in 2001. To emphasize her belief in extra-terrestrial travelers, Norman and styled herself the archangel Uriel. [78]

The Uranus society, like others, saw the return of the Nephilim (the "Sons of God") who would return to Earth to undo the sins of their forefathers. This led Heaven's Gate members and others in similar societies throughout the world to renouncing sex, sexuality, and even sexual organs. As with the followers of Heaven's Gate, many voluntarily mutilated or surgically removed all or part of their sexual organs. For others, the angels of today and for tomorrow will be their fantasies enacted.

---

[78] Cp. *The Gods Have Landed: New Religions from Other Worlds*, ed. James R. Lewis (Albany, NY: New York State University Press, 1995).

The quest for contemporary angels brought with it a bounty of erotic stories and even erotic art. Angels are pictured, without biblical precedent, as either big bosomed women or naked Greek statues. The majority of these images are usually in a relaxed (or dream-like) state. Many border on personal sexual arousal or implied determination to have sex with a mortal of either or both genders.

In each case of contemporary angels, the "divine being" reflects the image of angels found in Genesis 6: the "Sons of God" who copulated with the "Daughters of Men." This copulation, including the earthy interests in scratching oneself, drinking coffee and intoxicants, and matching the world's societal patterns does follow true biblical lines. It is most graphically pictured in the Hollywood production of the film *Michael* starring John Travolta.

What is unique about the contemporary angel, is that it has neither the medieval properties of being surrounded in layers of cloth, nor is it nude. Instead, the modern angel wears bracelets, garter belts, and high heels (if it is a woman), or it is attired grandly in a Stetson hat and cowboy boots, and in some instances a scarf (if it is a man).

The angel of today is independent, healthy in physical appearance, and quite attractive. Previously angels were feared because of their gortesqueness in appearance and in performance, What the angels of today have in common with the angels of the past is that all angels, yesterday's and today's messengers, sport wings.[79]

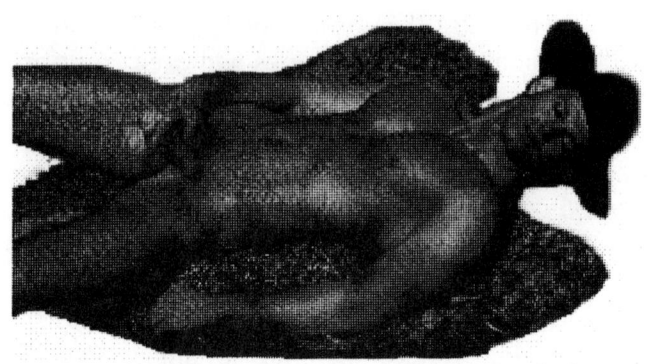

---

[79] Historically wings have been seen as a source of power, speed, and energy. Wings on angels was common during the Middle Ages in Western Europe, but not so prevalent elsewhere, or before, as the scriptures are silent concerning angelic movement apparatus. Wings first appear during the reign of Constantine, the first Christian emperor of Rome, and then were adapted from pagan thought and art, especially taken from the Nike (Winged Victory), coming from ancient Egyptian depiction of various imported gods, such as Nisroch from Assyria. From the fourth to the sixth century, wings slowly began to emerge. See: Gunnar Berefelt, *A Study of the Winged Angel: The Origins of a Motif* (Stockholm, Sweden: Almqvist Wiksell, 1968); cp. Clara Erskine Clement, *Angels in Art* (Boston, MA: L. C. Page, 1898).

# A

Aaron ............... 19, 104
Aaronic priesthood..... 265
Abaddon-Satan........... 155
Abel............57, 85, 86, 88,
   101, 106, 111, 151, 152
Abimelech............91, 217
Abraham1 ..........4, 25, 27,
   32, 45, 65, 68, 86, 87,
   91, 98, 100, 101, 102,
   104, 107, 108, 127, 138,
   145, 155, 204, 209, 211,
   212, 213, 215, 216, 217,
   219, 223, 225, 262, 263,
   274, 287
Accusing Angel.......... 160
Achaiah ...................... 260
Acts of the Apostles... 280
*Acts of Thomas*............ 156
Adam......5, 32, 33, 50, 57,
   82, 83, 84, 86, 89, 96,
   98, 101, 104, 105, 106,
   108, 120, 129, 142, 143,
   144, 151, 152, 160, 173,
   182, 189, 191, 201, 202,
   203, 204, 215, 233, 262,
   274
adultery ...................52, 61
Af.................................. 260
Agni .......................... 111
Agrat-bat-Mahlabt ....... 50

Ahura Mazda ......... 75, 76,
   149, 164, 165
Akkadian.............. 71, 205,
   210, 277
Akrasi-El............. 128, 129
Akriel .......................... 260
Alalus........................... 148
Allah ......... 39, 40, 42, 55,
   74, 96, 104, 166, 171,
   199, 200, 223, 261, 263,
   278, 287
Alphabet of Ben Sira .. 120
Ameretat ............... 74, 260
Amesha Spentas............75
Amitlai ..........................98
Amorite law .................. 60
Anael........................... 260
Ana-El........... 73, 127, 276
*anagaros* ..................... 277
angel ......4, 11, 12, 13, 14,
   15, 22, 33, 38, 41, 45,
   47, 50, 51, 54, 62, 65,
   67, 73, 74, 80, 81, 85,
   88, 96, 98, 103, 106,
   108, 111, 112, 113, 117,
   118, 120, 121, 123, 125,
   129, 130, 131, 135, 137,
   140, 142, 143, 147, 155,
   156, 160, 162, 169, 172,
   173, 178, 189, 195, 201,
   203, 206, 209, 213, 216,
   219, 223, 224, 229, 230,
   231, 234, 235, 237, 240,

241, 244, 247, 248, 251,
252, 253, 254, 263, 265,
268, 272, 275, 276, 279,
281, 283, 284, 286, 287
Angel of Carnal Desire 61
Angel of Carnal
  Knowledge ............... 58
Angel of Death ....... 14, 86,
  90, 96, 132, 137, 145,
  204, 247, 287
Angel of Fertility ......... 68
Angel of Insolence and
  Pride ......................... 48
Angel of Light ............ 160
Angel of Punishment ... 49
Angel of the Lord ........ 65,
  66, 67, 68, 70, 235, 251,
  267
Angel Princes ............... 71
angelic ...... 1, 2, 11, 15, 26,
  41, 47, 114, 128, 139,
  165, 222, 241, 248, 256,
  263, 283, 287
angelology ........ 11, 26, 29,
  53, 112, 154, 158, 172,
  239, 240, 274, 284, 287
Angel-Prince ............. 117,
  123, 125, 126
*Angeres* ...................... 277
Angra Mainyu/Ahriman
  ........................ 164, 165
Anmael ....................... 190
*An-Najm* (The Star) ..........
  40, 104, 201

*Annanage* .................... 189
Anus ........................... 148
Apocalypse ...... 37, 38, 47,
  89, 101, 106, 213, 272,
  287
apocrypha ........ 28, 59, 287
Apocrypha ....... 22, 85, 88,
  89, 101, 106, 111, 151
Apollo ........... 60, 156, 221
Apollyon ............. 153, 155
apostates ................ 79, 132
Apostle Thomas .......... 282
*Appu from Shudul* ....... 144
apsaras ................ 167, 263
Aquinas, Thomas ....... 279,
  287
Arael ........................... 260
Araquiel ...................... 190
Araziel ........................ 191
archangels ........ 15, 25, 26,
  30, 39, 42, 71, 73, 74,
  75, 76, 95, 100, 103,
  105, 106, 109, 111, 113,
  117, 127, 263, 287
Ardvi-Cüra ................. 123
Armaiti .................. 74, 260
Armisel ......,............... 260
Arsiel .......................... 156
Aryzyael ..................... 191
Asael ........................... 191
Asbeel ......................... 191
Ascension of Isaiah ...... 79,
  89
Asenath ................. 90, 100

*asha*............ 165
Asha............74, 260
Asmodeus............51, 105, 147, 153
Assyria........43, 115, 189, 287
Assyrian 10, 30, 115, 274, 276
Astarte............9, 52, 159
Atar............ 111
Athtar............ 52
Atuniel............ 112
Ausiel............ 260
Avenging Angels............ 197
Avites............ 114
Azael............41, 106, 171, 172, 173, 176, 178, 191, 212
Azazel............41, 81, 107, 147, 173, 212
Azza............191, 192

## B

Ba-al............ 150
Baal-beryth............44, 159
Babylon........88, 145, 155, 200, 273
Babylonian........5, 10, 16, 29, 53, 59, 62, 71, 73, 82, 84, 86, 92, 96, 101, 103, 108, 162, 176, 181, 204, 206, 208, 225, 227, 277
Balaam............ 66
Barakiel............260
Baraqijal............192
Barbelo............53
Bardiel............260
Bari-El............274
Beelzebul....153, 158, 159
Behemoth............87
Belial............38
Beliel............147, 156
Beliel-Satan............156
Beloved Son.........16, 161, 163
Benjamin............63, 228
*Beth-el*............227
Beth-El..........88, 92, 227, 231
Bethuel............102
Bible............6, 9, 10, 67, 166, 209, 215, 216, 221, 237, 246, 258, 287
biblical............10, 20, 34, 36, 80, 93, 127, 143, 164, 166, 174, 175, 185, 207, 214, 222, 223, 230, 231, 275, 282, 285, 286
Bodhisattva Avalokieteshwara...132
*Book of Astrology*.......192
*Book of Daniel*............67
*Book of Mormon*.........265
*Book of Noah*............42
*Book of the Angel Razi-El.* 129

Bottomless Pit 155, 156, 162
breast ........................ 46, 85
Buddha ........ 167, 270, 287
Buddhism ........... 132, 160, 167, 269
Buddhist .............. 132, 167, 168, 262, 269, 287
Butator ........................ 261

## C

Cabala ....................... 121, 287
Cain .......... 51, 85, 88, 140, 151, 152, 175, 182, 185, 190, 274
Cama-El ............... 275, 287
Canaanites ................. 8, 10
cannibalism ................. 180
Cassiel ......................... 261
Cave of Dudael .......... 107
Cervill ......................... 276
chaos ....................... 18, 53
chastity ................. 182, 238
Cherubim ......... 20, 25, 30, 35, 203
Chief of Demons ........ 139
childbirth .................... 151
Children of Israel ......... 66
Chitriel .......................... 50
Chosen One ................... 81
Christian ............... 6, 8, 15, 18, 22, 26, 51, 54, 57, 58, 79, 80, 81, 83, 89, 90, 93, 95, 110, 112, 125, 147, 148, 152, 154, 155, 158, 160, 163, 164, 165, 166, 182, 209, 222, 235, 240, 242, 245, 246, 249, 257, 258, 260, 264, 277, 278, 279, 281, 283, 284, 287
Christianity ...... 23, 36, 48, 62, 70, 77, 79, 89, 149, 155, 157, 160, 163, 164, 171, 179, 239, 244, 256, 281, 283, 287
circumcision .............. 7, 19, 101, 108
Colossae ........................ 28
Communion of the Sick (Last Rites) .............. 112
conception ............. 27, 151, 159, 233, 236
Creator ....... 47, 51, 53, 83, 85, 96, 117, 125, 128, 161, 193, 195, 205, 271
Creator God ................ 193

## D

*daemon* ............... 278, 287
Danamis ...................... 274
Daniel ........... 7, 11, 18, 22, 24, 25, 26, 28, 29, 35, 36, 39, 41, 67, 72, 80, 81, 95, 154, 173, 247, 259, 287
Dara ............................ 261

daughters of *adama*.... 182
daughters of Cain.............
   170, 179, 181
Daughters of Men............
   103, 106, 114, 141, 169,
   172, 181, 182, 285
David..........147, 192, 245,
   274, 276
Dead Sea Scrolls.......... 23,
   36, 156
death.............6, 27, 49, 57,
   61, 79, 85, 86, 90, 98,
   101, 107, 117, 132, 157,
   160, 161, 164, 167, 169,
   173, 176, 193, 236, 243,
   244, 248, 255, 257, 258,
   264, 287
deities..........5, 8, 9, 29, 72,
   84, 91, 99, 102, 156,
   171, 172, 173, 203, 211,
   212, 229, 287
Demon Princes............ 276
demons..........7, 10, 38, 45,
   51, 107, 139, 159, 167,
   173, 195, 242, 275, 278
Destroyer....................... 91
Devil...........3, 79, 82, 155,
   156, 159, 287
devils......................45, 195
Dinah.....................90, 100
ditheism...................... 281
Divine Advocate.......... 16
Divine Aid ................... 37
Divine Presence .......... 120
Divine Son ..................... 16
Divine Throne........31, 35,
   178, 202
Djibril..................261, 263
dog-priests ......25, 60, 222
Dominions ..129, 274, 287
*druj* .............................165
Dumah ....................45, 49

# E

Ecclesiastes..........20, 108,
   130, 248
Ecclesiasticus...........23, 36
Egypt......7, 45, 48, 52, 74,
   85, 88, 91, 100, 110,
   160, 215, 217, 222, 230,
   235, 237, 249, 271, 287
Egyptian............66, 85, 97,
   160, 162, 181, 217, 222,
   223, 224, 225, 287
Eisheth Zenunim.........261
Eleazar ben Judah of
   Worms ............130, 135
Eliezer........73, 84, 91, 92,
   93, 96, 97, 99, 100, 102,
   151, 154, 179, 182, 202,
   206, 213, 214, 217
*elohim* ..............7, 183, 280
Enforcers of the Laws.......
   ...............................139
Enlightened One .........269
Enoch...........5, 23, 29, 30,
   31, 35, 36, 37, 38, 39,
   41, 43, 44, 79, 81, 82,

87, 91, 101, 103, 104, 105, 106, 107, 108, 113, 114, 118, 129, 130, 132, 133, 135, 139, 147, 157, 174, 178, 180, 185, 186, 188, 189, 190, 192, 193, 195, 196, 197, 198, 204, 208, 262, 267, 271, 276, 277, 287
epigraphia ..................... 58
Er59
eroticism ..................... 269
Esau...........62, 92, 93, 103, 213, 214, 228
Essenes.....................23, 36
Esther .....................20, 237
*Ethiopic Book of Enoch* ... 6, 41, 81, 129, 139, 147, 157, 174, 178
Eurydice ...................... 222
Eve .............57, 58, 83, 85, 106, 140, 144, 151, 152, 182, 189, 193, 242, 274
evil ....... 12, 16, 17, 21, 38, 46, 48, 51, 57, 62, 77, 81, 87, 88, 109, 126, 137, 140, 148, 150, 153, 154, 155, 160, 165, 166, 178, 189, 195, 208, 224, 242, 275, 279, 280, 287
Exael .......................... 192
Exodus .........9, 24, 25, 26, 31, 38, 65, 66, 67, 69, 71, 72, 97, 118, 119, 120, 121, 125, 128, 130, 156, 211, 212, 230, 235, 237, 247, 264, 287
Ezekiel .........5, 20, 25, 30, 36, 57, 64, 71, 131, 161, 203, 223, 241, 247, 269, 287
Ezeqeel........................193

## F

face of God ....................68
Fallen Angels................37, 129, 132, 183, 185, 287
Fallen Ones ........ 103, 178, 179, 185, 275, 277, 287
fidelity (marital).............92
fifth heaven ...................30
Final Days...........115, 281
Fourth Ezra .............23, 36
Fourth Heaven ...............35
*fravashis*......................278
Friend of God..............128

## G

Gabriel .........3, 28, 67, 71, 74, 81, 84, 85, 87, 89, 91, 95, 96, 97, 98, 99, 100, 101, 102, 103, 104, 112, 114, 158, 189, 233, 235, 247, 261, 262, 287
Gabri-El .........71, 73, 274, 276
Gadreel........147, 176, 193
Gagiel..........................262

Galgallin ............. 131, 274
Gallizur ...................... 129
Garden of Eden ........... 17, 112, 193, 203
  Great Garden ............ 71
Garden of Gethsemane ..... ............................. 275
Gehenna ....... 45, 155, 157, 163
Genesis ........... 5, 7, 11, 14, 18, 19, 24, 25, 26, 30, 32, 43, 45, 51, 57, 58, 59, 60, 62, 63, 64, 65, 67, 68, 69, 70, 73, 83, 85, 86, 91, 92, 93, 95, 96, 99, 100, 101, 102, 106, 108, 109, 113, 125, 127, 129, 140, 151, 154, 164, 170, 171, 174, 175, 176, 178, 182, 185, 196, 201, 202, 203, 206, 209, 210, 211, 212, 213, 214, 215, 217, 219, 220, 221, 224, 227, 228, 229, 230, 231, 232, 235, 238, 239, 241, 247, 285
genii ........................... 273
Gentiles ... 11, 98, 183, 267
Gideon ......................... 66
Gnostic .... 53, 70, 108, 117
  Gnosticism ........ 54, 142
God ............. 3, 5, 6, 7, 8, 9, 10, 11, 12, 13, 14, 15, 16, 17, 18, 19, 26, 27, 28, 29, 30, 31, 32, 33, 35, 36, 37, 38, 39, 40, 41, 42, 43, 44, 45, 46, 47, 48, 49, 53, 54, 58, 59, 60, 61, 64, 65, 66, 67, 70, 71, 72, 73, 74, 76, 77, 79, 80, 81, 82, 83, 84, 85, 86, 88, 90, 92, 96, 97, 98, 99, 101, 102, 103, 105, 106, 107, 108, 109, 110, 111, 112, 114, 115, 117, 118, 119, 120, 121, 123, 125, 128, 130, 131, 132, 135, 137, 139, 141, 142, 143, 144, 145, 147, 148, 149, 150, 152, 153, 154, 156, 157, 158, 159, 160, 161, 162, 164, 167, 169, 170, 171, 172, 173, 175, 176, 177, 178, 180, 181, 182, 183, 185, 187, 188, 189, 190, 191, 192, 193, 194, 195, 196, 197, 198, 199, 201, 202, 203, 205, 206, 207, 208, 209, 210, 211, 212, 213, 219, 223, 224, 227, 228, 229, 230, 231, 232, 233, 235, 236, 239, 240, 241, 244, 247, 257, 258, 261, 265, 267, 268, 269, 271, 272, 274, 275, 278, 280, 281, 282, 283, 287
God of the Covenant ..... 44

Goliath ................274, 276
gospel...................163, 236
*Gospel of Bartholomew*.... 156
*Gospel of St. Matthew*...... 282
Grand Pontiff................ 45
Great Flood........107, 112, 197
Greek......9, 10, 11, 41, 52, 53, 88, 89, 92, 95, 99, 113, 117, 118, 125, 142, 154, 155, 157, 159, 163, 164, 173, 180, 205, 214, 234, 242, 256, 257, 285, 287
Greek Orthodoxy ....... 113
Gregory the Great ...... 279
Grigori.................172, 196, 197
Guardian angel........29, 63, 74, 227, 277, 278, 279, 280, 283

## H

Hadraniel...................... 33
*hafaza*.......................... 278
Hagar............45, 217, 223, 224, 225
Hami-El...................... 276
Harut ...................199, 200
Hasmal ...................... 274
Haurvatat...............74, 262
Hayyôth...........20, 36, 131

heathens ...................79, 90
heaven......5, 8, 12, 18, 24, 26, 30, 33, 39, 46, 50, 65, 66, 72, 75, 81, 88, 129, 131, 132, 139, 148, 149, 161, 164, 165, 166, 173, 180, 185, 188, 193, 196, 197, 199, 200, 202, 219, 238, 241, 247, 256, 260, 271, 272, 274, 277, 278, 280, 281, 287
Heavenly Host ............259
Heaven's Gate .....284, 285
Hebrew.............5, 7, 9, 20, 22, 24, 27, 29, 38, 46, 48, 58, 60, 71, 84, 95, 102, 106, 113, 125, 131, 137, 141, 147, 148, 152, 157, 158, 161, 164, 169, 170, 171, 178, 179, 182, 210, 235, 241, 257, 263, 271, 273, 274, 277, 287
Helel....................142, 183
Hell ......41, 42, 43, 44, 45, 46, 47, 49, 50, 52, 53, 55, 157, 159, 160, 163, 167, 257, 275, 276, 280, 281, 287
  fiery furnace..............44, 154, 155, 157
  Infernal Region .........47
henotheism......................6
Hereafter........40, 81, 143, 175

Herod ..................... 93, 237
Hindu .......................... 262
Hiwa .................... 172, 176
Hiya ..................... 172, 176
Holiness Code ............ 245
Holy Ghost ............. 20, 36, 234, 281, 282
Holy One ..................... 202
homosexuality ............ 220
horns ............. 10, 153, 174
Hosea .......... 9, 62, 70, 115
hymen ................. 150, 216

## I

*Iblis* ...................... 166, 173
Idris ............................ 262
Immaculate Conception ... 233, 269
Isa ............................... 262
Isaac ........... 27, 65, 85, 87, 204, 213, 214, 274, 287
Isaiah ....... 9, 11, 18, 19, 24, 28, 31, 34, 43, 45, 48, 54, 64, 67, 87, 89, 121, 140, 141, 142, 154, 157, 183, 214, 241, 245, 258, 259, 287
Ishmael .......... 45, 223, 224
Ishtar ............ 59, 162, 181, 210, 276
Islam ............... 54, 77, 103, 104, 166, 171, 189, 199, 261, 262, 263, 278, 287

Israel .......... 17, 60, 61, 65, 70, 74, 110, 115, 121, 140, 147, 192, 214, 227, 232, 237, 242, 260, 276, 287
Israelites .............. 8, 17, 44, 48, 119, 130, 147, 159, 160, 231, 258, 287
Israfel .......................... 262
Istahar ......................... 180

## J

Jabril ........................... 261
Jacob .......... 27, 62, 65, 86, 87, 88, 90, 92, 93, 100, 101, 103, 107, 113, 181, 211, 214, 216, 227, 228, 230, 231, 232, 275
Javan ........................... 264
Jehoel ............................ 54
Jehuel ............................ 54
Jeremi-El (Yerahme-El). ................................. 131
Jerusalem .......... 25, 29, 31, 32, 82, 83, 102, 104, 107, 145, 155, 157, 177, 203, 212, 222, 245, 249, 251
Jester of Hell ................. 52
Jesual .......... 161, 162, 163
Jesus ............ 12, 21, 27, 60, 63, 104, 109, 160, 162, 163, 164, 181, 212, 213, 221, 231, 233, 234, 235,

236, 237, 238, 239, 241, 243, 244, 245, 246, 248, 249, 251, 252, 254, 255, 256, 258, 260, 262, 266, 267, 275, 279, 281, 282, 283, 287
Christ.............3, 89, 165, 221, 236, 246, 260, 274
Second Coming........ 27
Jewish ..........8, 11, 23, 26, 29, 32, 35, 51, 54, 62, 83, 84, 88, 89, 92, 95, 96, 97, 100, 108, 111, 131, 142, 147, 157, 164, 166, 222, 240, 245, 262, 279, 287
Jibril ........................... 261
*jinn* ........................21, 278
Job.........7, 8, 9, 12, 13, 14, 16, 18, 20, 24, 25, 28, 33, 53, 54, 87, 105, 125, 139, 147, 154, 163, 166, 169, 199, 240, 248, 258, 287
John......12, 14, 17, 20, 23, 28, 63, 75, 85, 104, 109, 112, 129, 158, 164, 212, 215, 233, 234, 236, 238, 240, 242, 246, 248, 249, 253, 254, 255, 256, 260, 283, 287
John of Patmos........... 283
John the Baptist.......... 104

Joseph ............63, 91, 101, 104, 113, 228, 234, 237, 251, 252
Josephus..............6, 10, 23, 36, 182, 185, 186, 208, 219
Joshua ..........7, 11, 16, 24, 25, 45, 48, 51, 66, 107, 178, 179
Jubilees ......22, 36, 37, 38, 39, 85, 185, 227
Judaeo-Christian ..........53, 65, 79, 120, 127, 164, 169, 185, 195, 201
Judah.................43, 45, 51, 59, 60, 61, 62, 135, 179
Judaism ............36, 57, 69, 72, 77, 117, 149, 157, 160, 164, 171, 179, 239
Jude.....................5, 11, 15, 19, 20, 25, 82, 240, 242, 287
Judgment Day..............263
Judith .......................23, 36
Jung, Carl....................284

# K

Kabbalists ...................277
Kali ...............................52
*kami* ...........................279
Kasdaye ...............194, 264
Kashdejan ...................194
Kemu-El..............275, 287
Kharsag Epic........186, 188

King of the Demonic
   Locusts .................... 156
Kohathite .................... 113
Kokabel ...................... 194
Kshathra ................ 75, 264
Ksiel ............................. 49

## L

Laban ......................... 102
Lahatiel ........................ 49
Laila ........................... 264
Last Day ................ 15, 107
Last Supper ........... 63, 212
Lazarus ......... 63, 154, 155,
   217, 249
Levi ....... 37, 39, 107, 205,
   231, 287
Leviathan ......... 53, 87, 95,
   153, 154
Liliel ........................... 264
Lilith ..................... 50, 51
Liwet .......................... 264
Lord ....... 8, 12, 14, 16, 37,
   38, 40, 44, 49, 65, 68,
   70, 118, 120, 128, 139,
   141, 147, 158, 159, 161,
   189, 196, 197, 198, 199,
   210, 219, 231, 234, 235,
   245, 253, 254, 273, 282,
   287
Lord of Spirits ........... 196,
   199
Lot ........ 68, 127, 215, 219,
   220, 221

Lubhudha .................... 152
Lucifer ......... 47, 141, 142,
   147, 150, 153, 155, 159,
   160, 161, 162, 264

## M

Maccabees ....... 23, 36, 37,
   38, 85
Magdalene (Mary) ............
   ........ 253, 254, 255, 256
Magnificent Seven ...... 276
Maimonides ................ 131
Makkiel ........................ 49
*malak* .......................... 280
Malakim ..................... 274
Malik ............................ 54
Mamre .......................... 69
Manasseh .............. 69, 157
manna .................... 29, 180
Manna ........................ 264
*Ma'on* ........................... 29
Mara ........................... 167
Mark ............... 15, 20, 63,
   109, 154, 157, 160, 163,
   165, 196, 212, 231, 234,
   239, 240, 242, 243, 244,
   245, 246, 248, 249, 250,
   251, 252, 253, 254, 257,
   287
marriage ............... 52, 151,
   183, 233, 234, 238
Marut ................. 199, 200
Mary (mother of Jesus)

181, 233, 234, 253, 254, 255, 256, 283, 287
*massar sulmi* ............... 278
Mastema ................. 38, 147
Matesma-Satan ........... 160
Matriel ........................ 264
matrimony .......................
  *See* marriage
Matthew ............ 10, 12, 13, 14, 15, 20, 26, 27, 28, 48, 63, 64, 89, 109, 125, 153, 154, 157, 160, 163, 165, 196, 203, 212, 233, 234, 235, 237, 238, 239, 241, 242, 243, 244, 246, 248, 251, 252, 253, 254, 257, 282, 287
Mehabiah .................... 264
Mercury ..... 10, 88, 90, 287
  Hermes ...... 88, 262, 287
Meririm ........................ 47
Merkaba ..................... 125
Mesopotamian ........... 7, 50
messengers ............ 3, 6, 11, 26, 31, 139, 142, 205, 219, 221, 244, 246, 263, 277, 286
Messiah ........................ 60
Metatron ............ 54, 73, 98, 117, 118, 119, 120, 121, 128, 178, 192, 235, 272, 276
Michael ...... 23, 25, 28, 29, 32, 67, 71, 73, 74, 79, 80, 81, 82, 83, 84, 85, 86, 87, 88, 89, 90, 91, 92, 95, 96, 103, 112, 114, 132, 158, 189, 221, 231, 246, 262, 263, 264, 286, 287
Micha-El ........ 71, 73, 118, 274, 276
Middle Ages .......... 11, 35, 58, 80, 130, 155, 268, 277, 279, 287
Mithra ......................... 117
monotheism ........ 6, 72, 76
Moon God ................... 148
Mormonism ................ 265
Morning Star .......... 16, 52, 162
Moroni ....... 264, 265, 266, 267
mortals ......... 6, 11, 14, 17, 24, 26, 28, 29, 32, 45, 49, 72, 74, 83, 91, 97, 108, 111, 112, 144, 145, 160, 171, 172, 174, 175, 176, 177, 185, 190, 193, 194, 195, 199, 200, 233, 239, 241, 245, 265, 269, 274, 277, 287
Moses ........... 9, 19, 33, 38, 48, 65, 79, 83, 86, 89, 90, 97, 100, 101, 104, 106, 107, 119, 120, 121, 128, 130, 131, 132, 138, 145, 160, 181, 204, 211,

230, 235, 260, 262, 271, 280, 287
   burning bush ....... 65, 66
Moslem ...... 26, 39, 42, 74, 95, 278
Mother Earth .......... 84, 88, 96, 183
Mother Goddess Hel .. 162
Mount Hermon ........... 186
Mount Hira .................. 103
Mount Horeb .............. 130
Mount Moriah ....... 83, 227
Mount Olympus .......... 10, 72, 287
Mount Saphon .............. 88
Muhammad ............ 21, 55, 104, 166, 261
Mulla Nasru-din ........... 42
Mulla Nassr Eddin ....... 42
Mumiah ...................... 267
myth ........... 33, 53, 85, 93, 112, 113, 121, 135, 142, 144, 148, 173, 178, 189, 205, 214, 219, 222, 223, 227, 229, 230, 242, 287
mythology .......... 8, 19, 29, 50, 65, 113, 123, 137, 141, 157, 160, 161, 273, 276, 284, 287
   mythological ......... 175, 183, 283

## N

Naamah ................. 51, 191
Nabu .............................. 88
Nasr' .............................. 42
Nasr-ed-Din ............ 41, 42
Nephi .......................... 266
Nephillim .... 171, 178, 285
Nephites ...................... 265
New Testament ........ 9, 11, 13, 14, 15, 20, 25, 26, 27, 60, 63, 82, 157, 161, 162, 163, 212, 213, 233, 238, 258, 287
Nimrod .................. 98, 154
nirvana ........................ 167
Nisroc ..................... 42, 43
Noah ........ 35, 51, 91, 107, 108, 112, 114, 130, 205, 206, 207, 208
Norman, Ruth ............. 284
nudity ......... 239, 245, 246, 248, 287
   naked body .............. 245

## O

oak of Moreh .............. 209
Och ............................. 267
Old Testament ........ 7, 8, 9, 11, 14, 18, 20, 28, 30, 45, 62, 70, 76, 83, 85, 88, 89, 95, 101, 106, 111, 130, 132, 148, 150, 151, 157, 163, 201, 211, 215, 224, 233, 244, 246, 280, 282, 287
Ophanim ............. 131, 274

Ophannim ...............20, 35
oracular oak .................. 68
Order of Principalities.. 43
Origen ................257, 279
Orpheus's wife ........... 222

**P**

pagan...........11, 17, 62, 99,
    102, 154, 209, 210, 228,
    281, 287
Paradise...............122, 203,
    208, 244, 272, 287
Parasiel........................ 267
passion .................91, 172,
    269
patriarch .............101, 107,
    113, 118, 213, 216, 228
Pegasus .................35, 104
    Buraq...................... 104
Penance ....................... 102
Penemue...................... 195
Penemuel.............194, 195
penis.............51, 140, 141,
    170, 179, 181
    phallic ..............69, 162,
        180
    phallus...............57, 153,
        268, 270
Persia..............67, 73, 117,
    235
Persian..............10, 20, 77,
    117, 123, 137, 149, 157,
    203, 242, 277

Peter...........11, 15, 20, 58,
    89, 158, 162, 165, 241,
    242, 251, 254, 287
Phanuel .........81, 189, 267
pharaoh ........11, 160, 215,
    216, 237
ˌPharaoh .........................48
Pharmoros....................196
Phoenix ..............25, 35, 36
pillar of fire.........119, 211
Pirqe Rabbi Eleazar ....131
Pistis-Sophia .................53
Plato ............................222
pleasure........18, 114, 178,
    199, 225, 269, 278
Pliny....................281, 287
Poteh ...........................268
Potiphera..............91, 101
Powers ....15, 16, 275, 287
prayer....12, 171, 177, 205
Priapus ........................268
Prince of Darkness............
    16, 155, 159
Prince of Light...............16
Prince of Sheol............156
Prince of the World.....117
Princes of Hell ..43, 44, 45
Principalities ..........15, 16,
    129, 276
Prometheus .........111, 112
promiscuity ..............52, 91
prophet.............34, 75, 89,
    115, 223, 231, 237, 267,
    287

prophets............19, 69, 76, 104, 210, 230, 263, 287
Proserpine.......52, 53, 159
prostitutes..........50, 60, 61, 210, 213, 222
prostitution.......51, 62, 90, 91, 182
Proverbs.........20, 31, 154, 163, 236, 287
Psalm........7, 8, 12, 18, 19, 24, 29, 30, 31, 48, 53, 54, 63, 64, 67, 87, 118, 121, 125, 154, 163, 183, 192, 202, 225, 240, 241, 242, 257, 258, 280, 287
Psalms..............23, 36, 209
Pseudepigrapha......22, 85, 88, 89, 151
Pseudo-Dionysius....... 26, 279
punishment.......13, 42, 67, 82, 138, 157, 163, 196, 197, 200, 221, 260
purgatory.............164, 257
Puriel............................ 50

## Q

Qelimath.................... 152
Queen of the She-Demons 52
Queen of the Stars........ 52
Queen of the Underworld 52
Qumrân..................23, 36

Qur'an........25, 26, 27, 39, 40, 42, 74, 85, 97, 102, 104, 171
Koran...........39, 42, 54, 55, 166, 223, 261, 263

## R

Rabbi Jehoshua ben Levi.. 145, 204
Ragu-El........73, 127, 128, 129, 276
Raguil..................108, 135
Rahab.............47, 48, 271
Ramiel...........41, 271, 272
Rampel................272, 287
Raphael......28, 71, 74, 81, 85, 89, 103, 105, 106, 107, 108, 109, 110, 114, 158, 189, 287
Rapha-El........71, 73, 131, 133, 274, 276
Rashiel........................272
Rasuil..........108, 128, 135
Ratzi-El....................129
Raziel..................108, 135
Razi-El.........73, 127, 129, 130, 276
Rebekah..............213, 217
rebellion in heaven 138, 140
Red Sea...........48, 66, 271
Rediyao.................73, 123
Regent of God.............147

reincarnation ............... 167
Remi-El .........73, 127, 131, 132, 276
Renaissance ............11, 203
resurrection .............28, 81, 157, 238, 239, 249, 256
*Revelation* ........12, 13, 14, 15, 16, 17, 25, 28, 33, 47, 60, 82, 88, 125, 129, 149, 156, 157, 162, 163, 164, 236, 241, 242, 247, 258, 259, 260, 267, 283, 287
Rofocale ........................ 47
Roman Catholicism ..........
 ........................112, 149
Roman Mass .....34, 79, 90
 Litany of All Saints 112
Rufa-El........................ 128

## S

Sachiel.......................... 272
Sachluph ..................... 272
sacrifice ..........29, 65, 101, 109, 211, 212, 274
Sadducees .........23, 36, 93
Sahaquiel..................... 272
saints ................7, 79, 160
Samael............88, 98, 137, 138, 139, 141, 142, 143, 144, 147, 148, 151, 169
Samal ..........148, 149, 150
Sam'al......................... 150

Sammael ........14, 85, 137, 139, 141, 147
Samson............66, 97, 223
Sandalphon ..........73, 125, 126, 272, 287
Saoshyant......................81
Sarah .............68, 91, 105, 109, 215, 216, 223, 224, 225, 287
Saraosha.........................75
Saraqael .......................190
Saraqu-El ............129, 132
Sariel.............................45
Sari-El..........73, 127, 132, 133, 276
Satan ..........16, 17, 38, 46, 50, 51, 81, 85, 114, 140, 142, 147, 148, 150, 151, 152, 153, 154, 155, 156, 158, 159, 160, 161, 164, 165, 166, 167, 169, 179, 199, 202, 213, 230, 239, 241, 243, 248, 272, 274, 277, 280, 287
 Mephistopheles ........46, 47, 155
 Satanas ....................156
Satanail .......................196
Satan-El .............147, 155, 161, 274
Satan's Brides.................50
Saul of Tarsus ...................
 *See* St. Paul.
sbires............................54

scapegoat.............107, 177
scrotum ....................... 140
Semil....................108, 135
Sennacherib..........43, 132, 272
Seraphim........20, 34, 132, 147
serpent........17, 35, 85, 87, 139, 142, 150, 153, 156, 162, 189, 236, 287
Serpent in the Garden 142
Seventh Heaven.......... 30, 35, 104, 276
sex........18, 25, 30, 44, 51, 52, 57, 58, 59, 61, 62, 91, 103, 106, 129, 143, 151, 158, 170, 171, 172, 178, 185, 186, 190, 207, 217, 220, 225, 235, 269, 277, 285, 287
   coitus..........25, 59, 140, 159, 190, 191, 197
   copulate............206, 285
   copulation ............... 285
   cunnilingus........50, 151
   fellatio .......50, 143, 151
   fertility .........9, 46, 118, 150, 170, 194, 210, 269
   frigidity ................... 153
   illegitimate .............. 220
   impotency .........12, 153
   infertility ................. 153
   intercourse .......57, 151, 179, 185, 191, 193, 194, 215, 216, 233, 234, 277
   masturbation ...1, 50, 59
   oral....51, 159, 178, 179
   orgasm ....150, 180, 194
   orgies .................22, 182
   procreation..............114, 178, 180, 269, 276
   sodomy.......60, 69, 143, 222
Shaftiel..........................49
*Shahar*........................183
*Shaitin*........................165
Shakziel .....................272
*Shalem* ........................183
Shalgiel ......................272
Shalmaneser................114
Shamsiel.....................272
Shateiel ......................272
Shechem..........68, 90, 100, 210
*Shehaqim* .....................29
Shelah ..........................59
Shem .........................107
Shemal ...............137, 150
Shemhazai............91, 171, 172, 173, 175, 176
Sheol ...................156, 257
Silence of Death............45
sin ........14, 38, 45, 48, 58, 143, 164, 183, 186, 193,

194, 195, 199, 200, 214, 220, 221, 239
transgression ......37, 42, 51, 53, 143, 171, 183, 185, 199, 215, 216, 217
Sixth Heaven...........31, 35
Smith, Joseph.............. 267
Sodom...............68, 69, 97, 127, 219, 220
Sofiel.......................... 272
Solomon........9, 23, 31, 36, 63, 96, 101, 107, 109, 130, 135, 145, 192, 202, 211, 214, 236
Son of Dawn .......142, 150
Son of God.........6, 16, 38, 282
Sons of God ...........37, 91, 103, 106, 114, 169, 170, 282, 285
sons of judges.............. 183
Sons of the Sons of Light 133
Sophia ........................... 53
sorcery........................ 200
Spenta Mainyu ............ 77, 164, 165
sperm...................180, 201
Sphinx .......................... 10
spirit
  daevas ..................... 165
Spirit ........20, 36, 77, 164, 197, 281, 287

St. Paul.............22, 28, 93, 158, 164, 219, 233, 236, 237, 242, 249, 256, 257, 280, 282
Strabo..........................219
stupidity ......................195
succubi..........................51
Sumerian........10, 71, 106, 137, 210, 277
Sun God........46, 150, 156
Suriel...........................107
Suriy-El.......................132
Suwa ............................42

## T

Tabris ..........................272
*Tale of the Two Brothers* 217
Talmaiel......................197
Talmud........29, 39, 62, 82, 84, 86, 92, 96, 101, 103, 118, 140, 145, 204, 271, 287
Talmudists ....................63
Tamar................58, 59, 61
tamarisk tree ...............209
Tamiel..................41, 176, 198
*tantras* ..........................269
Tantrism......................269
Targum ............85, 91, 92, 108, 118, 130, 214
Tarshish ......................274
Tarshishim ..................274

Tartak ............................ 114
Tartarus ................. 114, 158
*Tehomoth* ..................... 123
Teiaiel .......................... 272
terebinth tree ................. 68
*The Thanksgiving Hymns* 156
theology ............ 75, 77, 95, 111, 148, 163, 165, 197, 201, 235, 256, 263, 268, 287
Third Heaven .............. 204
Thoth ...................... 88, 287
Throne of God ............... 34
Thrones ......... 36, 131, 274
  Erelim ..................... 131
Tobias .......... 28, 105, 109, 110
Tobit ............ 23, 36, 37, 38, 39, 105, 109
Tomb
  empty ...................... 248
Torah .............. 39, 72, 140, 178, 181, 287
Tower of Babel ........... 171
transvestitism .............. 143
Travolta, John ............ 286
Tree of Everlasting Life 274
Tree of Immortality ...... 43
Tree of Knowledge .... 203
Tree of Life .......... 43, 106, 180, 189
Trinity .......... 89, 281, 282, 283, 287
Trisagion ..................... 273
tritheism ...................... 281
Tubal-Cain .................... 51
Turel ........................... 198
Typhon ......................... 88

## U

Uriel ........... 22, 71, 74, 81, 89, 91, 103, 111, 113, 114, 139, 158, 189, 267, 272, 285, 287
Uri-El ....... 71, 73, 128, 276
Usiel ........................... 198
Utnapishtim ........ 205, 208

## V

Vedic ..... 77, 111, 262, 287
virgin ............... 3, 163, 181
Virgin Mary .....................
  *See* Mary
virginity ...................... 216
Virtues .................. 85, 274
Vohu Manah ......... 75, 272

## W

Wadda .......................... 42
war ......... 9, 11, 59, 72, 77, 88, 91, 103, 112, 118, 148, 158, 167, 174, 192, 210, 241, 269, 272, 275
  celestial battle ........ 188, 228

*Wars of the Sons of Light against the Sons of Darkness* .................. 133
Watchers ........ 29, 30, 176, 185, 186, 187, 190, 191, 196, 197, 198, 199, 222, 247
wings ............. 3, 10, 22, 25, 34, 118, 131, 139, 150, 188, 248, 261, 262, 263, 286, 287
Wisdom .......... 17, 36, 108, 205, 236, 287
woman in heaven .......... 52

## Y

Yaghuth ......................... 42
Yahweh .......... 7, 8, 16, 18, 43, 45, 46, 49, 51, 53, 66, 68, 69, 70, 84, 85, 87, 88, 117, 119, 120, 129, 130, 138, 142, 147, 148, 151, 169, 170, 199, 205, 208, 210, 216, 222, 233, 258, 281
Yahweh's wife ............... 69
Yahwists ....................... 45
Ya'qu ............................ 42
yazatas ...........................

*See* angels
Yezidics ........................ 42
Yroul ........................... 273

## Z

Zaa'fdiel ...................... 273
zabayniya ...................... 54
Zacharias .................... 233
Zadkiel ................ 273, 287
Zagzag-El .................... 132
Zarobii ........................ 273
*Zebhul* ............................ 29
Zechariah ..... 7, 16, 22, 24, 25, 36, 64, 66, 67, 68, 70, 156, 239
Zerachi-El ................... 132
Zeruel .......................... 273
Zethar .......................... 273
Zeus ......... 31, 88, 92, 118, 183, 221
Zoroaster ..... 72, 75, 76, 77
Zoroastrian ............. 74, 75, 81, 111, 148, 164, 165, 166
Zoroastrianism ............. 76, 77, 149, 158
Zoroastrians ................ 278
Zulphas ....................... 273

**Arthur Frederick Ide** is a writer and lecturer by profession. He is the author of more than 350 books. Many are on religious topics. They include *Qur'an on Woman, Marriage, Birth Control and Divorce* (Tangelwüld, 1996), *Marriage, Divorce, Remarriage, Woman & the Bible* (Tangelwüld, 1995), *Battered & Bruised: All the Women of the Old Testament* (Monument Press, 1993), *Catechism of Family Values Based on the Bible* (Liberal Arts, 1993), *Zoar & Her Sisters: Homosexuality, the Bible & Jesus Christ* (Minuteman, 1991), *Evangelical Terrorism: Censorship, Falwell, Robertson & the Seamy Side of Christian Fundamentalism* (Scholars, 1986), *Teachings of Jesus on Women* (Texas Independent Press, 1985), and *Jews, Jesus and Woman* (IHP, 1984), to mention but a few. Dr. Ide's books have been reviewed in *Playboy*, *New Testament World*, *New Testament Abstracts*, *This Week In Texas,* and numerous papers and journals.

Dr. Ide regularly appears on radio, television and cable coast-to-coast presenting what is and not what people are told exists. He is a sought-after speaker on the lecture circuit. His specialty is ancient languages, religions and their sacred texts, and the environment in which they were written and enforced as law.

A native of Iowa, Dr. Ide holds advanced degrees in history, religion, education, and psychohistory. Starting in his hometown of Cedar Falls, he attended the State College of Iowa, University of Northern Iowa, University of Cincinnati, University of Illinois at Urbana-Champagne, Arizona State University and Carnegie-Mellon University, and various other institutions. He served on the counseling staff at the University of Cincinnati, and taught a plethora of courses ranging from Economics and Sociology to the History of Women and a course in Death and Dying. His teaching career was born at the University of Northern Iowa, migrated to Iowa Lakes College, and from there to the University of Illinois, Mauna Olu College of Maui (Hawaii), University of San Diego, and Eastfield College (Dallas).

For several years Dr. Ide worked at Bridwell Library, Perkins School of Theology (SMU), where he became a close friend of its Director: Dr. Decherd Turner. Dr. Ide has since returned to his native state of Iowa where he makes his home.

When not pursuing his own writing career, Dr. Ide teaches creative writing in his home; he is the author of *Writing Plain English* (Tangelwüld, 1994), or working on human rights issues. Arthur Frederick Ide's biography appears in *Who's Who in America*, *Who's Who in the American South and Southwest*, *Directory of American Scholars*, *Who's Who in Education*, and other sources. Later in 1997, Monument Press will release his *Preaching Prejudice, Hallowing Hate*, a study on the radical religious right.

**John Paul Smith** was born in Irving, Texas. Growing up in northern California, he completed his education there, and subsequently joined the United States Air Force. He served in Japan. After a short stay in Arizona, he returned to Texas, and later became a close confidant and highly valued assistant to Dr. Arthur Frederick Ide.

John Paul Smith has a rare and sterling rapport with everyone. He possess an extraordinary ease with primary material and a fertile enthusiasm to help stimulate scholarly research, a talent that has motivated Dr. Ide to write this treatise on angels. The powerful personality of Mr. Smith brought quick fruition, for within three weeks (the start of their research into primary sources until the finish manuscript was submitted to the publisher who quickly contracted for the book rights) *Angels* was completed.

Robustly, Dr. Ide has endorsed John Paul Smith's exceptional skills, extraordinary talents, and persuasive abilities. He has asked his publishers to commission Mr. Smith to work with him in completing the research for future books. John Paul Smith, Dr. Ide noted, agilely adapts himself to the mastery of the topic, thoughtfully considers all issues and marshals magisterial material to support the thesis under consideration. Monument Press immediately concurred with Dr. Ide's assessment of the value of Mr. Smith to his writing needs and endorsed his recommendation. Given Mr. Smith's *im Geist der Zeit*, Dr. Ide has already nearly completed a lengthier volume for the press. The book is scheduled for publication winter 1997.

**Decherd Turner** earned a Bachelor of Arts degree at the University of Missouri, and a Bachelor of Divinity degree at Vanderbilt University (where he won the Founder's Medal for Highest Scholarship), and attended George Peabody College of Teachers to study Library Science.

From 1946-1950, Decherd Turner was First Cataloguer and later Librarian of the Vanderbilt Divinity School Library. In September 1950, he became the Librarian of Bridwell Library of Perkins School of Theology at Southern Methodist University, and retained that post until 1980. "There," Valerie R. Hotchkiss, current Director of the Bridwell Library, has written, "*ex nihilo*, he gathered together one of the country's best theological libraries and assembled one of the world's finest collections of rare books ranging from incunables to important Methodisticus, to the art of the book. His reputation and renown are tremendous, verging on legendary. His famous "deals" and amazing acumen in the book world have earned him the respect, and the envy, or every major collector and library in the world."

On 1 June 1980, Decherd Turner became the Director of the Humanities Research Center at The University of Texas at Austin. He retired 1 June 1988, and since that time has been quite busy doing book appraisals and library consultation.

Mr. Turner was a founder of the American Theological Library Association, and later served as its president. He is a member of the Grolier Club, Texas Institute of Letters, and the William Morris Society.

Mr. Turner is married, and has two adult children and two grandchildren. With his wife, Margaret Ann Turner, Dr. Turner became a close friend of and authored introductions to many of Dr. Ide's published books.

Of a limited number of 500 copies

this is copy number  *458*